Gardening on the Edge

Drawing on the Cornwall Experience

Conceived by **Neil Armstrong**

General Editor
Philip McMillan Browse

Alison Hodge

First published in 2004 by Alison Hodge
in association with Neil Armstrong
Alison Hodge, Bosulval, Newmill, Penzance,
Cornwall TR20 8XA
info@alison-hodge.co.uk
www.alison-hodge.co.uk

ISBN 0 906720 33 8

A catalogue record of this book is available from
the British Library.

Designed and originated by BDP –
Book Development and Production,
Penzance, Cornwall.

Cover designed by Christopher Laughton,
based on a photograph by Susanna Heron ©

Front endpapers: *Colocasia esculenta* 'Burgundy Stem' with
Tetrapanax papyrifer.
Back endpapers: *Dicksonia squarrosa.*
Facing title page: View from The Island Hotel, Tresco,
Isles of Scilly.

Printed and bound in Italy.

Contents

Introduction

Philip McMillan Browse

Those of us who live in the extreme south-west of England, or in similar climatic conditions – in the north-western tip of Brittany, or the south-west of Ireland, for instance – have the opportunity to garden in circumstances that others would regard as particularly favourable, for we are able to cultivate a much wider range of less hardy exotics than is the normal palette. In bald statistical – but nevertheless selective – terms, the climate of the far south-west is advantageous in terms of higher mean temperatures; minimal levels of frost incidence; above-average humidity, and sufficient – if not excessive – rainfall. The one major problem is wind, which means we must either develop protection, or simply ride with this particular element. However, there are many unanswered questions in the way various advantages coalesce to provide particularly favoured niches, and it is difficult to characterize all of the contributory factors.

Left: *Ensete ventricosum* 'Maurelii', Tremenheere, near Penzance, Cornwall.

Bosahan, one of Cornwall's famed valley gardens, enjoys natural shelter from the full force of the wind. It became celebrated for its early plantings of *Chamaerops*, *Trachycarpus*, *Phoenix canariensis*, and tree-ferns.

Since just after the Second World War, the bible for those wishing to be adventurous, and to select more unusual plants for gardening in such advantageous conditions, has been W. Arnold-Forster's *Shrubs for the Milder Counties*, published in 1948, and also Edgar Thurston's earlier, less well-known, and less easily obtainable *Trees and Shrubs in Cornwall* (1930). These volumes have been the inspiration for the present work.

It has become evident that the number of plant introductions, and the associated hybridization which has occurred over the last 50 years, have been so extensive that neither of these volumes now provides a sufficiently comprehensive coverage. It is equally clear that one author could no longer cope with all the possibilities that are now available. Thus, rather than duck the issue, in *Gardening on the Edge* some prominent gardeners and botanists, who work and garden in Cornwall, provide contributions on their own particular interests or specializations, from their own particular perspective.

The authors have been chosen, primarily, because of their high reputation as practising gardeners, but also because between them they contribute individual and personal segments on a wide diversity of subject matter, which is related to their particular specialist interests and knowledge. This also adds up to a harmonious whole, which, as a complete volume, pays tribute to their progenitors Arnold-Forster and Thurston, and once again emphasizes that Cornwall is still at the cutting-edge of horticultural endeavour.

Any discussion that defines climatic advantage depends on many factors, and then on their particular confluence in a specific place. Cornwall is a diverse county in both topography and climate, but these notes are effectively limited to the southern and far western, lowland, coastal areas – for it is in these areas that the mitigation of the sea, in reducing the incidence of frost, and the development of higher mean temperatures throughout the year, brings maximum advantage. In particular niches, the confluence of these advantages, plus the natural shelter from the full force of the wind, created by the shape and position of land masses, brings exceptional advantage, as can be seen at Lamorna; on the Helford River in gardens such as Trebah, Glendurgan; and Bosahan, and at St Mawes, where Lamorran House Gardens provide a stunning example. But gardening is also very much on the edge along the northern coastal belt, which is substantially advantaged by the sea, but is nevertheless very much battered by the wind – sometimes a particularly cold wind.

The components of this advantage – of gardening on the edge – reflect the southerly geographical location (latitude) that implies better light intensity, and a less variable pattern of day-length from summer to winter, and so may well suit those plants from positions nearer the Equator; and the fact that Cornwall is virtually surrounded by sea – this,

Native gorse and heather on the coast, west Cornwall.

as a 'warm' body of water, in itself affecting the basis for higher than average, ambient temperatures. However, the considerable disadvantage to plant growth is the wind – which arrives, virtually unimpeded, off the sea, at a land mass that no longer has a great deal of tree cover to provide protection.

Despite these comments, which emphasize 'the far south-west', there is much in *Gardening on the Edge* that is relevant to anyone gardening in a coastal location, where the sea provides a mitigation against extreme temperature fluctuations. It will have even more relevance to those who garden in the more favoured areas on the west coasts of Scotland and Ireland.

Wind

Gardening on the edge has one major problem: the incidence of higher wind velocities than elsewhere. Strong winds can be mind-numbingly frightening in exposed places, and have the potential to cause high levels of physical damage to plants.

Wind is the major influence on plant growth and development in almost all parts of Cornwall – limiting growth through water loss; the loss of buds and leaves through the abrasive action of wind-blown sand, and leaf-scorch from the effects of salt carried on the wind. It is not nec-

essarily the normal wind pattern that creates any significant problem, as this is usually manageable, but rather the effects of abnormally high wind speeds, which often emanate from unusual and unexpected directions. Even in very brief gusts, high wind speed can cause great damage by the energy imparted and, in extreme conditions, may cause the uprooting of trees or the breaking off of major limbs. Such occurrences do not need to be very frequent to cause lasting damage – as is evidenced by the hurricanes of late 1987 and early 1990, the repercussions of which are evident up to 15 years later. It is therefore important to understand the mathematics associated with the 'force' of the wind. The commonest misunderstanding is that this force – the energy imparted

The hurricane of early 1990 destroyed trees in west Cornwall.

A mixed *Escallonia* hedge grown in a low garden wall. The outer windbreak includes *Camellia* 'St Ewe', *Cupressus macrocarpa* and *Pinus radiata*. Inner wind-filtering shrubs include *Berberis* and *Olearia macrodonta*.

– is simply proportional to the speed of the wind. Unfortunately this is not the case: force increases dramatically as wind speed increases.

Much advice is available about the planting of windbreaks to provide shelter; however, the positioning and structure of such plantings also has a major impact. Simply creating a fairly solid, evergreen windbreak may create an impermeable structure that causes the wind to be guided up and over – thus increasing its speed and the likelihood of significant eddying of high velocity on the leeward side. The trick is to create a windbreak in which the pattern of planting, and the type of plants used, effectively filter the wind, and although not eliminating it, reduce its speed over useful distances.

An increase in wind speed causes an increase in the rate of evaporation from the leaf surface, and this in turn causes a reduction in the temperature of the leaf. This negates much of the benefit of an otherwise generally improved ambient temperature, which is thus only a real advantage when enhanced by protection from the wind.

The effects of wind-blown sand and salt are also proportionally more damaging as wind speed increases. Sand, by its abrasive effects, can cause unexpectedly high levels of damage, especially to buds, and this factor emphasizes the distortion of tree and shrub growth in exposed areas. Similarly, salt may be deleterious because of the 'scorch' created on leaf surfaces.

The perpetual presence of wind, even at low speeds, means that where natural topographical shelter is generally good, it may nevertheless be wanting from a particular quarter, and it becomes necessary to provide protection by the judicious siting and planting of trees and shrubs to create effective shelterbelts. This can be seen at its most effective on Tresco, and in the Isles of Scilly generally; at Trewidden and Trengwainton in the far west; at Caerhays and Heligan in mid-Cornwall, and at Antony and Mount Edgcumbe in the east.

Where a particular site is exposed to the full force of the wind – and this is usually associated with soils that are acidic and low in nutrients – either the shelter has to be built up in stages, using subjects such as gorse and sea buckthorn, which improve the soil as well as establish the first rank of shelter; or this height of shelter is used in conjunction with the natural depressions in the very local topography to give protection over much more limited areas, as was achieved by Arnold-Forster at Zennor.

Distortion of trees in exposed areas.

Temperature and the growing season
The advantage of being so far south, together with the ever-present effects of the sea in maintaining higher ambient temperatures, has potential

significance for the growth of plants. The growing season starts earlier, and lasts considerably longer than elsewhere. The primary and crucial factor in plotting this assessment is the occurrence of the 'first day of spring'. It is the received wisdom that this date is the date at which plant growth will begin and be sustained. It is usually accepted that this is when the average ambient temperature reaches 5°C. In west Cornwall, this average date is normally assessed, in climatological statistics, as the fourteenth day of February.

Second, the maintenance of a temperature level above this base determines the season available for growth – i.e., the length of the growing season. For the western half of Cornwall, long-term climatological tables – which are averages – show this to exceed 300 days, which means that in favoured locations, the growing season could be longer, and indeed may not cease at all.

Latitude and day-length

Although the southerly latitudes of the far south-west – the southerly tip of The Lizard peninsula clips the fiftieth parallel, and the Isles of Scilly lie below it – bring obvious benefits of improved light intensity, and hence higher temperatures, the often unrecognised benefit to the successful growth of the warmer-climate exotics is provided by the reduction in variation between the extremes in the cycle of annual day-length.

This feature is probably more significant in its relation to winter day-lengths, for even on Midwinter Day it is still light enough, in plant terms, for the day-length to exceed eight hours (conversely the length of the dark period is less than 16 hours). This figure is normally critical, as it is often a contributory factor in triggering the onset of dormancy, or a dormant-like condition. The converse scenario is that on Midsummer Day, the day-length is shorter than up-country, especially north of the Border. However, the sum of these differences constitutes a more even growth pattern in these southern latitudes.

The most noticeable advantage for many of these less-hardy and evergreen subjects is the increase in the setting of flower buds engendered by this conditioning, which is seen to consider able advantage in the greater flowering potential of such genera as *Camellia* and the Asiatic species of *Mahonia*.

Temperature and the incidence of frost

What really limits the suitability of a particular site for growing less hardy plants is the susceptibility of a particular subject to low temperatures, and the duration of those temperatures.

Generally speaking, plants are hardy – i.e., can withstand freezing temperatures – or they are not: there is very little grey area. It is not easy to summarize the physiological conditions that enable frost-hardiness, but this depends principally on a plant's ability to develop 'antifreeze' in its cells, which is achieved by the increase of soluble materials in the cell sap – usually sugars. This is triggered by the advent of short days, and lowering temperature, and is most obvious in deciduous

Mahonia benefits from winter day-lengths exceeding eight hours in the far south-west.

plants. The depth of temperature drop that can be withstood by a plant depends on the degree to which this ability is developed.

It is not unusual for some plants from the cooler areas of, say, Mediterranean climates to survive transient frost – i.e., a degree or two for an hour or so around dawn – and this is probably more attributable to their leaf structure. In nature, although an unusually severe frost may kill off part of the stem system, these plants will regrow as long as the root system has not been damaged, and some stem buds survive.

The incidence of frost in a Cornish garden is less easy to categorize, but more than any other feature of the local climate, it is the limiting factor in what may be grown successfully.

Cold temperature, which causes freezing, may be delivered by a cold, below-freezing wind, usually from the north, but also often from the east. Alternatively, and not uncommonly, freezing temperature occurs as a result of radiation conditions. On still, clear nights when the surface of the earth loses heat fairly quickly to the upper atmosphere, this loss continues until after daybreak, when the temperature begins to rise in the sun. If the amount of heat loss causes the surface tempera-

Camellia 'Drama Girl': plants from subtropical climates benefit from year-round rainfall and relatively high humidity.

ture to drop below freezing, then we have a radiation frost. If this surface happens to be a leaf or a stem, and unless the plant has 'antifreeze', disruption and death of the tissues ensue, the degree of damage depending on the level of penetration.

In Cornwall the ever-present sea helps to mitigate the occurrence of these frosts, by contributing heat to, and reducing the cooling loss from, the immediate land surface. Distance from the sea, and aspect in relation to the sea, are therefore of paramount importance. Yet the prediction of frost incidence for a particular site is difficult, and occurrence may vary from year to year; but within reasonable limits it is possible to predict the likelihood. However, none of this takes into account freak years when severe cold may occur at critical times, and at unexpectedly low temperatures – as happened in April 1891, when the Great Blizzard affected the whole of Cornwall and south Devon, and caused very considerable damage;

and in April 1987, when a severe frost crippled the Isles of Scilly and west Cornwall. The critical feature was not just the low temperature, but that it occurred when plants were in their full spate of soft growth, and therefore at their most susceptible, whether hardy or not. It might be expected that such occurrences in midwinter would not be so damaging. All in all, the incidence of frost is the most unpredictable of all the parameters that are to be considered.

Temperature and global warming

Any discussion of gardening in the future ought to take account of the trends of climate, and in this context the effect of global warming cannot be ignored.

Although it is fairly self-evident that the south-west benefits from generally higher ambient temperatures than the rest of the UK, the features that allow warmer winter temperatures also keep the summer temperatures from reaching the extremes experienced further east in the country, and so provide a more equable and advantageous climate.

However, dealing in straightforward averages often misses the point, as the climate tends to be cyclical, both in the short term and in the longer term. It is fair to say that the last decade, since the early 1990s, has been generally warmer than the longer-term averages, but whether this is a reflection of a general, longer-term, warming trend, or part of a 'normal', short- or medium-term cycle is difficult to know. It may be part of a more significant, longer-term, man-made global warming pattern, but this is still very much a subject for debate, as the trend has not yet had time to provide any conclusive manifestation. Have we forgotten about the drought of the mid 1970s, or the cold winters of the late 1970s and early 1980s? These were very much exceptions to the general trend, and created much discussion concerning the future!

It is difficult to predict what would happen in Cornwall if the pattern of warming continued for a longish period. It is not sufficient to say that the climate would get warmer – although strictly this might be true – because this might unleash the possibility of drastic changes in weather patterns. The severity of the extremes might increase, together with the likelihood of increased winter rainfall and storms. Alternatively, it is postulated that the climate could become colder as a result of the melting of the polar ice-cap, and the increasing southward movement of cold water could cause a substantial change in the pattern of the North Atlantic Drift – the Gulf Stream – leaving the west coast with climatic conditions more like those experienced at present in Norway.

All of this has implications for gardening on the edge in the medium term. Will the climate warm, and if so what are the implications for weather patterns; or will the climate cool? It is anyone's guess!

Rainfall and humidity

Year-round rainfall and conditions of relatively high humidity are both an advantage and a disadvantage when it comes to selecting the palette of suitable plants. It is obviously of benefit for plants from warmer areas with high rainfall, such as New Zealand, and for those from subtropical climates – particularly the lower reaches of the Himalayas and south-western China, such as *Rhododendron* and *Camellia* – but is less suitable for those from Mediterranean-type climates, which experience only winter rainfall naturally. Such plants often have grey foliage – *Lavandula*, *Phlomis*, and *Santolina*, for example – and do not appreciate water on their leaves. However, in exposed situations the effects of high rainfall may well be mitigated by the drying effects of the wind.

The amount of rainfall experienced in Cornwall varies with the topography: up on the moors it can be quite high, while down west it may be drier; but even here, the average rainfall is from 100cm to 110cm. Again, averages mask short-term trends, and since the early 1990s, it has not been uncommon to see totals as high as 150cm per annum. This relatively high rainfall causes leaching of soluble materials, such as lime, from the soil, and so acidic soils with low nutrient levels are the norm in the county.

Conclusions

What conclusions can be drawn from these observations? Undoubtedly, almost all of Cornwall has some climatic advantage in terms of gardening on the edge; but one cannot be dogmatic about the site, nor about the position or apparent hardiness of any particular plant. The occurrence of favoured niches or, indeed, microniches is virtu-

ally unpredictable: the only recommendation can be to observe, to experiment, and to be brave! One example that typifies this approach is a specimen of *Lonicera hildebrandiana* (the Giant Burmese honeysuckle), which has flourished and flowered profusely on a pergola in the Melon Yard at Heligan since 1996.

The emphasis in the practice of gardening as we see it today in the far south-west began in the grounds of the large country houses towards the end of the eighteenth century. Collection and hybridization were encouraged and sponsored by the owners. Families like the Foxes, Williams, and Tremaynes had the money to indulge their interests, and are examples of those who were pre-eminent in this field. By the Edwardian era and into the 1930s, smaller country houses had joined the fraternity; and after the Second World War this interest trickled down to the larger village and suburban gardens, as the general wealth of the population began to increase. The trend accelerated from the 1960s, and continues day.

The Giant Burmese honeysuckle, *Lonicera hildebrandiana*.

This interest in gardening, fuelled by improved incomes and the leisure to indulge it, has provided the impetus for the massive collection and importation of plants into the UK in recent years. Among these has been an extraordinary variety of what are regarded, in this country, as less hardy subjects, and which are therefore more difficult to manage in general cultivation, except in favoured localities such as Cornwall. Thus this book carries on a tradition in which Cornwall continues to be gardening on the edge.

1 Gardening at the Edge of the Sea

Peter Clough

Two threads have drawn me through life. The first, and strongest, has been the desire to be always with plants. Plants connect everything, and everything depends on them. I have no doubt that plants are the most important living things on Earth. To plants, I hope, I will remain a humble servant. The other thread has been that which draws me to the edge of the sea. I have been captured by wild coastlines, and I have never wished to escape. This thread was strong enough to pull me away from the wonders of fields of bog asphodel on the West Pennine Moors to seek my good fortune in gardens on the Isle of Gigha in the Hebrides, followed by a sojourn on Tresco in the Isles of Scilly, then a return to Scotland at Inverewe in the empty lands of the North-West Highlands. Currently I farm and garden, as a hopeful traveller, on the savage, beautiful cliffs of West Penwith in Cornwall. Always plant-led, and always drawn to the coast.

Left: *Libertia*, *Brachyglottis*, and *Griselinia* established happily in wild, windswept Cornish moorland.

Agapanthus on the beach, Tresco, Isles of Scilly.

Choices

Let us consider the alternatives for those lucky enough to live in sight of the sea who, like me, have the need to surround themselves and live with plants. There are two courses for those wishing to develop seaside gardens: the first is to plant shelter to try to remove the effects of salty winds on desirable plants; the second is to use only plants capable of standing coastal situations without shelter.

The provision of shelter

The provision of shelter of the first course does allow a wider range of plants to be grown which, although usually benefiting from the generally milder climate of the coast in winter, are actually not suited to the limitations of normal coastal conditions, particularly salt-laden gales and sandblasting. It is curious that the most famed coastal gardens of the British Isles rely on these dense salt- and wind-combing shelterbelts to enable them to grow glorious spring-flowering plants native to sheltered valleys a hundred or a thousand miles from the sea. In such gardens, particularly in Cornwall, natural topography of the land was used in addition to the provision of shelter, and deep valley sites running down to the sea were favoured. *Rhododendron, Magnolia, Camellia* – these were the exciting genera that Victorian estate-owners were desperate to grow – all with only a few members that, in the wild, have to cope with high winds, let alone high salt concentrations. Our coastline is ringed by great woodland gardens formed against the odds by determined – and often eccentric – owners, all planting shelter against the winds to allow them to grow their favoured woodland choices, and often, because of the protecting shelterbelts, sacrificing their views of the ever-changing sea. The names have made British coastal woodland gardens famed throughout the world: we are, in the British Isles – and sometimes even the tourist boards forget it – the envy of the civilized garden world. Names like Penjerrick and Caerhays, Inverewe and Muncaster, Ilnacullin and Dereen, Brodick and Benmore, Gigha and Colonsay, are held in greater awe and reverence in California or New York than in Scotland or London. Ever since the 1790s, plant-crazy British garden-builders have set the world standard for the temperate coastal woodland garden. We visit now, and wonder at, these creations in their glorious maturity, and sometimes remember how lucky we are not to have to travel thousands of miles to marvel at them.

A hedge of *Escallonia macrantha* provides shelter.

Writers

Many writers have contributed to the subject of coastal shelter. In my journey of discovery I have found the three books of Christine Kelway (1962, 1965, 1970) very helpful, and Fred Shepherd's RHS Handbook, *Seaside Gardening* (1990) is concise, practical, and excellent. An American book, *Hedges, Screens and Windbreaks*, by Donald Wyman (1938), is interesting for its insight into New World garden thinking. J.M. Caborn's *Shelterbelts and Windbreaks* (1965) is fascinatingly scientific, full of technical value on both the climate's effects on plants, and garden choices, as are the reports of the Rosewarne Horticultural Research Station – now sadly defunct – on their experimental work on coastal shelterbelts for Cornish growers. W. Arnold-Forster's brilliant *Shrubs for the Milder Counties*, first published in 1948, is still, over 50 years on, the ultimate gospel for the aspiring coastal gardener anywhere in the temperate world. All these works list suggested species suitable for wind and salt defences for those who wish to keep their garden treasures from the rigours of the sea.

The early days

Coastal gardeners who decide to employ sheltered strategies in their garden plantings nowadays can, and should, draw on the experience of 200 years of trial and tribulation by the builders of the great gardens that ring our coastline. Remember too that they had no prior experience to draw on in determining their planting choices for shelter from the sea. Study their successes and apply their methods of observation – nature itself has all the answers. Osgood Mackenzie at Inverewe, for example, saw that native gorse produced enough shelter by the sea, even in impoverished soil, to allow less salt-resistant plants to establish themselves inside its defences. So he scattered gorse seed around his coastal perimeter. He noticed that native Scots pine grew occasionally very close to the sea, so behind the establishing gorse he planted seedlings of the Caledonian pine. 'If Scots pine grows, will other pine species be successful?', he asked himself, and obtained and tested any other pine species he could lay his hands on at that time (1853), from all over the world. Behind and among the gorse frontline he selected the Mountain pine, *Pinus mugo*, to form the shelter for the next row of taller-growing pines selected from the maritime Corsican pine, *P. nigra* ssp. *maritima*, and the tough,

slower-growing Austrian pine, *P. nigra* ssp. *nigra*, which proved over the years to be totally wind-hardy and brilliantly salt-resistant. Later, following the lead of Tresco and the gardens of southern Ireland, the windbreaks were further strengthened by the addition of salt-resistant coastal plants from the Southern hemisphere – particularly *Griselinia littoralis* from New Zealand; and *Drimys lanceolata*, and *Escallonia macrantha* from the wild coasts of Chile around Cape Horn. Osgood Mackenzie's pioneering work was continued after his death by his daughter Mairi who, after reading Arnold-Forster's recommendations from Cornwall, continued the good work by the addition of two front-line defenders from New Zealand – *Olearia traversii* and *O. macrodonta*.

From 1834 onwards, on the island of Tresco in the Isles of Scilly, Augustus Smith had looked to the equally wild Pacific coast of California for his windbreak trees and, with slightly milder win-

Osgood Mackenzie's Scots pine windbreak, protecting the garden at Inverewe from westerly gales.

Pinus thunbergii clings to the rocks on the coast of Japan.

ter winds, achieved almost instant success with his chosen defenders – the Monterey pine, *Pinus radiata*, and the Monterey cypress, *Cupressus macrocarpa*. Both are quick to establish and fast-growing, and proved to be immensely successful in the milder climates of the west coast gardens. In less favoured climates, a coastal planting in sand-dunes on the Culbin sands of Morayshire using the Beach pine, *Pinus contorta* – the coastal form of Lodgepole pine – soon proved the value of this species for both successful quick coastal windbreaks, and the stabilization of moving sand-dunes. Experience has shown that its phenomenal growth rate can result in a later lack of stability in high winds, but the species has enormous value as a nurse plant to protect slower-growing, but longer-lived windbreak plants in their early, more vulnerable years of establishment.

Some of the finest coastal plantings in Britain were stimulated by the need for gardens to attract tourists to coastal holiday resorts. Here hedges, shelterbelts, and windbreaks were often needed to afford protection from the winds off the sea – not only for the benefit of delicate, unprofitable plants, but also for the delicate and definitely profitable visitors coming to admire them. As

early as the 1830s, the Fox family of Falmouth in Cornwall realized that the milder coastal climate allowed plantings of a more exotic nature to be used to delude visitors into feeling they were holiday-makers in a 'subtropical' paradise. At Rosehill garden (now Fox Rosehill Gardens) in Falmouth, their experimental work formed the foundations of the 'Cornish Riviera' image, and before long the palm-fringed promenades of Torbay were started, ready for Mr Brunel to deliver the visitors on his wonderful Great Western Railway. Further east, the great resorts also wished to plant colourful coastal gardens, and here different shelter choices were made, using slightly hardier hedges and shelterbelts. The trees they selected needed to be extra tough to deal with the colder winds from the English Channel. The Maritime pine, *Pinus pinaster*, proved a popular choice in the south coast resorts, as did *P. strobus*, the Yellow pine, better known now as the Weymouth pine, due to its frequent use in coastal Dorset. In the holiday resorts of the south-east and east coast, the greater wind chill factors demanded a little more hardiness in hedge plant selection, and popular choices were the supreme coastal hedge champion *Elaeagnus × ebbingei*; two of the toughest olearias – *Olearia*

× *haastii* and *O. avicenniifolia*; and the salt- and wind-invincible *Euonymus japonicus* from the windy coasts of Japan. These plants provided the foundation for garden shelter by the sea: none has outlived its usefulness, and mercifully their use and value have not been influenced by garden fashion changes advocated by the somewhat mephistophelean persuasions of today's garden media.

The twentieth and twenty-first centuries

Interest in finding new acquisitions to help deal with the adverse effects of salt winds did not diminish after the nineteenth century. Newer plants to add to the coastal gardener's armoury are still appearing and proving their merit. Good examples are two pines of great value: *Pinus muricata*, the Bishop pine from British Columbia, which has proved immensely valuable, due to its spreading branches supporting the plant, as it were, 'on its elbows', and making it particularly difficult to be blown over sideways by the strongest winds; and *P. thunbergii*, the Japanese Black pine, which shares with Austrian pine the gale-proof advantage of a vast spreading root system, and is particularly useful in difficult, shallow soils on cliffs. It is the classic pine of Japanese paintings, clinging so dramatically to vertical rock faces. Its stalwart qualities in severe exposure can be seen on the rocky tip of St Michael's Mount, where it is planted in a suitably dramatic place. When I lived on the Isles of Scilly, I used to describe their geographical location as a half-mile within the warm temperate zone of the world. This, at least, may explain why here is the only place in the British Isles to grow successfully one of the great flowering trees of the world, the Pohutukawa, *Metrosideros excelsus*, from the North

Metrosideros excelsus, from North Island, New Zealand.

Island of New Zealand, where it grows happily on rocks and shores, even overhanging the high-tide line. On Tresco, the scarlet of its late July flower can be seen from St Mary's two miles away. Its salt- and gale-resistance are equally phenomenal, and it has been selected on Tresco as a major windbreak replacement for the ageing remnants of Augustus Smith's original windbreaks of Monterey pine.

At Inverewe, 600 miles north, it is not warm enough in winter to grow Pohutukawa to any respectable age, but here gardeners discovered the sheltering qualities of another spectacular *Metrosideros* from the cooler South Island – the Southern rata *M. umbellata*, which also possesses great salt- and wind-tolerance, and is highly recommended for future coastal shelter on the western perimeters of the coastline of the British Isles from Land's End to Cape Wrath. Another surprising discovery at Inverewe was the success, as a coastal windbreak in severe exposure, of the beautiful natural hybrid *Olearia* 'Henry Travers' – one of many fine introductions from the Chatham Islands by Major A.A. Dorrien-Smith of Tresco in 1911.

A garden in severe exposure: St Michael's Mount, Cornwall.

Brachyglottis rotundifolia planted on a rocky shelf high on a moor in west Cornwall.

Choosing plants for shelter

Anyone interested in the tolerance of coastal garden plants should read Arnold-Forster's writings. He gardened at Eagles Nest, perched above Zennor on the north coast of west Cornwall in the teeth of the elements, lashed annually by 100 m.p.h. salt gales of full Atlantic fury. His philosophy has become mine over the last 40 years of dodging the wind: seek out the plants that actually prefer to be in exposure. A good example would be yet another fine New Zealand coastal plant, *Brachyglottis rotundifolia*. Its thick, leathery leaves are perfectly adapted to windy conditions. At Eagles Nest it moulds into low domes that almost follow the landscape; it forms tight, hard clumps, and the wind has to go around it or be slowed down. On the Isle of Gigha I made the mistake of planting it in sheltered woodland. I thought it deserved it – its foliage was so beautiful. Every plant in the favoured shelter grew lank and tall, pined away, and died. The lesson? Choose plants for shelter that seem to despise not being exposed to cruel winds: avoid the prima ballerinas of the Himalayan valleys – their petal tutus blow off, and they suffer terribly from the cold draughts blowing around their knees. Leave it to the likes of the pines and olearias – they are the tough guys.

Plants that can withstand coastal situations without shelter

With so many fine examples of gardens by the sea protected by magnificent shelterbelts, it is not surprising that people with more modest aspirations of building their personal paradises feel that hedges, fences, and shelterbelts are essential to the successful planning of a coastal garden. But this is not necessarily the case, unless the garden-owner wishes to specialize in the plants whose natural habitat is in sheltered woodland situations. Gardening at the edge of the sea does not need to be based on a woodland theme, and it is by no means compulsory to be extravagantly exotic. It could be argued that anyone living within sight of the sea should be prepared to share the storms and furnish the garden with plants that endure the onslaught.

British coastal plants

Anyone with a love of plants who walks the shores of the British Isles knows that the native flora of the foreshore, sand-dunes and cliffs provides seasonal flowering spectaculars enough to grace any garden. Proximity to the sea brings superb light intensity and brilliance of colour. Natural coastal plants have evolved to survive the conditions of wind and salinity that shelterbelts attempt to reduce, and there is a clear logic in choosing them in the hope of successful establishment in gardens by the sea. So let's walk the British coastal path to find the sane first choices for a British seaside garden. The clues are easy – sea campion, sea-kale, sea heath, sea-pea, sea holly, sea milkwort, sea bindweed, sea lavender, sea-pink, sea buckthorn, sea spleenwort – all British natives with particu-

Sea bindweed, growing in sand.

Wild asparagus, Kynance Cove, The Lizard, south Cornwall.

shores, as well as becoming one of our most frequent denizens of bedding schemes.

There is a quite understandable belief that all the plants we use in our rock gardens are plants from high Alpine regions. In fact, many are coastal plants, often from the Mediterranean shores, and even, in some cases, from our own shores. Anyone growing *Frankenia laevis*, for example, could be forgiven for imagining its grey-green mats of needles studded with pink flowers gracing mountain ledges, but it is actually a coastal plant of sand and salt marshes from Kent to Norfolk. It would be most interesting to construct a rock garden by the sea using only native coastal plants, or indeed to build a native heather garden using varieties discovered in the wild close to the coast. This would include the dwarf forms of *Calluna*

lar qualities in different coastal situations. In the botanical Latin of plant nomenclature, *maritima* gives similar confirmatory clues, as does *littoralis* – 'of the seashore'. *Armeria*, *Crambe*, *Eryngium*, *Glaux*, *Otanthus*, and *Mertensia* all provide us with native *maritima* choices, as does *Asplenium* with *marinum*. Apart from these tough coast-lovers, whose names proclaim their delight in growing by the sea, there are a host of other garden-worthy natives that feature in the rich tapestry of flowering plants around our shores. The lesser celandine, *Ranunculus ficaria*, thrives in coastal grasslands, and would enrich any exposed coastal garden. It is available in many selected garden forms: *The RHS Plant Finder* lists over 70 garden forms with wonderful names like 'Coppernob', 'Jane's Dress', 'Fried Egg', 'Double Mud', and even a choice between 'Brazen Hussy' and 'Coy Hussy'. The horned or sea poppy, *Glaucium flavum*, loves sand and salt, and has large, bright flowers of yellow or orange, jagged foliage, and most unusual seed-heads, each like the twisted horn of a unicorn. In similar sandy situations grow two British species of the genus *Matthiola*, better known to all as 'stocks', which were developed by the plant breeders to produce the many garden forms, all carrying the wonderful scent of the wild sea stocks and all, hardly surprisingly, thriving in sand by the sea. The British flora is beset with what could be described as 'legal immigrants', many imported by the Romans from the Mediterranean. The common 'sweet alyssum', *Alyssum maritimum*, for example, has established itself on sea-

Wild chives growing on the cliffs above Soapy Cove, The Lizard, south Cornwall.

Nature's garden: thrift on the edge of the sea, The Lizard, south Cornwall.

a typical example: commonly found next to the sea; usually associated with poor, rocky soils; even standing salt-water immersion twice a day in salt marshes in the inter-tidal zone, and also found again on similarly poor soils on mountain screes between 600 and 1,000m. As a garden plant, thrift is easy and free flowering, as long as it is not coddled in any way, and given full Spartan exposure to sun, drought, and wind. One of the best garden sights of Newquay in Cornwall is a stone Cornish 'hedge' outside a small house where every crevice is covered in sea-pinks, providing in May a flowering spectacle that certainly equals many more exotic wall plantings. At Inverewe a splash-zone rock garden was built just above the high-water mark, exploiting the beauty and hardiness of this, and many other examples of the sharers of mountain and seaside habitats. Others used here were *Silene acaulis*, the moss campion found on Britain's highest mountain ridges, and by the sea in the Shetland Islands. Much rarer, and a much greater challenge in cultivation, is the very beautiful *Oxytropis uralensis*, a purple-flowered vetch relation found in the Ural Mountains, and also, very surprisingly, in Britain in cliff-top grassland on the north coast of Scotland around Dunnet Head, growing alongside one of Britain's rare endemics, the tiny *Primula scotica*. Mountain avens, *Dryas octopetala*, occurs on both high limestone plateaux and alkaline coastal machair. *Potentilla fruticosa* is a commonly planted shrub in British gardens, with many garden cultivars. Few gardeners know that this is a British native plant from high moorland Teesdale, but also found coastally in south-west Ireland, yet another native addition for our coastal heather garden.

vulgaris from St Kilda, and the many selections from the south-west of the Cornish heath, *Erica vagans*, and the Dorset heath, *E. ciliaris*, together with Miss Waterer's delightful *E. cinerea* 'Eden Valley', and all the hybrid finds of P.D. Williams and D.F. Maxwell. These, together with the prostrate coastal form of *Juniperus communis*, which grows 'a stone's throw from the sea' near Lizard Point, and the flat coastal form of gorse, *Ulex* 'Mizzen Head', from the south-west tip of Ireland, would produce a garden of native species by the sea to emulate the famous Heather Gardens of Wisley, or even Adrian Bloom's so aptly named Foggy Bottom in deepest Norfolk.

Gardeners near the sea can exploit in their rock gardens the similarity of habitat experienced by plants of mountain ledges, screes, and rocks with the maritime conditions of the seashore or sea cliffs. The clues here are the surprisingly large number of species in the British flora that appear in both mountain and coastal habitats. Thrift is

Potentilla fruticosa – a native of high moorland Teesdale.

Geranium maderense with *Echium candicans.*

Plantings from other shores

Few gardeners in Britain would wish to confine their choices to British natives alone, especially when there are so many cool temperate coastlines around the world to increase immeasurably the available plant diversity. Our gardens are enriched with these treasures from other shores. The Atlantic coastline brings us wonderful salt- and wind-resistant plants from Brittany, Spain, and Portugal, together with plants from the maritime island floras of the Canary Islands, Madeira,

and the Azores, many of which are well established in coastal gardens in the milder counties of the British Isles. Many of our most aromatic garden plants, and so many of our herbs, grow naturally on the shores of the Mediterranean. North America offers plants of its western seaboard from Alaska to mid-California, and Japan's coastal plants offer further choices. The Southern hemisphere adds enormously to the variety. New Zealand and Tasmania have produced an enormous range of the most salt- and wind-resistant plants imaginable, and the bulk of the finest plants for coastal shelter. Chile and Argentina have presented us with a range of suitable plants for our gardens by the sea – Tierra del Fuego and the Falkland Islands are rich in low-growing plants for real wind exposure. Another rich contributor to our coastal gardens has been South Africa – particularly Cape Province – which has provided so many colourful challenges to our mildness, many with surprising hardiness now they have become acclimatized and are selected for hardiness.

New Zealand coastal plants

New Zealand has a maritime climate much like our own, and since their relatively late introduction to gardens in the Northern hemisphere towards the end of the nineteenth century, its plants have provided a terrific range of wind- and salt-tolerant hedge and shelter plants for gardens by the sea. Their importance in sheltering crops from the effects of wind and salt, particularly in the south-west, allowed the development of the daffodil industry on the Isles of Scilly and the Cornish coast. Shelter plants such as *Olearia traversii*, *Griselinia littoralis*, and *Pittosporum crassifolium* enclose the tiny fields, allowing more delicate plants to thrive against the odds.

Kniphofia, from South Africa, growing in coastal grassland, 10m from the sea, on St Michael's Mount, Cornwall.

Olearia 'Talbot de Malahide' shelters a garden on the north Cornish coast.

The use of New Zealand shelter is not confined to the 'milder counties', however. Tough, leathery-leaved olearias, such as *Olearia avicenniifolia* and *O.* 'Talbot de Malahide' shelter gardens along the south coast, and even into the winter coldness of the east coast. Many of these traditional shelter plants could be used equally well to give hardy substance as single shrubs in a garden by the sea that did not seek to cut out the sea views. Among the coastal range are some of the showiest and most desirable shrubs imaginable. From the Chatham Islands, for example, *O.* 'Henry Travers' covers itself with large, daisy flowers of pale lilac with purple centres; in the full sun and exposure that it loves, it forms an attractive green- and silver-

foliage addition to any garden by the sea with maritime climate advantage. A little more tender is *O. chathamica*, with larger flowers. Olearia in general are white-flowered, and include some whiter than white, like the disputedly named *O.* × *scilloniensis* – now regarded as a form of *O. stellulata* – and some of the finest white-flowered garden shrubs in glories like *O. cheesemanii*, and the fine-foliaged *O. macrodonta* – musk-scented, and tough as old boots. The hard, sinuate leaves of *O. paniculata* are a wonderful light green colour, which goes well with the colours of the sea. *Olearia* also provide us with perfectly formed smaller garden shrubs, such as *O. moschata*, and the many forms of *O. nummulariifolia*, with leaves as hard as nails, and a salt-resistance second to none. Another brilliant success in the teeth of any gale is *O. solandri*, with tiny hard leaves, and small cream flowers, growing to 2m high and providing perfect wind protection.

Griselinia littoralis, with its clean, apple-green foliage, does not always need to be cut to form a hedge, and as a specimen can provide a handsome, shapely tree in the teeth of the winds. It can also be used as a significant accent plant in its striking variegated forms, such as *G.* 'Bantry Bay'. There is another rare species not often seen in Britain – *Griselinia lucida*, with larger leaves shining with gloss, and known in New Zealand as the 'Maori Looking-glass Tree'.

Alongside the olearias, New Zealand has given our gardens the glories of the genus *Brachyglottis* – still probably better known as the shrubby senecios, with the aptly named, grey-foliaged *B.* 'Sunshine' surely the brightest, and certainly the most cheerful yellow-flowered shrub for the normal sunny garden, and one of the most reliable shrubs for successful flowering by the sea. There are other, more compact forms, and the wavy, silver-edged foliage of *B. monroi* is especially attractive for the frosted rims of its leaves. For those wishing to push the climate to

Olearia 'Henry Travers' covered with large, daisy-like flowers.

the extreme, try *Brachyglottis repanda*, the 'Rangiora', whose large leaves with white, felted backs led to its odd epithet – the 'Maori Postcard Tree': apparently it was used for inscribing messages in charcoal. Don't scoff: I have sent a stamped, addressed leaf successfully through the British post – so it does work! It is surprising that such a large-leaved shrub can stand salty winds, but it is a coastal native and will take full exposure.

Hymenanthera crassifolia is a low-spreading, densely foliaged shrub that grows tightly by the sea, bearing small yellow flowers that place it surprisingly in the violet family. *Muehlenbeckia complexa* is immensely successful as a coastal plant – a brilliant sand-binder, but its tiny leaves are carried on wiry, pliable stems that can overpower anything it touches. In the Isles of Scilly, on St Mary's it expanded over a tangled, impenetrable acre down to the edge of the sea, and its wiry stems will stop the most powerful chainsaw in seconds, as it winds around the drive shaft. On Tresco, it climbed and almost obliterated a 12m Holm oak, known, from its strange mushroom shape, as the 'Atom Bomb'. You have been warned! Two fine-leaved myrtles from New Zealand are excellent in coastal conditions: *Lophomyrtus bullata* has, as its name suggests, hard 'bullate', or puckered leaves of pale green, which can stand fierce gales; *L. obcordata* makes a neat, wiry shrub with delightful, small spatulate leaves. These have hybridized to produce the more often used garden forms of *Lophomyrtus* × *ralphii*, which include the delights of the variegated 'Versicolor' and 'Gloriosa'; the bronzy, puckered foliage of 'Kathryn', and the purple-foliaged 'Red Dragon' – all great recent additions to the foliar armoury of the garden.

Another group of hard-leaved, handsome-foliaged shrubs and trees consists of *Neopanax* and *Pseudopanax*, which have shown considerable coastal tolerance in the south-west, as have the members of the genus *Corokia*, best known in British gardens from *C. cotoneaster*, aptly named the 'wire-netting bush' from its intricate tangle of branches carrying narrow, grey-backed leaves. Another coastally rewarding genus is *Coprosma*, now available in many coloured foliage cultivars to suit the smaller garden. *Coprosma repens* is suitable for only the mildest winter climates, but perfect by the sea: it forms close-packed, salt-resistant, low bushes with supremely glossy leaves, which shine and flash, reflecting the sunshine.

New Zealand coastlines also offer our gardens by the sea some lovely perennial plants. *Geranium traversii*, with white flowers, and *G. traversii* var. *elegans*, with pink flowers, would grace any coastal rock-garden, as would a lovely white gentian, *Gentiana saxosa*, which thrives a couple of metres from the high-tide line at Inverewe. We tried it first unsuccessfully on a woodland peat bank, where other high mountain gentians grew happily, but where it soon let us know its distaste, pining as it was for the salt and sand of its native New Zealand beach.

Pseudopanax crassifolius.

'Halo-' as a prefix indicates salt tolerance, as in halophytes (salt-marsh plants, such as *Salicornia*), and the succulent foliage of *Haloragis erecta*, particularly in the bronze-pink-leaved form 'Wellington Bronze', which makes an excellent contribution by the sea. It is used unusually, and as far as I know, uniquely, at Pine Lodge Gardens near St Austell, in Cornwall, as a low-growing hedge, surely the softest hedge possible. *Haloragis* is the type genus for the family Haloragaceae, which includes the genus *Gunnera*, best known for the giant-leaved *G. manicata* from the swamps of Brazil, which is definitely not a good choice for windy positions by the sea. But New Zealand does have two other dwarf species of *Gunnera*, which there inhabit sand-dunes. *G. arenaria* forms dense mats of small, attractive leaves, and *G. hamiltonii* forms slate-grey mats of foliage, and carries superb spikes of red berries in late summer. It is a rare and endangered plant in the wild – difficult

New Zealand scree garden, with *Olearia stellulata*.

to believe when you see it surviving and spreading magnificently by the sea at Inverewe, 10,000 miles away from its native home.

Fuchsia one would normally associate with South America, and *Fuchsia magellanica* is certainly one of nature's greatest flowering gifts to the coastal gardener. But New Zealand shares the genus, providing evidence of a common origin before the shifting of the continents of Gondwanaland, and *Fuchsia procumbens* crawls in turf at the sea edge, bearing dark red and purple tubular flowers, and tolerating, like the sea-pinks, a twice-daily immersion in salt water. One of its great features is the bright blue pollen borne freely on its anthers – reputedly used by Maori maidens as eye-shadow, and so doubly valuable to grow for the reduction in cosmetic bills! The other fuchsias from New Zealand are larger and more normal, but *Fuchsia excortica* forms a small tree with most attractive pale brown, flaking, peeling bark, and is also good by the sea.

One of the finest of prostrate berrying plants, *Nertera depressa*, the bead plant, comes from the New Zealand coast where, in coastal turf, it produces its complete cover of red or orange berries

in late summer. Another good coastal sprawler is *Pimelea prostrata*, a tight shrub with silky, hairy flowers and white or red berries rather like those of the yew tree.

Occurring in New Zealand both coastally and in the high mountains, the genus *Celmisia* offers many challenges, and many great beauties to the coastal gardener. The fine, silver foliages, and their purest white daisy flowers look well by the sea, especially when planted in rough scree. Their nomenclature is a minefield, confusing particularly because of their tendency to hybridize. At Inverewe I had a collection of 30–40 recognizably different types, nearly all of which bore names that were questionable. Certain species, such as *C. coriacea*, *C. hookeri*, *C. holosericea*, and *C. semicordata*, are coastal in origin, but at Inverewe we found that the montane species were all equally salt- and wind-tolerant. *Cotula* is another tough coastal addition to the rock-garden by the sea, forming tight mats, and surviving extreme drought. *Cotula squalida* has been used as a suitable turf for aircraft landing strips in dry areas, and would make a fine lawn on dry sand.

The Chatham Island Forget-me-not, *Myosotidium hortensia*, is one of the loveliest of all perennial garden plants. It is found in the wild

Celmisia in the coastal rock-garden at Inverewe.

Myosotidium hortensia – the Chatham Island Forget-me-not.

among coastal rocks, and on sandy beach margins on only one or two of the Chatham Islands. It forms domes of large, deeply veined leaves, and carries huge clusters of large, forget-me-not blue flowers, usually in May and June. It is a challenge to grow successfully, and is usually placed in some shelter, but Mairi Sawyer at Inverewe established it close by the sea without protection, where it thrived for many years on its diet of seaweed and dead fish applied as a mulch whenever possible. Another New Zealand endemic well worth trying by the sea is *Jovellana sinclairii*, a small, shrubby calceolaria with creamy, purple-spotted flowers.

The shrubby veronicas, now gathered together as the genus *Hebe*, provide a host of choices for flowering shrubs by the sea, and are a major summer-flowering feature of the gardens of seaside resorts around Britain. There are over 100 species, and many garden hybrids, all of which are likely to succeed by the sea, and tolerate salt- and wind-blasting. There is a wide flowering colour range

of white, purple, pink, and blue, and a habit range from ground-hugging to 3–4m high. They are all evergreen, with foliage of every hue from silver-grey, through emerald green, to reds, deep purples, and bronzes. There are fine variegated forms. The group with reduced sized leaves, known as the 'Whip-cord hebes', are found naturally in mountain habitats, but are perfect for difficult positions close to the sea. Of the larger-leaved hebes, the most naturally coastal species are *H. elliptica*, *speciosa*, and *salicifolia*, but all species and cultivars are worth trying. In Allan's *Flora of New Zealand* (1961), the habitat of *H. chathamica* is described as 'maritime cliffs, where there is a maximum of spray'. What better qualifications could there be for its inclusion in the wildest of coastal gardens? And what a lovely plant anyway – it forms dense ground cover with pure white flowers.

Previous mention has been made of the 'Rata', *Metrosideros excelsus*. Try it, if you like to gamble with plant hardiness, but the odds are very unfavourable, even in the very mildest areas. Other gambles are the 'Ngaio', *Myoporum laetum*, a great evergreen coastal tree with shelter potential in the very mildest areas, and the tree verbena, *Vitex lucens*.

The genus *Aciphylla* comprises viciously spined, wind- and salt-resistant plants very suitable for the coast. Only a few species are actually coastal in the wild, but their hard-wearing nature makes them very suitable for tough conditions by the sea. Although they look like armoured grasses – their common name is 'spear grass', or 'wild Spaniards' – they are members of the Umbelliferae, and carry flowers rather like our wild carrot. They look their best planted in loose scree with *Celmisia*, as pioneered at Inverewe.

The New Zealand rock lily, *Arthropodium cirrhatum*, is found coastally, and makes a beautiful, elegant plant, with star-like lily flowers, and strap-like, glaucous leaves. It is slightly frost tender, but has been established well in Cornwall and south-west Ireland. The best form to try is 'Matapouri Bay', which has taller flowering stems, and leaves of a bluish-grey cast.

Grasses and sedges are being used increasingly in gardens, and many are particularly suited to the coastal garden. New Zealand has provided us with two or three sedges that are excellent by the sea. *Carex comans* is low-growing, with drooping, arching leaves, which look as if they could be combed

Cordyline australis 'Purpurea'.

like hair – and this is actually quite achievable to anyone who wishes to try. In the cultivar 'Frosted Curls', the leaf-tips are of a curled blonde, providing an even more exacting hairdressing challenge. *Carex buchananii* is straight and upright, with reddish-brown foliage. It thrives in full sun and wind. Another sedge that has achieved great popularity recently is *Uncinia rubra*, with very strong red to reddish-brown foliage, which is enhanced in the high light intensity close to the sea. New Zealand abounds in beautiful strong grasses. *Chionochloa conspicua* is particularly handsome, forming tussocks over 1m high, with arched, flowering panicles to 2m high. Its flowering stems age to pure white, and can be retained through the winter until the next year's flower spikes appear.

In the forefront of the 'exotics' that gave the 'Riviera' image to the coasts of South Devon and Cornwall is the New Zealand Cabbage palm *Cordyline australis*. This used to be known as *Dracaena*, and lends its old name to the ceremonial Dracaena Avenue leading to Falmouth's beach resort. Its remarkable, honey-scented, cream-flowering clusters are stunning along the promenades and in the gardens of the south-west coast resorts. There are many colour forms and variations: 'Albertii', with yellow-striped varie-

gation; 'Purpurea', with deep purple foliage; and the excellent new selections of the Palm Farm at Torquay, including 'Torbay Dazzler', and 'Torbay Razzle-Dazzle', which is more compact and broader-leaved. *Libertia* – a member of the iris family – grows wonderfully by the sea, and New Zealand offers the lovely *L. grandiflora*, with pure white flower, *L. ixioides*, known for its bright yellow seed pods, and *L. peregrinans*, lower growing, and enjoying starvation diet in sand, which accentuates its unusual, bright orange leaf midribs.

One of New Zealand's most striking plants ideal for the coastal garden is *Phormium* – the New Zealand flax – which, in many ways, is the coastal plant *par excellence*. Growing in dry or wet conditions, withstanding salt and strong winds, and frost-hardy, these striking plants of the coast have now produced foliar variation of an enormous range of colour, and variegation, with dwarf and giant forms abounding. There are over 200 cultivar names, many of them Maori. They bring bold architectural strength to most coastal garden plantings. It would be difficult to be without them by the sea.

From the coasts of the temperate world

The extent of the New Zealand coastline is of similar scale to that of our own British Isles. I have used it in some detail to give an impression of just how much a garden choice can be generated by one coastline. The temperate coastline of the world is a thousand times greater, and beckons temptingly, but here I can attempt to give only

Fascicularia bicolor – from Tierra del Fuego.

a few examples of the potential riches of the rest. South America – particularly Chile and Argentina – has furnished many of the great tried and tested plants for growing by the sea. Escallonias, from Chile, have provided some of the best windbreaks and the showiest evergreen shrubs; and where would we be without the colourful *Fuchsia magellanica* and its variants for summer colour by the sea? Berberis, with hundreds of species and cultivars, are generally ideal by the sea. *Gaultheria mucronata* – as yet better known under its old name of *Pernettya* – produces some of the best berried shrubs with salt and wind tolerance. Growing at Inverewe, almost into the sea, is *Bolax glebaria* – tight, spiky low hummocks, with tiny cream flowers, that brought the Falklands War closer to me, seeing it at Goose Green in the television pictures. Tierra del Fuego ought to produce pretty salt- and wind-tolerant plants, and it does so spectacularly with *Fascicularia bicolor*, and *F. pitcairniifolia*, which both stand salt and blown sand brilliantly. The wonder of the flower and leaf coloration – sky-blue flowers deep in the rosette of crimson leaf bases – being produced within an inch of the high tides on St Mary's, on the Isles of Scilly, remains for me one of nature's miracles.

And then South Africa – think of the coastal delights from there: all plants natural to the sea's edge. From the sand-dunes of the Cape, agapanthus in every shade of blue and white; gladioli, and watsonia; and from the shingle beaches of the Garden Route, gazania and lampranthus. From Australia, wonderful callistemons and leptospermums, and closer to home, the plants of the true Mediterranean shores – erica, cistus, halimium, helianthemum, lavender, rosemary, and the fan palm, *Chamaerops humilis*, which accompanies them to the sea's edge.

True coastal plants on the edge

The choice of true coastal plants for coastal gardens is enormous, and spans the temperate world of both hemispheres. Choosing from them offers the best chance of success to those fortunate enough to garden by the sea. My advice to the lucky owners of coastal gardens would be to love the light, and the salt, and the wind blowing through the grasses, and to live with the plants that

Gazania – from the shingle beaches of South Africa.

thrive at the ever-changing edge, where the land meets the sea.

To me, one plant symbolizes this edge, where land plants finally give up their battle with the sea. It is the strangest of all pioneer species, and the only component in the flora of the Isles of Scilly that occurs on every island and named rocky outcrop capable of supporting higher plant life. Far out on one of the Western Rocks, it is the only species present. It is not tiny – in fact it is one of the larger of coastal perennials – with large flowers of deep pink as good as any hollyhock. It is the tree mallow, *Lavatera arborea* – the first-choice emblem for gardeners on the edge who believe anything is, or at least may be, possible.

The tree mallow – *Lavatera arborea*.

2 Recent Woody Plant Arrivals in Cornwall

Tom Hudson

It was with some trepidation that I undertook the task of compiling a list of new woodland plants in Cornwall. I have been gardening in the county only since 1987, and as the winter of 1986–7 was the coldest in some parts of Cornwall for 100 years, and we have had a run of relatively mild seasons since, I have not experienced temperatures as low as -10°C in the garden. Therefore, many of the plants mentioned in this list have survived outside since the spring of 1987.

Left: *Michelia yunnanensis.* (See page 49.)

Within the last 30 years there has been a tremendous upsurge of interest in the flora of eastern Asia. Many gardeners have had the opportunity to visit these parts, and many plants have been introduced for the first time. As a result, many plants listed in this chapter come from this region. Areas that botanical science had not reached have been the source for many of the plants that venturesome gardeners of milder counties are growing. Many of the plants mentioned in 1948 by W. Arnold-Forster in his *Shrubs for the Milder Counties* (Chapter XV 'Some Uncommon, Untried, or Tender Shrubs') were at that time untested in gardens in the west of Britain, although Cornwall had been at the forefront of new plant introductions since the great interest of the Victorian era.

Unfortunately, there has been a dramatic decline in interest in new woodland plants in Cornwall. This is the result of a number of factors: the decline in interest of owners of traditional Cornish woodland gardens; the attitude that all worthwhile plants are already in gardens; the fact that so many woodland gardens are run by committees; and the odd notion that it is more important to garnish woodlands to gain more visitors than to experimentally plant untested and new material.

But there are people who are venturesome with new plants, many of whom realize that it is not necessary to have a large area in order to create the right sheltered conditions. Hopefully this chapter will inspire more gardeners to try many beautiful but little-known plants, and to re-establish the proud record of Cornish gardeners that made the last chapter of Arnold-Forster's book such an inspiration. I shall follow his example, emphasizing mainly the species, and hope that this chapter will complement that excellent list.

Acer

There is probably no other genus of small trees that provides such variety and beauty of leaf and habit for planting as understorey trees in the sheltered woodland. Acers are happiest in sunny glades, with shelter from wind, which can damage the young growth. The short list below includes some of the more exciting species, but the keen gardener will enquire further. The taxonomy of maples is particularly confusing at present, as the latest definitive work was published without a key.

A. campbellii and its numerous subspecies form part of a group of around 30 species from eastern Asia. *A. flabellatum*, *A. wilsonii*, and *A. sinense* are all included under *A. campbellii*. They are deciduous, with from three- to seven-lobed leaves, green stems, and weeping branches. They make excellent small specimens, although in the wild they can reach 30m.

A. laevigatum is a tender, simple-leaved evergreen species from south-east Asia. It has a green stem when young, but this feature is reduced to the branches with age. *A. fabri* is a close relative, with shinier leaves and less toothing on the margins.

A. laurinum is a very showy maple, on account of its simple leaves being shiny green above, and highly glaucous below. It is a very widespread large tree in the Far Eastern tropics, but an introduction from northern Vietnam is relatively hardy, having flowered and fruited at only 3m high in Cornwall. *A. jingdongense* is a similar-looking plant, but with red petioles and larger leaves up to 15cm long.

Acer laurinum.

A. oblongum is a small, evergreen tree with simple leaves. Very unlike what is thought of as being a typical maple, the leaves are glossy green above, whitish below, and the young growth has a coppery tint. If possible, try to grow a plant from

Acer pentaphyllum.

China, as these seem to be hardier than those of Himalayan origin. Other maples in the same alliance are *A.* spp. *albopurpurascens*, *coriaceifolium*, and *paxii*.

A. pentaphyllum is a very rare maple in the wild, discovered in western China in 1929, and not seen again by botanists until the last years of the twentieth century. The outstandingly ornamental leaves are divided into five completely dissected leaflets with red petioles, which come into growth very late in the season. Tender when young.

A. sikkimense now includes *A. hookeri*, but that does not matter as any plant will be an asset to a moist spot in the woodland garden. This maple is from eastern Asia, and is tender, especially as it flushes its lovely coppery-red young leaves early. It is evergreen in a mild winter, and has a striped trunk, but is not noticeably striped on the branches.

A. wardii is a very ornamental, small, weeping tree from the Burmese-Chinese border regions. It has showy, tri-lobed leaves, with each lobe ending in a drip tip. The introductions of George Forrest proved to be tender, so it is hoped that those of more recent origins will be hardier.

Alangium

Mainly a tropical group of trees, but with two species seen in cultivation in milder zones. In the forest, they are marked by their noticeable and attractive sympodial branching habit. Both the species below prefer full sun in our maritime climate.

A. chinense tends to make only a shrub, as it is the more tender of the two. The flowers are similar to *A. platanifolium*, but have more scent, and their petals recurve fully to reveal the yellow stamens.

A. platanifolium, from the Far East, makes a small tree with variably (up to seven) lobed simple leaves, rather like a *Platanus*, as its name suggests. The white, very narrowly tubular flowers appear in cymes in summer, and make a quiet spectacle when the plant is tall enough for them to be viewed under the branches.

Alniphyllum

A. fortunei is likely to be the only hardy member of this small genus from the Far East. It has a wide distribution from south China to Korea, giving the gardener a chance to find a plant of hardy origin. It grows into a small tree up to 12m high, with whitish-grey bark, rather like some species of birch. In late spring, it produces large, showy panicles of up to 16 white flowers, which can be as much as 2.5cm across. It is an ideal foil for heavy, textured, evergreen company in the woodland.

Anneslea

A. fragrans is from the Theaceae family, and is therefore related to the camellia. It comes from subtropical regions of south-east Asia, at a reasonable altitude – which provides some measure of hardiness. Often seen in dry, even rocky positions, in open pine forest, it also occurs in moister spots. The habit is somewhat reminiscent of a *Daphniphyllum*, with clusters of leaves at the ends of branches. The white flowers occur in clusters near the ends of twigs, and form ornamental, woody, orange-red, jug-shaped fruit.

Arbutus xalapensis.

Arbutus

There are a few species in southern USA and Mexico that have been introduced recently.

A. spp. *arizonica, texana,* and *xalapensis* are all closely related and thrive in the more xerophytic nature of their origins. But this does not mean they shouldn't be tried in maritime Britain. However, any position must have full sun and a relatively free-draining soil to help ripen the wood, whence they will make small trees with terrific reddish, peeling bark, and small, dark red fruit.

Aristotelia

A group of some ten interesting species of shrubs and small trees from the Southern hemisphere.

A. chilensis, from Chile, is very similar to *A. serrata,* the New Zealand wineberry, but will stand a more exposed position. *A. macqui,* also from Chile, has small, edible fruits, which the locals use for flavouring drinks and, when sugared, as sweets.

A. peduncularis, from Tasmania, is a lax shrub with sparse flowers, larger than the preceding species and fairly hardy, even though its native habitat is damp gullies.

A. serrata is the popular wineberry from New Zealand, which likes a sheltered spot. It is a small, weeping tree, with heart-shaped leaves, and showy pink flowers in the spring. *A. fruticosa* is hardier, less ornamental, but interesting on account of its divaricated foliage – a feature of many plants from New Zealand.

Aucuba

A. omeiensis is a terrific foliage plant, closely related to *A. chinensis.* The heavy, dark green, toothed leaves can reach 30cm in length. From western China, this species can reach 5m in height. It really needs a warm spot in the garden, to prevent the leaves from yellowing, and is quite happy in shade.

Betula

The birches are an excellent group of trees for any garden, especially when planted in thickets to accentuate their bark. Of particular interest for gardeners in milder areas is the following group that belong to subgenus *Betulaster,* which are from the warm temperate areas of eastern Asia.

B. alnoides, B. cylindrostachya, and *B. luminifera* are all fast-growing, large trees in the wild, with brownish shining bark. The male catkins are very ornamental, hanging in slender small groups up to 20cm long, and appear with the leaves in early spring. The leaves and twigs contain methyl salicylate, and when crushed, emit a strong winter-green smell. It is very difficult to identify the differences in this group, and when the topic arises it is always likely to generate a lively debate among enthusiasts.

Caldcluvia

A component of evergreen forests of the Southern hemisphere, whence originate many trees and shrubs that seem to grow just as well in Cornwall as in their homelands.

C. paniculata, from Chile, looks rather like the more often encountered *Weinmannia*. It grows into a small tree in wet areas, and produces masses of fluffy white flowers in summer. *C. rosaefolia*, from New Zealand, is more tender, coming from the Kauri forests of the North Island, where it is happy in quite shady positions. It is a handsome tree, with hairy pinnate leaves and many-branched panicles of white flowers.

Camellia

In 1948, Arnold-Forster honoured the camellia with a whole chapter. Much of what was known then is applicable today. Camellias were still regarded as rather scarce and expensive, but today they are found in nearly all gardens. Many new species have been introduced, some of which are worth a more detailed description. Most of the species tend to flower in the winter, but do not mind some overhead shelter, which helps to keep away the frost. Virtually all the hardier species new to cultivation come from southern China.

C. japonica has made such an impact on gardening in the milder counties that it needs looking at separately from the other species. There has been an explosion of *C. japonica* mutations (sports), since 1948 – well over 10,000 – most of which should have been destroyed upon discovery, but the temptation to those of a train-spotting disposition to put a label on another one has been too great. This has led to far too many scarcely separable sports being labelled. However, certain breeders have created some careful selections, which are top-class woodland plants, and these should be separated from the chaff and given a shady position, in exposure or woodland, to prevent the foliage from yellowing.

C. reticulata and its hybrids are the loveliest large shrubs for the mild garden. They succeed in dappled light, but are even more at home in full sun, where the growth is much tighter and more upright. Initially, the large flowers are too big for the small bushes – especially as they are often grafted – but these plants do make small trees, and when seen flowering the proportions look splendid. There are many venerable specimens protected around temples in China, which are hundreds of years old, many of them pruned up on trunks. There is a lovely form that is pink in bud and opens white in cultivation, and this selection is ideally suited to woodland as it is rather more subtle than *C. japonica*.

Many hybrids of *C. reticulata* also have *C. saluenensis* in their parentage, which brings hardiness into the offspring. Many of these hybrids, as well as the seedlings of the straight species, originated in the USA, where fashion has tended towards a large flower size. The red-pink flowers are up to 15cm across; semi-double to peony in shape, and rather blousy when young. Careful selection is needed to avoid any with a harsh pink tone.

C. × williamsii involves a huge number of hybrids of *C. saluenensis* and *C. japonica* varieties. The resulting plants have proved to be the most reliable for the average garden in the UK. They are very free flowering, even in north-west Scotland, and their flowers tend to drop after flowering, unlike many *japonica* varieties. They are reasonably sun-tolerant, and their buds open in succession over a couple of months, giving another show if initially frosted. J.C. Williams of Caerhays was a pioneer, and his family name was given to the whole group. Several of his early hybrids are better than many registered today, and are worth seeking out. Gillian Carlyon of Tregrehan continued this Cornish tradition, and bred a number of excellent varieties. There are thousands of varieties registered, and there is a mass of literature available to the gardener who needs to sort out the desirable cultivars.

Other breeding work

Many people – initially in the USA, and latterly in Australia and New Zealand – have devoted much effort to imparting scent to camellias. Using mainly *C.* spp. *lutchuensis*, *oleifera*, *sasanqua* and *yuhsienensis*, there are now more fragrant camellias available to the gardener in mild areas, but these species are of a tender nature. The degree of success achieved has been somewhat limited so far, and the fragrance produced is mainly akin to that of a sweet pollen.

As well as fragrance, breeders in Australia and New Zealand have been using slow-growing and dwarf species to produce the so-called miniatures. These plants are ideal for gardeners with limited space, or for pot cultivation, and can be kept outside unless there is hard frost.

Camellia crapnelliana, left, and the fruit, above.

Other species

Unfortunately, none of the recently described yellow species shows any likelihood of being hardy outside, which is partly due to their insistence on growing at the times of equinox. They grow at low levels in the tropics and, sadly, attempts by hybridizers to transfer the yellow colour genes into hardier stocks have failed.

C. chekiangoleosa occurs in south-east China, in mountainous areas. It makes a large, sprawling shrub with glossy leaves and deep red flowers – a thoroughly desirable addition to a collection.

C. crapnelliana, from Hong Kong, needs a very sheltered position, but is worth a chance on account of its superb, chestnut-brown bark, and similarly coloured fruit, which reaches tennis-ball size.

C. granthamiana, another tender Hong Kong rarity, has superb large, shiny, rugose leaves, and large, poached-egg flowers in late winter.

C. grijsii makes a small tree with tough leaves. The scented flowers are delicate, white, with lobed petals in early spring.

C. irrawadiensis forms a small tree, with bright green, shiny foliage and white, scented flowers in early spring. Close to *C. taliensis*.

C. lutchuensis has particularly attractive, weeping foliage, with the young growth emerging a russet colour. The masses of fragrant flowers are exceptional in a cold greenhouse, and have attracted the hybridizers.

C. pitardii is a bush or small tree, with flowers that vary from red, through pink, to white. It occurs in certain places in north Yunnan and south Sichuan, at high elevations up to 2,800m. It is very similar to *C. reticulata*, and may justify merging.

C. rosiflora has lovely small, pale pink flowers on a small bush. Initially it was confused with *C. maliflora*; now it is considered to be of natural origin.

C. salicifolia, from eastern China, is a large shrub with arching branches, and small flowers appearing in winter.

C. sinensis and its variety *assamica* are the tea plants of commerce. The variety *assamica* is more tender than the type, and has larger, glossy leaves. The type has miniature flowers in winter, and is of curiosity value really. Grown mainly by people who wish to brew their own 'cuppa'!

C. transnokoensis, from forests in Taiwan up to 3,000m above sea-level, is similar to *C. lutchuensis*, but smaller in all its components. The clusters of decorative pink buds open into masses of miniature flowers, making a striking picture.

C. tsaii is a superb, graceful large shrub with coppery-coloured young growth, and masses of small white flowers. An essential camellia for the woodland, it would not matter if it didn't flower.

C. vietnamensis is allied to *C. oleifera*, and is used for the production of oil from the large seeds. The flowers are slightly scented, pink in bud, and white when fully open. Ornamental and worth showing off in a sunny, sheltered corner.

C. yuhsienensis is a small shrub, up to 2m, with sweetly scented white flowers in the winter.

C. yunnanensis is a top-class large shrub, with scented flowers appearing in the autumn, which comprise white petals and a large boss of yellow stamens. The fruits are large – up to 6cm across – and contain oil-bearing seeds.

Camellia yunnanensis.

Camptotheca acuminata.

Camptotheca

C. acuminata, a member of the Nyssaceae family, is a medium-sized tree from China, where it is often planted as a street tree. It is tender when young, needing shelter from hard frosts, but grows best in full sun. The young leaves are an attractive pink shade when in full growth, and the hanging fruit clusters are showy in autumn. Scientists are studying the foliage as it is thought to have anti-carcinogenic agents.

Cardiandra

Of Hydrangeaceae, the *Cardiandra* are sub-shrubs with alternate leaves, from eastern Asia. The flowers comprise both sterile and fertile parts, as in many hydrangea species.

C. formosana grows to 40cm high, with bright green, glabrescent leaves, and blue-pink flowers forming a large terminal corymb up to 20cm across.

C. sinensis, from eastern China, has dull green, serrate leaves, with very attractive, shell-pink flowers up to 15cm across. It is often seen in damp areas and along shady ditches, where it grows up to 60cm high, and spreads by root rhizomes.

Cardiandra sinensis.

Carpinus

The hornbeams – a group of graceful small trees – do not stand out in the crowd, but have a fine distinction, which makes them more attractive with observation. Many of the 40 or so species deserve description, but just a few are mentioned here:

C. fangiana, from west Sichuan, has large leaves and long, pointed buds. The fruiting catkins are also impressive, reaching 30cm in length. A must for any gardener if it appears in a nursery.

Carpinus fangiana.

C. londoniana, from south China and Vietnam, is a very ornamental tree, with lovely shades of pink and red in the young growth, so a position sheltered from strong winds is a good idea.

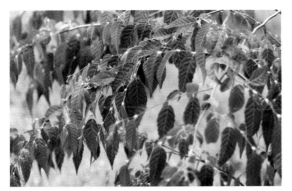

Carpinus londoniana.

C. pubescens has been collected many times recently from Yunnan. It makes a 15m tree in the wild, with a fine weeping habit.

C. rankanensis is a rare tree in Taiwan, worth growing because of its detailed foliage. Its leaves have up to 24 pairs of lateral veins in only 8–10cm.

Choerospondias

C. axillaris, from south-east Asia, is a medium-sized tree, with pinnate leaves and small, dark red flowers. The wood seems to be brittle in strong wind. Widespread in subtropical zones, it may need more heat in cultivation to set fruit, whereby the plant gets its vernacular name, 'hog plum'. The plum is, in fact, a large, bony stone with an edible fleshy coat.

Choerospondias axillaris.

Citharexylum

C. spicatum, from the *alto plano* in Bolivia, is a subtle evergreen shrub in the UK, with small, fragrant, mauve flowers in a spike rather like a verbena. The dark green, glossy foliage can be harmed in severe winters.

Clethra

The C*lethra* are superb flowering large shrubs and small trees, which should be planted in the garden more often, as their fragrance in summer is a treat. They extend into the Old- and New-World tropics, where some grow at quite high altitudes, and therefore would be worth a try.

C. cavalerei, from southern China, is a lovely shrub with characteristic reddish young wood, and greyish-green leaves.

C. mexicana is possibly more suited to hotter climates, as the upright racemes of flowers do not ripen until the autumn.

Clethra mexicana.

C. poilanei, from north Vietnam, is a strong, open shrub with very hairy young leaves and stems, and long flower stalks on which the individual flowers open in succession.

C. pringlei, from Tamaulipas in Mexico, has long racemes of cinnamon-scented flowers in the summer. It makes a small evergreen tree, with showy bronze young foliage. From about 1,500m, it may be hardy in south-west England.

Cornus

A well-known, mainly temperate genus, from which there are many outstanding garden shrubs and small trees. However, others from warm temperate climates are worth trialling in milder areas.

C. chinensis was introduced initially from Assam in 1950 by Frank Kingdon Ward. This collection has been difficult in cultivation, but recent seed from

Cornus chinensis.

Yunnan has led to a much more vigorous plant. The young stems are green, and merge with the attractive leaves, which are large, with conspicuous veining and a long drip-tip. The sessile, small, bright yellow flowers are produced in the late winter, rather like *C. mas*. The overall effect is of a splendid plant from the rain forest.

C. floccosa, from Mexico, has leaves rather like a hairy *C. capitata*, and is obviously suited to xerophytic areas.

C. kousa angustata is an evergreen form of *C. kousa*, with outstanding bronze-coloured young growth.

Correa

The *Correas* are beautiful, small, evergreen shrubs, and all need a sheltered spot apart from in the mildest zones. They are native to south-east Australia and Tasmania, and all have showy flowers among small leaves.

C. alba is common in sandy soils by the coast, and the leaves have developed a leathery texture to cope with these conditions. The flowers are white and funnel-shaped, with reflexed lobes.

C. decumbens has narrow leaves, and a narrowly tubular flower, crimson with a green tip. It likes to cover the ground, and looks well on a bank where it can grow downwards.

C. lawrenciana can make a small tree in its native montane habitat, growing in shady spots under the tree canopy. Its flower colour varies from yellow-green through to pale red.

C. reflexa is called the native fuchsia, and with good cause, as its green to red-green flowers hang under the branches in a like manner. The leaves and branchlets are relatively coarse, making it a shrub adaptable to most conditions.

Craibiodendron

C. yunnanense is from a small group of south-east Asian species, recently seen in cultivation. It is a relatively common small tree in central Yunnan, and once seen is certainly not forgotten, due to the brilliant coppery-red colour of its young foliage. Initially, it looks like a pieris, to which it is related, but the flowers are quite different, sitting erect on the branch tips. It is proving to be relatively hardy.

Decaisnea

D. insignis was recently successfully introduced into the UK from Bhutan by Keith Rushforth. It seems to grow at a lower elevation than its cousin *D. fargesii* (which is widespread in gardens), and so is likely to be more tender. The pinnate leaves are up to 60cm long, and turn yellow in autumn, even in Cornwall. The edible fruits are also yellow, and leathery to touch, not brown and glossy as described in the *Flora of Bhutan* (Grierson & Long, 1983). The flowers are insignificant, but this plant has distinct appeal due to these other ornaments.

Deutzia

The *Deutzias* are neglected in many mild gardens, rather unfairly as they compliment the spring-flowering shrubs, with their airy aspect and masses of flowers in early summer. Any unattractive old wood can be taken back hard, but many have

Decaisnea insignis.

Dichroa febrifuga.

lovely, brown-orange peeling bark, which makes a feature in itself.

D. calycosa is closely related to *D. longifolia*, and has flowers of variable colour, from white to pink, which are freely produced.

D. nitidula is a recently introduced plant from Sichuan, with corymbs of white flowers and interesting, small leaves, which have a glaucous reverse.

D. pulchra is a tough, large shrub (considering its origin), from the Philippines and Taiwan. The very showy white flowers are in long racemes, and an added attraction to this first-rate shrub is the orange, peeling bark.

D. staminea, from about 2,500m in the Himalayas, needs a sheltered spot as it dislikes hard frost. It bears showy white corymbs of flowers in June.

Dichroa

Mainly of tropical origin, there are two *Dichroa* species that seem to be hardy enough for growing in milder counties. They are both very ornamental, evergreen, upright shrubs of Hydrangeaceae, coming from the Himalayan foothills, and south and east as far as Vietnam. They flower at a young age, even as cuttings.

D. febrifuga grows up to 3m on forest margins, and at the edge of thickets, where it can get enough light. The star-shaped flowers are arranged in large panicles, and are followed by ornamental, dark blue berries quite unlike hydrangea. Apparently the locals use it in a febrifuge.

D. versicolor, from eastern China, was named by Fortune, and seems to be remarkably similar to the material from Yunnan province, which has been grown as *D. febrifuga*.

Dipentodon

D. sinicum is scarce in cultivation, which is curious as it was collected by Forrest in Yunnan province in the 1920s. There it grows into a small tree (at around 2,500m), with simple, glossy leaves, and wonderfully curious, sparkler-shaped, fragrant

Dipentodon sinicum.

Edgworthia papyrifera.

off-white flowers, 3–4cm across, on vertical stalks, which perch along the branches. When sited in a sunny position, the leaves show autumn colour.

Dodecadenia

D. grandiflora, from the Himalayas, is an evergreen member of the Lauraceae, closely related to *Cinnamomum*. This tree has pale yellow flowers in clusters along the branches. The young leaves are silky at first, needing shelter from prevailing winds, but toughen over the growing season into coriaceous, long-pointed entire leaves.

Dracophyllum

There are approximately 50 species of *Dracophyllum* in Australia, North Caledonia, and New Zealand, many of which are of montane origin, and form shrubs and small trees. The generic name refers to the resemblance of the leaves to those of the *Dracaena*. These are fascinating plants, curiosities to most gardeners, and have gained the name 'grass trees' in New Zealand. They appreciate an open position with good drainage.

D. fiordense, usually with a single trunk, and only to 3m tall, has leaves that can grow to 70cm long.

D. traversii is the most spectacular, reaching 10m, with ascending branches bearing leaves up to 60cm long. Flowers occur terminally on the branches, as panicles 15cm long, in summer.

Others to watch for include *D. latifolium*, *D. longifolium*, *D. menziesii*, and *D. milliganii*, but they are all interesting to the keen gardener.

Edgeworthia

Edgeworthia are Asiatic shrubs allied to *Daphne*.

E. papyrifera is a deciduous shrub from east Asia, well known for the wood being supple enough to tie into knots, and for its use in making paper. The flowers arrive in late winter, packed into a yellow, globose-shaped head, approximately 4–5cm across. *E. gardneri* is a native of the Himalayas; generally similar, but evergreen, and less hardy.

Elaeocarpus

Essentially a tropical genus, where shifting cultivation and logging have pushed over 50 species on to the *World List of Threatened Trees*!

E. hookerianus, from New Zealand, is fascinating and worth growing as it exhibits a complete change in foliage type, from small, saw-toothed leaves 2cm long, to simple, leathery leaves up to 10cm long. This happens at 2–3m in height, just above moa-grazing level.

E. reticulatus is a large shrub, but makes a small tree in mild localities as it is from south-east Australia. The leaves are simple, tough, and show a pink tinge when forming. The flowers are formed in white panicles up to 8cm long in early summer, and are followed by blue berries, hence its vernacular name – blue olive-berry. Watch out for the lovely pink-flowered form.

E. sylvestris, widespread in the Far East, makes a small tree, with coriaceous, simple leaves, and racemes of white flowers up to 8cm long from the leaf axils.

Enkianthus

Outstanding shrubs with exceptional beauty in flower, a few are evergreen, but most are deciduous, and show some of the best autumn coloration for west-country gardens. The smallish leaves lighten the effect of the more familiar, heavy woodland shrub planting. These shrubs are best seen in small groups. *E. serotina*, from southern China, is virtually evergreen in its native habitat, but likely to be deciduous in cultivation. With larger, stiffer leaves than its more temperate cousins, it has a similar appearance to *E. quinqueflorus*, which was introduced *c*.1800 from Hong Kong.

Escallonia

E. leucantha is a large, weeping shrub, with small leaves up to 2cm long, which become crowded with panicles of white flowers 15cm long in midsummer.

E. tucumanensis was introduced to Kew in 1961 from the foothills of north-west Argentina, and seems to be relatively hardy, though appreciating some shelter. It makes a large, arching shrub, with leaves up to 10cm long. The flowers are large for the genus, at around 1.5cm across. They appear in late summer and have a sweet scent, which can be likened to toffee.

Euonymus

The *Euonymus* mostly have little beauty in flower, but their habit, fruit, and autumn colour are an essential foil for all the confident shrubs that tend to dominate in planted woodland areas.

E. cornutus is fishing-rod shaped, with lanceolate leaves. It is an extraordinary sight in the autumn when planted in groups, and laden with fruit the shape of pink jesters' hats. The seeds are orange, and hang by arials from the hats.

E. porphyreus is similar to *E. cornutus* in fruit, but it is a stronger-growing shrub, with thicker branches and wider leaves.

E. tingens makes a small evergreen tree with oval leaves. The flowers have interesting detailing, being white with a purple network of veining, and when fully open they give the plant a subtle beauty.

E. echinatus and *E. wilsonii* are both scandent shrubs, and worth growing for the pink-lobed fruits, which are covered in spines rather like a hedgehog.

Exbucklandia

E. populnea is an arresting sight when first encountered. It resembles a large poplar tree on growth steroids, and in fact its leaves tremble like one – hence its local name, Malayan aspen. In fact it is a Hamamelid, with large, evergreen cordate leaves, and large stipules folded against one another protecting the buds. It grows at up to 2,500m in evergreen, broad-leaved forest in south-east Asia, so hardy provenances would be the key to successful cultivation. It was introduced by Forrest and probably Ward, but never became established.

Exbucklandia populnea.

Fieldia

F. australis is a first-rate Gesneriad from rain forests in eastern Australia. It is a lover of any wet, mossy situation, including trees and tree-fern trunks, where its creamy-white, hanging flowers are best seen. In fact, it doesn't really flower at all until it is off the ground.

Gomortega

G. keule has appeared in cultivation recently, thanks to the work done at the Royal Botanic Garden Edinburgh with its programmes in Chile to help protect endangered trees, especially the conifers. The Queule is rare in the wild, but still a valuable plant on account of its various uses, including timber, and the fruits, which are used in beverages and jams. It makes a large evergreen tree in the wild, but is likely to need some protection from cold in cultivation.

Gordonia yunnanensis.

Gordonia

G. szechwanensis has leaves up to 24cm long, and is common in gullies at low altitudes in western Sichuan. The flowers are sweetly scented, and the plant has withstood some frost in Cornwall without damage.

G. yunnanensis makes a large tree in wet forests of southern China, and when flowering in the autumn *en masse* the sight is memorable. The flowers are like large poached eggs, and give way to bullet-shaped fruits containing maple-like seeds. Other plants, from northern Vietnam, have a pink coloration when the flowers are opening.

Halesia

H. macgregorii, when discovered as late as 1924 by Professor R.C. Ching in south-east China, made the day for the geophysicists, as prior to this discovery there were only a few species, all confined to eastern North America. Like many other Styracaceae, it grows into a medium-sized deciduous tree suitable for mixed woodland. The white flowers form axillary clusters in late spring.

Heptacodium

H. jasminoides is a superb, late-flowering, large shrub for a sunny position in the west. The flowers are creamy-white and fragrant, and move on to produce distinctively coloured fruits that go from green, to rose-pink, to purple, and then light brown when ripe.

The bush, if pruned, shows a lovely stringy bark, and the overall appearance is of a large, shrubby honeysuckle.

Huodendron

H. biaristatum is likely to be the most ornamental of three species of *Huodendron* for the gardener. All are based in south-east Asia, and owing to the profusion of small flowers produced virtually next to each other at a young age, the small trees will be very valuable for a sheltered spot. Two other features make this tree stand out: the lovely pink, glossy young leaves, and the smooth, mahogany-coloured stems.

Hydrangea

Arnold-Forster sums up well the value of the hydrangeas to the summer display. However, a few have made an impact since.

H. angustipetala, from eastern Asia, is a lovely small shrub growing in clearings on the edge of thickets, with pink flowers in late summer.

H. indochinensis is a delicate, small shrub, up to 1m tall. It has attractive blue lacecap flowers in summer, and some forms have purple foliage, which is finely serrated.

Hydrangea indochinensis.

H. lobbii is sometimes included in *H. scandens*, but as it bears the name of Thomas Lobb, a Cornish botanist, the name should be kept! From lower forests in Taiwan and the Philippines, it is a glabrous small shrub, with showy white flowers.

Hydrangea lobbii.

H. longipes, from western China, would be worth its place in open woodland even if it did not flower. The leaves are ovate, and the leaf petiole is longer than the blade, making a very lax habit. The flowers are white and large – up to 30cm across.

Hypericum

H. canariensis makes a large shrub, 2–3m high, and has yellow flowers with attractive long, protruding stamens.

Hypericum revolutum.

H. revolutum, from Africa and south-west Arabia, is an unbelievable sight when covered in orange-red flowers and 10m tall. As with many other genera – for example, *Senecio* and *Lobelia* – from very high altitudes near the Equator, the local species have developed into giant forms of what is regarded as the norm in more equable climes. The flowers are up to 7cm across, cup-shaped like tulips, and hang from the branch ends. To grow well, this plant likes intense radiation, some rain or snow, a frost every night, and heat by day – i.e., extremes of all conditions. It has flowered in the UK, so it is possible!

H. roeperianum, from Zimbabwe, is a shrub up to 2m tall, with yellow flowers, and worth growing on account of the curry scent of the foliage, which is detectable metres away on a hot day.

Illicium

It must have been an oversight that no *Illicium* were mentioned by Arnold-Forster, as they are large shrubs and small trees out of the top drawer. Several well-known species are found in most publications, but the following are less common.

I. dunnianum makes a spreading shrub to 2m. It has very narrow leaves, rather like a *Podocarp*, very unlike what is usually expected.

I. majus, from central Yunnan, has thick, fleshy leaves and pink-white flowers, which are showy in the spring.

I. simonsii has pale yellow, starry flowers, and deep green, matt foliage, and should be hardy in the south-west as it grows with other plants introduced and doing well.

I. verum is the star anise of culinary use. It forms a tree in southern China, but in order to succeed in cultivation it is likely to need a very protected spot.

I. yunnanensis is a terrific small tree. Upright and vigorous, it has heavily scented flowers that perfume a wide area and last right through early spring. The growth is dark red, and the leaves are an attractive lanceolate shape.

Illicium yunnanensis.

Iochroma

A genus confined to the northern Andes, *Iochrama* has the reputation for producing very ornamental plants for the coldhouse, but several species are proving to be relatively tough outside. They rather like the extra warmth generated by a south-facing wall.

I. australe, from the Bolivia/Argentina border region, is probably the hardiest in the genus. It is a deciduous shrub reaching 5m, with lanceolate leaves up to 8cm long. The flowers, which are usually of a deep blue-purple colour, occur in bunches of up to five, hanging under the branches. There is also a lovely white cultivar, called 'Andean Snow'.

I. cyaneum is possibly of hybrid origin, as self seedlings are variable, producing various colour-shades of corolla, from pink to purple. Cultivars include 'Album', 'Apricot Belle', and 'Trebah', the latter having magenta-purple flowers.

I. gesnerioides and *I. grandiflorum* are both tender, but as the seeds germinate readily, and cuttings root easily (as with all the *Iochroma*), keeping stock is no problem.

Itoa

Itoa comprises two species only, from south-east Asia, belonging to Flacourtiaceae, which is a large family combining such disparate members as *Carrierea* and *Azara*.

I. orientalis is a small tree with magnificent foliage, for the sheltered woodland. It grows in south China in moist gullies, and produces simple leaves over 40cm long. However, the flowers are not showy, having to compete with such bold foliage.

Itoa orientalis.

Jovellana

Jovellana are lovely, small shrubs, which are happy in sun or shade, but dislike hard frost. They are subtle in disposition, but on close examination the *Calceolaria*-like flowers can be seen to have wonderful detail.

J. punctata, from southern Chile, is a shrub up to 1m high, with largish leaves, up to 10cm long, and pale lavender flowers, 2cm across, in early summer, standing proud of the foliage.

J. sinclairii is really a sub-shrub, up to 1m high, liking a well-sheltered and free-draining position. It has white flowers, with purple spotting. It grows in damp places in New Zealand.

J. violacea, from Chile, is a suckering shrub up to 1.5m high, with upright branches, neat, small leaves, and masses of pale violet flowers in early summer. This species seems to be the easiest to establish.

Lagunaria

L. patersonii is an interesting ornamental tree from the subtropical Norfolk and Lord Howe Isles. It has simple leaves, up to 8cm long, which are somewhat leathery, with a white reverse. The real beauty is reserved for the flowers, however, which are pale pink and open in succession over the summer. The fruit capsules are covered in a hairy irritant (*Lagunaria* belongs in Malvaceae), so it is lucky that it is easy from cuttings.

Laurelia

A small genus of only a few species from New Zealand and South America, which when given shelter can make sizeable trees, such as the lovely weeping examples at Penjerrick, and Kilmacurragh in Ireland. The *Laurelia* are not showy in flower or fruit, but have lovely stature as evergreen background.

L. novae-zelandiae makes a forest tree in wet zones in New Zealand, with the trunk showing flange-like buttresses when grown in swampy places. The simple leaves are serrate, and make an attractive, glossy, green-coloured foliage.

L. philippiana is similar to *L. sempervirens*, but generally grows at a higher altitude. The small flowers are produced earlier; the leaves have an even more pungent smell, and the bark seems to be paler and smoother.

L. sempervirens has been grown in milder places for a long time, and makes handsome specimens when grown in woodland. The serrate leaves are bright green, and when bruised give off an aroma akin to malt extract.

Leycesteria

L. crocothyrsos was introduced by Ward in 1928. The story of its botanical discovery is part of plant-hunting legend. An arching shrub with attractive golden-yellow flowers, it succeeds in milder counties, but is tender elsewhere. A good spot is under another shrub, where its lax branches can get support and the frost is kept off.

Lindera

Both *Lindera* and *Litsea* from Lauraceae are very underrated genera for the woodland garden. Many of the deciduous plants flower on naked stems in late winter, creating an unusual pattern. They can be deciduous or evergreen small trees in warm temperate forest, so appreciate some shelter.

Lindera erythrocarpa is a large, deciduous shrub from east Asia. The leaves turn a lovely yellow in the autumn, and combine well with the small red fruits.

L. glauca grows to about 8m. Its leaves are glaucous on the undersides, and turn all colours in late autumn. The fruit is black and shiny.

L. neesiana, from south-east Asia, has yellow flowers in globose heads, and deciduous leaves that are aromatic when crushed.

L. pulcherrima is seen as high as 2,700m in south-east Asia. It has a distinctive three-paralleled leaf with a long drip-tip. The buds are silky-haired, and the flowers greenish-yellow.

Litsea

The leaves of *Litsea* and *Lindera* contain alkaloids, which are used in many ways, including incense manufacture, silkworm and animal fodder, and insecticides in seed oil.

Litsea cubeba.

Maesa montana.

Litsea aestivalis, the pond-spice from south-east USA, is a deciduous shrub, with yellow flowers opening in late winter before the leaves.

L. cubeba is a fast-growing tree from south-east Asia, with small, narrow, scented leaves creating an open habit, suitable for sun or shade.

Maesa

M. montana is a bold-leafed tree from western China, worth a sheltered spot on account of its foliage. The lightly scented small flowers tend to be covered by the large, bullate, paddle-shaped leaves.

Magnolia

W. Arnold-Forster's *Shrubs for the Milder Counties* included a chapter on magnolias, compiled by the great Cornish gardener, G.H. Johnstone. Since then (1948), there have been a number of introductions, and a wealth of very garden-worthy hybrids and selections flooding into cultivation, many of which make top-class plants for the woodland. Numerous publications deal with these. Some are worth mentioning here, a few of which were raised in Cornwall.

Hybrids

Work undertaken at Caerhays, mainly by the former head gardener Philip Tregunna, has produced several very good hybrids using the large-growing Asiatic species. 'Caerhays Belle' and 'Caerhays Surprise' are both excellent hybrids, among many raised, for the gardener with space.

The hybrids from the Jury stable in New Zealand are outstanding plants for the Cornish climate. Most flower at a young age, but a few, including 'Vulcan', take time to produce fully developed flowers. Plants such as 'Apollo', 'Athene', 'Atlas', 'Lotus', and 'Black Tulip', all flower early, and are available from specialist nurseries. Os Blumhardt, also from New Zealand, has produced some recently popular hybrids, including 'Early Rose' and 'Star Wars'.

Breeders in the USA have worked hard to produce a good yellow magnolia in cultivation. The Brooklyn Botanic Garden brought many into cultivation, their efforts culminating in 'Lois', an intense yellow-flowering tree, registered in 1998. Subsequently, August Kehr has registered the fruits of many years' work on excellent yellows with 'Sunburst', 'Sun Spire', 'Hot Flash', and 'Golden Endeavor'. These hybrids are worth searching out for their later-flowering ability, and suitability for a smaller position. Most of the yellow hybrids are formed using *M. acuminata* in the parentage, so are hardy. The intensity of colour seems to vary with soil pH: in this case, the more alkaline the ground, the deeper the flower colour.

Species

M. amoena is a deciduous small tree from eastern China. The fragrant flowers are 5cm across, with up to nine pink tepals. Seed received in cultivation has produced variable offspring, hinting at some hybridity. This may have occurred within the botanic institutes in China that distributed the seed, or it may be an unstable species as it shares its range with *M. cylindrica* and *M. denudata*. It may be some time before the situation is resolved.

M. biondii is a hardy, deciduous tree from central China, introduced to the USA as recently as 1977. The white flowers are fragrant, and about 10cm across, appearing in late winter. It belongs to section Buergeria, so is closely related to *Magnolia* spp. *salicifolia*, *kobus*, and *cylindrica*, but it has yet to prove itself superior to any of these.

M. coco is a large, upright, evergreen shrub from southern China. The cup-shaped flowers measure a few centimetres across, and are very fragrant. A slow-growing, small magnolia, it would be worthy of pot cultivation: it is tender, and can withstand indoor treatment where the perfume can be fully appreciated.

Magnolia coco.

M. cylindrica, from east China, makes a small, very floriferous tree. The first introduction to Hillier's was from Lu shan B.G. seed, and is presumed to be a hybrid with *M. denudata*. These plants are now in many gardens, and have been given the clonal name 'Pegasus'. The real species now in cultivation has characteristic cylindrical fruits and flowers, similar to those of *M. denudata* in shape, with a purplish tinge at the base of each tepal.

M. kachirachirai, from Taiwan – where it grows into a large evergreen tree – has not yet been tried in West-Country gardens. It may be hardy, and would certainly be worth a sheltered position, as it is in the same section as (and possibly may become a variety of) the superb *M. nitida*.

M. lotungensis, M. omeiensis, M. robusta, and *M. yunnanensis* have all been described recently by Chinese botanists. They belong to the section including *M. nitida*, but there seems much doubt as to whether their differing characteristics warrant specific status, due to the lack of sufficient material. There is a little difference in some of their vegetative characteristics, but from the gardener's point of view, all would be top-class small trees, and worth

a place in woodland. Sometimes it is best for the botanists to fret over the labels!

M. macrophylla subsp. *ashei*, from Florida, grows in poor, sandy soils, which perhaps explains its dwarf nature when compared with the type species that grows in forests. Essentially *M. macrophylla* in miniature, it is useful for smaller gardens, where it will appreciate a sunny position and flower at only 1m or so.

M. macrophylla subsp. *dealbata* comes from the wet forests of eastern and southern Mexico, and is geographically distinct from *M. macrophylla*. It seems to be much happier in Cornwall than the type, growing very quickly, flowering earlier, and seemingly more robust. A 'must have' plant for people with enough room and some shelter, the size of the leaves – and flowers – will astound onlookers.

M. pacifica, M. schiedeana, M. sharpii, and *M. tamaulipana* are all large, evergreen species related to *M. grandiflora*. They represent disjunct populations in Mexico, and to the adventurous gardener have a certain appeal. However, such aesthetic information as is available does not reveal any significant horticultural advantages over *M. grandiflora*.

M. zenii is a small, deciduous tree from east China. Rare in its local habitat, it has been grown in the UK since only about 1990. Its scented flowers, about 12cm across, are white, with an attractive purple base to the tepals.

Manglietia

Mentioned by Arnold-Forster under *Michelia*, the *Manglietia* from south-east Asia has become more prominent recently, with further introductions of different species. All are likely to make remarkable large-foliage trees, and are evergreen apart from one. The cold winter of 1963 defoliated the trees at Caerhays, but they have since recovered. Shelter from strong winds is vital for a vigorous tree.

M. decidua, from a very limited distribution in south-eastern China, is by name deciduous, but looks anything but, with lovely metallic-coloured young foliage. Grown in cultivation only since 1999, it may prove to be hardier than the others on account of its deciduous nature. The flowers have up to 16 petals, and are creamy-white.

Manglietia insignis.

M. duclouxii makes a small tree, and is recognizable due to its slender twigs and small leaves. The flowers are reddish-purple.

M. fordiana is a widespread species, and this has resulted in a number of varieties. It succeeds well in cold areas of the USA, and so would be a useful tree in the western UK. One variety – *M. yuyuanensis* – has attractive, narrow, boat-shaped leaves. The flowers are pure white, and fragrant.

M. insignis is another widespread tree, which is already reaching a large size in Cornwall. However, it is worth looking for forms from southern Yunnan that show spectacular, strong pink-red colour on the outer sepals of the flower.

M. szechuanica looks a promising species from Emei shan in Sichuan, where it grows at heights of up to 1,800m, and should be worth a try in mild spots. The flowers vary from white to pink and purple-red. Woodland gardeners should be clearing a space now!

Meliosma
Summer-flowering small trees, with either pinnate or simple leaves, essential to the make-up of the woodland, *Meliosma* are happy in shade, but flower more effectively in sunny glades. The genus is most often represented in cultivation by the eastern species, but for the plant-searcher it would be worth seeking out specimens of half-hardy origins from Mexico and South America.

M. rigida, from the Far East, has large, simple leaves up to 30cm long. A fast-growing, small tree, with terminal panicles of creamy, scented flowers on lateral branches.

Melliodendron
M. xylocarpum was named as a genus only in 1920, from material collected in south-east China. It is one of the larger-flowered members of the Stryracaceae, with flowers – either solitary or in pairs – up to 5cm in diameter. It is a deciduous small tree, which seems relatively hardy and suitable for a sunny or shady position.

Michelia
The *Michelia* are separated from *Manglietia* primarily in having axillary flowers. They are a large genus, and have colonized many different niches, hence providing more variety for the gardener than *Manglietia*, although many will only be hardy in the milder counties. *Michelia* are exceptionally ornamental plants in habit and flower, and many an unexciting old magnolia hybrid should be tidied up by the adventurous gardener, to make way for a *Michelia*.

M. cavaleriei is widespread in southern China, and makes a branched tree with white, fragrant flowers in early spring.

M. compressa is hardy, but has only relatively small flowers, which are well scented. It will perhaps be of use to the hybridizer.

M. floribunda makes a large tree in south-east Asia, and some forms are relatively tough. The flowers are white and scented, and the forms where they overlap with *M. doltsopa* have possibly hybridized, leading to some confusion.

M. foveolata is another large tree in the wild, but likely to be smaller in cultivation in the UK. Worth growing for its foliage alone, it has leaves up to 30cm long – green above and silver below, both sides being covered in short, brown hairs.

M. maudiae has bold green leaves, which are whitish underneath. The large, well-scented flowers are held above the leaves, making a really showy spectacle. The original plants were thought to be very tender, but this is not so, and a sheltered position in sun would help the flowers to develop.

Michelia maudiae.

M. velutina, from the Himalayas, has very pubescent stems and elliptic leaves, and scented, pale yellow flowers in late spring. It makes a small tree, which is showing reasonable hardiness, but needs good light to flower.

M. wilsonii is vigorous, and makes a free-flowering tree. The scent from the smallish flowers is musky, and really needs warm air to set it going. Often planted in parks and temples in China, where the fragrance is highly rated.

Michelia wilsonii.

M. yunnanensis is a gem of a plant. Can tolerate dry or damp positions, sunny or shady, and

is seen from a dwarf shrub to a small tree. The freely produced, sweetly scented flowers can be detected several metres away, and they open in succession over a month or more. Nurserymen have had a field-day, and there are many cultivars in commerce. One proposed use is for a clipped hedge – why not? (Photo page 28.)

Nyssa

A first-rate group of trees that are happier in full sun than woodland, especially in maritime zones. Two species, *N. sylvatica* and *N. sinensis*, have been very successful in cultivation for some years, where their autumn colouring is as good as any deciduous tree. They transplant badly, so should be planted in their final positions when young.

N. aquatica is called the 'Water Tupelo', and is often seen growing in water along southern rivers of the USA, such as the Mississippi. The trunk forms a swollen base at a young age, and with maturity (up to 35m high), a buttressed base.

N. ogeche, from further east in the south-eastern USA, is probably more tender than *N. aquatica*, and is different mainly on account of its red fruits, which are flavoured and sometimes used as a substitute for limes – hence the vernacular name, 'ogeechee lime'. *N. ogeche* forms only small trees to 10m in bogs and swamps.

Ormosia

A large group of mainly tropical trees belonging to Leguminosae. There are, however, a few species that extend above the tropics in eastern Asia. George Wilson described the two species he came across in central China as being very ornamental, but not often seen.

O. formosana is an evergreen tree, with odd-pinnate leaves, from central and southern Taiwan. The axillary yellow flowers are formed in dense terminal racemes.

O. henryi forms a small evergreen tree, which bears yellowish-white flowers.

O. hosiei is rare in western China, as its red-coloured wood is highly esteemed for top-grade cabinet-making. It grows to a large size with a massive bole, and fragrant white-pink flowers.

Osmanthus

O. fragrans is a plant whose scent, once encountered, is never forgotten: it is full of tropical overtones, especially on a warm evening. It is not as strong-growing as most of the others, making a medium sized bush. Except for their scent, the flowers are almost incidental, although there is a variety called *O. fragrans* 'aurantiacus', which has yellowish-orange flowers. It likes a sheltered spot on a warm wall.

Paeonia

These are magnificent plants for woodland gardens. Among the 30 or so species is a handful of shrubby, or 'tree peonies', which are an excellent foil for other, evergreen shrubs in woodland clearings. Classification has been a complicated affair, as *Paeonia* have been cultivated in China for millennia for medicine and ornament, and are known as the 'King of Flowers'. Suitable for West-Country gardens, but their shoots are often harmed in colder zones by late spring frosts. Two of the best species are:

P. ludlowii, a superb plant growing to 2m, with large, golden yellow flowers up to 10cm across opening with the leaves in spring. The foliage consists of deeply cut leaves, placing this shrub in the indispensable category.

P. ostii, named only in 1992, after the Italian peony expert Gian Lupo Osti, has lovely, simple flowers, white with yellow stamens. It is a vigorous plant, therefore often cultivated for pharmaceutical use. Flowering when young, and relatively easy to grow from seed, it should become popular with time.

Paeonia ostii.

Peumus

P. boldus is a small tree from central Chile, with simple, tough leaves, which are useful in an incredible number of ways: as an infusion to strengthen the stomach and relieve pain; to cure earache and head colds, and to treat sores. The fruits can be pickled like olives, and the scented wood has many uses, including the lining of wine barrels in order to impart flavour. The leaves can be used in place of tea, but the aroma from the crushed leaves is intense, and takes some time to adapt to.

Philadelphus

Philadelphus are top shrubs for a sunny position, where their summer-flowering habit can lighten areas when the main garden is over. The following few species are all a little tender, and are from New Mexico and Mexico.

P. affinis has scented flowers, which are white with yellow stamens. If well placed, it can scramble up into other bushes.

P. argyrocalyx is a graceful shrub for a warm position, where the scented flowers, each 2–3cm across, cover the branches.

P. mexicanus is a loose shrub with fragrant flowers, which are white with a purple blotch.

Picconia

P. excelsa has made a large tree at Abbotsbury in Dorset, but is little seen, which is surprising as it was introduced from the Canary Islands in the eighteenth century. The fragrant flowers appear in summer in racemes at the ends of the branches. Related to the olives, the tree looks more like a small-leafed evergreen oak.

Pinckneya

P. pubens is monotypic, and originates from the south-eastern USA. It makes a small tree in its wild state, with a downy covering on the branches and oval-shaped leaves – hence the species name. The flowers are rose, purple-spotted, and up to 7cm-long corymbs. The large, pink bracts, combined with the corolla, create a decidedly ornamental effect. The plant needs as much sun and heat as possible in the western counties.

Pittosporum

Pittosporum have long been popular in milder gardens for windbreaks and hedges. These have been based mainly on species from New Zealand, but many others are now in cultivation from southeast Asia. These prefer some shelter, rather than providing it, as they are not fully hardy. Unostentatious plants, they are easily missed in the forest understorey, unless flowering, when their scent is often detected before the plant is noticed.

P. brevicalyx, from the Yunnan plateau, grows to 6m and is a very worthwhile addition to the woodland garden, its scented yellow flowers bunched together in terminal clusters.

P. illicioides makes a large shrub under broad-leaved forests in Japan and Taiwan. The flowers appear in small groups of up to four, but are highly fragrant.

P. omeiensis is a small tree with narrow, shiny leaves. It is much grown in the temples on the famous Emei Shan (Mount Omei) in China, where it is valued for its highly coloured yellow flowers.

Pittosporum omeiensis.

Polygala

P. arillata, from eastern Asia, is a widespread shrub of up to 2m or so, which is most often seen growing in scrubby, cut-over areas. The yellow, pea-like flowers form terminal racemes over the summer. These are followed by quite striking red-purple fruit capsules in the autumn. It can cope with quite low light levels, but performs better in cultivation with at least half sun.

Polygala arillata.

Polylepis

Polylepis are amazing shrubs and trees from the Andes, which grow at altitudes above 5,000m, thereby making them the highest-growing arborescent angiosperm genus. The highest-growing species form pure stands of dwarfed trees, due to the extreme location. The thin, exfoliating bark, and thick trunks with twisting branches are very characteristic, and can be seen even from a distance. There are about 15 species in the family Rosaceae.

P. australis, from north-west Argentina is in cultivation, forming a shrub up to 3m high. The leaves are pinnate, with around six toothed leaflets clustered around the growing point. The flowers form racemes, but are not prominent, and occur in late spring.

Reevesia

Reevesia form a small group of trees not often seen in cultivation. However, they are well worth tracking down by the keen gardener, as they are one of the few genera of Sterculiaceae that can be grown in the milder counties.

R. pubescens has reached tree size in Cornwall, but is damaged in really severe winters. It has evergreen, coriaceous leaves, which are uninteresting apart from the vivid tints of the young growth. The flat heads of the flowers are creamy-white, with each individual showing a distinctive staminal column protruding 3cm clear of the corolla.

R. thyrsoidea is from south-east Asia, and seems to be less hardy than the Himalayan *R. pubescens*, but similar in most parts. Both like a sheltered spot in woodland, but need sun to produce any flowers.

Rehderodendron

R. kweichowense, from Vietnam, is proving to be hardy so far. It seems to be evergreen in these mild winters, but has not yet produced flowers.

R. macrocarpum has made a lovely small tree in many Cornish gardens. Another member of the sublime Styracaceae family, it was named by Professor Hu after the botanist Alfred Rehder of the Arnold Arboretum. The white flowers are cup-shaped, with a lovely lemon fragrance, and hang in clusters with the leaves in late spring. The intriguing fruits are sausage-shaped, up to 7cm long, and can take a number of years to germinate. There are five species from south-east Asia, all of which are likely to be ornamental, but some may be tender, so siting will be important.

Rehderodendron macrocarpum.

Rhabdothamnus

R. solandri is a small shrub of Gesneriaceae, found only in the North Island of New Zealand, where it grows in dry, shady, shingly gullies, along creeks and edges of bush. The flowers are usually red, uncommonly yellow, bearing some semblance to *Gloxinia* – hence its vernacular name, New Zealand gloxinia. Tender, it really needs the growing conditions above in a mild locality.

Rhododendron

This genus was another that occupied a whole chapter in Arnold-Forster's book, and since then there have been many publications devoted to rhododendrons (see Further Reading), and many advances in taxonomy and field exploration. However, this work has not greatly affected gardens in Cornwall, as there has been a falling in favour of planting new rhododendrons. They are no longer in fashion – perhaps because of their domination of woodland gardens for so long. A large garden full of rhododendrons does lack appeal to all but the real enthusiast, and they should be used carefully, in conjunction with many other woodland shrubs to please the eye. Sourcing of new planting material from reputable growers is easy though, and important for larger collections. If the plant is grown from wild seed, so much the better, as this prevents bastards from confusing the visitor, and adds scientific interest to the garden. The taxonomy of the genus is complicated and warrants a small dissection.

Taxonomy

First, the genus is tricky to identify correctly, due to natural and garden hybridization. There are many more natural hybrids than was realized when plants were first introduced, and many of these were thought of as species until recent fieldwork. Second, the whole system of classification has changed since 1980 with 'The Revision', from the Royal Botanic Garden Edinburgh, which supersedes earlier reference material. There are also many people working on the genus in various parts of the world, who are giving different interpretations of individual species. Third, too many species were named initially, and these have had to be abandoned, beginning the ongoing debate between the 'lumpers' and the 'splitters', and leaving the poor gardener in the middle. In addition, recent work using DNA analysis often has the gardener reaching for new plant labels!

For these reasons, numerous introductions since 1950 have yet to be named. A short selection of the species most suitable for Cornish conditions is listed below by region, showing where most of the present field-work is concentrated. Detailed descriptions needed for planting requirements are available in many recent publications (see Further Reading).

Bhutan

R. *bhutanense*, a recently named shrub, is very hardy, with a deep pink full truss.

R. *kesangiae* is a recently described, handsome, rose-coloured, large-leafed species, not wind tolerant.

Central China

R. *coeloneuron* is a large plant with attractive rufous branchlets and leaves, and pink flowers.

R. *haofui* was introduced in 1985 by a Royal Botanic Gardens Kew trip to Fanjing shan. It has white to pink flowers on a small tree.

R. *liliiflorum* is another species related to R. *Lindleyi*, which was introduced from Fanjing shan in 1985.

R. *oligocarpum* is a red-flowered species, which will stand exposure.

R. *platypodum* has very limited distribution in the wild. It has pink flowers, and should be hardy in the west.

Eastern China

R. *championae* is a tender, white-pink flowering member of the R. *choniastrum* section, with distinct, bristly hairs.

R. *kiangsiense* likes a similar position to R. *levinei* (below), but is more straggly in habit, with larger flowers.

R. *levinei*, a small, neat plant, is suitable for rocky, well-drained banks.

Western China

R. *glanduliferum* is a superb, scented species, with handsome, long-leafed foliage.

R. *gongshanense* is a red-flowered small tree with very rugose leaves.

R. *hancockii* is a fine, underrated species, with scented white flowers.

R. *valentinianum* var. *oblongilobatum* bears lovely, bright yellow flowers on a small shrub.

R. *viallii* flowers very early. It is tender and rare, but worth tracking down on account of its bright red flowers.

North-east India

R. *santapauii* is a tender dwarf plant, with creamy-white flowers, and is suitable for an old mossy stump.

R. *subansiriense* makes a small tree, with scarlet flowers. It needs a sheltered position from late frosts.

R. *walongense*, an epiphytic *Maddenia*, has shiny, peeling bark and scented flowers.

Malaysia

R. *wrayi* may be hardy in very mild areas, due to having *Irrorata* blood. It is white-flowered.

Taiwan

R. *ellipticum* has lightly fragrant, pink-white flowers, and grows up to 3m. It likes a sheltered position in full sun.

R. *formosanum* needs careful siting to show its white, sometimes spotted, flowers without spoiling.

R. *kawakamii*, a superb wee shrub with yellow flowers, is usually seen as an epiphyte in the wild.

R. *pachysanthum* is an excellent foliage plant that withstands windy positions.

Thailand

R. *ludwigianum* is a straggly shrub with white flowers sometimes flushed pink, which needs a very sheltered corner.

R. *veitchianum* is similar to R. *ludwigianum*, but in some forms has an attractive frilly edge to the flowers.

Tibet

R. *dekatanum*, a lovely, yellow-flowering low bush, flowers early in the season, so will need some frost protection.

R. *luciferum* is a hardy, outstanding foliage plant with white flowers.

R. scopulorum, a scented *Maddenia* with loose habit, has waxy narrow leaves, and white flowers with a yellow blotch.

Vietnam

R. excellens is happy as an epiphyte in the wild. Drainage is important to ensure a spectacular performance of up to ten scented white flowers.

Rhododendron excellens.

R. grandia sect. is of exceedingly limited distribution in the wild. This unnamed species has large leaves similar to *R. protistum*, and cream flowers.

R. leptocladon, a terrific small, greenish-yellow-flowering shrub, is seen in the wild growing in the branches of the *R. grandia* listed above.

R. nuttallii, whose origin has already proved to be much hardier than the eastern Himalayan form, flowers later, but will still need careful siting to show its spectacular flowers.

R. rushforthii has showy yellow flowers, and is distinct on account of its pale, glaucous leaves.

R. serotinum was initially confused with *R. hemsleyanum*, with which it shares an auriculate leaf and scented white flowers.

R. sinofalconeri should be hardy in the south and west, as it grows at over 3,000m in northern Vietnam. It bears well-proportioned, yellow flowers on a tree up to 20m tall.

R. spanotrichum is a large-growing plant with red flowers, in the *Irrorata* section.

Vireya Rhododendrons

The *Vireya* section of rhododendrons is of a very tender nature, and the plants have trouble adjusting their flowering and growth cycles to a warm temperate climate as they are native to the tropical latitudes of south-east Asia. But if the seasons remain warm, it may be possible to attempt some of these plants in very favourable corners of the far south and west. The flowers on many are spectacular in size and colour, which will no doubt tempt the adventurous gardener.

Richea

The *Richea* have evolved in Tasmania (one species in south-east Australia), rather like the *Dracophyllum* in New Zealand. Both genera actually belong to the heath family, Epacridaceae, and are well suited to handling rugged weather conditions and stony, peaty soil. In foliage, they resemble certain monocotyledons, such as *Cordyline* and *Pandanus* (which is the species name for the largest *Richea*).

R. dracophylla is an erect, slightly branched shrub, which grows up to a few metres tall, with white flowers packed into large, dense terminal spikes, in spring.

R. pandanifolia is a wonderful foliage plant, a must for all people who don't like flowers, as the leaves can be up to 1.5m long, and steal the show. It is slow growing, but eventually makes a single-stemmed small tree, with the dead leaves clothing the stem.

R. scoparia is a hardy small shrub, up to 2m tall, with hard, sharp-pointed leaves, which remain on the plant even when dead, rather like a miniature monkey-puzzle. The flowers are showy, and vary in colour in the wild from white, to pink, to dark red.

Sarmienta

S. repens is a lovely sub-shrub from Chile. It produces masses of *Mitraria*-like, orange, tubular flowers in early summer. It prefers a cool, moist spot in the shade, where it can climb mossy trunks and banks.

Sassafras

S. randaiense, from Taiwan, is scarce in its natural habitat, and has been introduced only recently.

The leaves are deciduous and can be either entire or three-lobed, with a glaucescent lower surface. It has a lovely green trunk when young, and this colour remains on the branches.

Sassafras randaiense.

S. tzumu, from central China, is widespread, but never abundant in the forest as it is used locally for timber. A very ornamental tree with an open branching structure, it is a quick grower, with varying lobed leaves, which have lovely tints of pink when growing, and red later in the autumn. The flowers are creamy-yellow, and small, but combine on the naked branches in late winter to make a show, especially against a dark background.

Saurauia
S. nepaulensis, from south-east Asia, makes a small tree rather like a loquat. The leaves are heavily parallel-veined, and up to 30cm long. The flowers, though small, are a pleasing shade of pink, forming clusters among the leaves. Worth growing for its subtropical foliage effect, in a sheltered spot as it dislikes hard frost. A plant called *S. subspinosa*

at Tresco is growing back strongly after the 1987 cold snap.

Schefflera
A genus that is becoming more popular as people realize that many are relatively hardy outside, and not just useful for low-light situations inside as house-plants. The foliage effect is tropical, with palmately compound leaves on elongated petioles up to 60cm long. Shelter is necessary as the long petioles can sometimes be bent and broken in wind.

S. delavayi is widespread in southern China, and makes a small tree with large, often incised leaflets (four to seven), when young.

S. digitata, from New Zealand, is commonly found in damp, shady parts of the forest, and along stream edges. The inflorescence is large – up to 30cm across – with dull, greenish coloured flowers, which give way to masses of white fruit.

S. impressa, from the Himalayas, is one of the hardiest species, even surviving in the Hillier garden at Ampfield, near Romsey, for some time. It has

Schefflera impressa.

a lovely pale brown covering on the emerging leaves, which over the season turn dark green.

S. taiwaniana is a fast-growing, branching species, with light green, fine foliage, making a small tree.

Schima
Arnold-Forster mentioned *S. khasiana* and *S. argentea* in his *Shrubs for the Milder Counties*, and there are others worth noting, as they are superb, late-flowering, evergreen trees related to *Camellia*. The taxonomy does vary though, with several sources giving only a single variable species, *S. wallichii!* All have white flowers with a boss of yellow stamens. The fruits mark the tree, as they form a distinctive five-valvate, round, woody capsule.

S. noronhae may possibly warrant varietal status, on account of its superior bunches of flowers produced in the axils of the terminal leaves.

S. superba, as seen from south China and Vietnam, looks very similar to *S. argentea*, with the characteristic glaucous leaf reverse. *S. yunnanense* looks as though it may be synonymous.

S. wallichii var. *liukiuensis* has been distributed from Korea, and looks like an upright grower. It could be hardier than some others as it is from so far north.

Sinocalycanthus
S. chinensis is a monotypic genus, closely related to *Calycanthus*, with which it has been hybridized. Only recently introduced to cultivation from eastern China, it first flowered in England in 1989. The flowers are about 6–8cm across, pale pink in

bud, opening white with yellow stamens. It is a medium-sized, deciduous shrub, with glossy green broad leaves, which turn yellow in autumn.

Sorbus
The range and variety of these beautiful plants is spread right across the temperate Northern hemisphere. Included below is one from each section, as a taster for the woodland gardener, especially as there are so many excellent species from which to choose.

S. harrowiana is a remarkable small tree from the *Aucuparia* section, with from two to four pairs of leaflets on leaves up to 30cm long. It is commonly seen in the wild in south-west China, growing on other trees, where, after a number of years, its roots find their way down the trunk to the ground. In autumn it turns all shades of red, and has bunches of fruit that start red and turn white.

S. hedlundii, from moist areas in the Himalayas, is a medium-sized tree of the *Aria* section, with striking foliage. The leaves are large, and have a

Sinocalycanthus chinensis.

Sorbus hedlundii.

silvery-white reverse, and a conspicuous golden-brown vein system. It likes an open position, and makes an eye-catching statement when seen from a distance.

S. rhamnoides belongs in the *Micromeles* section. It is a small tree with leaves up to 15cm long, which colour brilliantly in the wild. Given an open place in the garden, it would be a colourful autumn show.

Stuartia
S. pteropetiolata is an evergreen tree, introduced by Forrest, but it has never become widespread. This is unfortunate as it has ornamental, glossy, dark green leaves with bright red petioles, and white flowers in late spring. After the flowers drop, they continue to turn cream, and then yellow, making a carpet on the ground.

Styrax
The *Styrax* are among the best groups of trees and shrubs for the garden, being particularly beautiful when in full flower. Even when not in flower, they have poise and style. There is one to fit any position.

S. confusus has a rather stately *Rehderodendron* look, with droopy leaves, and showy terminal racemes of flowers.

S. formosana is a neat, upright shrub, with dainty leaves, and white, scented flowers in the spring. A lovely plant for a sheltered corner.

S. glabrescens is quite a large tree in Mexico, but is not likely to reach that in cultivation. Its large fruits are of interest.

S. grandiflorus makes quite a spectacle when in flower (July), not because of the size of the flowers, but because of the mass of smallish racemes, in which each flower has a distinctively reflexed corolla.

S. hookeri has toothed, rough leaves, and hairy young branches. Its flowers are white, some 2.5cm long, in lax clusters in June. It comes from wet forest in the Himalayas, where it makes a small tree.

Styrax confusus.

S. huanus is a recent introduction from south-east Sichuan, which has leaves up to 15cm long, and large racemes of scented flowers in late spring.

S. limprichtii is a suckering shrub from dry banks in central Yunnan. The leaves are grass-green, and look well with the masses of flowers, which start when the bush is only 60cm high. It was originally grown as *S. langkongensis.*

Styrax limprichtii.

Ternstroemia nitida.

S. perkinsiae, from north-west Yunnan, makes a small tree with purple-brown branchlets, and leaves with a glaucous under-side. The flowers are white, in racemes of three or four.

S. platanifolia subsp. *mollis*, from north-east Mexico, has large, nodding flowers and silver-green foliage. It makes a medium-sized shrub.

S. roseus makes a small tree with large, pink-white flowers in late summer. It should be hardy as it is from reasonable altitude in central China.

S. tonkinensis is a fast-growing tree, which is semi-evergreen in a mild winter. The leaves are papery and large – up to 18cm long. The flowers are white. It is from quite low altitudes in south-east Asia, so a sheltered site is important.

Ternstroemia

Part of the Theaceae family, the *Ternstroemia* are mainly a tropical genus. The two below extend into warm temperate regions, and are quiet but effective plants for woodland situations.

T. gymnanthera is a stiff shrub, with thick, ever-green leaves. It does not mind a shady corner, where the bunches of flowers appear at the ends of the shoots in summer.

T. nitida makes a large shrub with big, coriaceous leaves. A really first-rate foliage shrub for a situation in the understorey.

Tutcheria

Tutcheria, or possibly *Pyrenaria*, is the correct genetic name. They are a group of small trees, closely related to the camellia. It is only in the fruit structure that they are differentiated.

T. spectabilis withstands some frost in Cornwall, but needs a sheltered site to produce flowers in the autumn. The flowers are white with yellow stamens, and have a slight pollen scent. The habit and foliage is very camellia-like, with the young growth appearing pink in spring.

Vallea

V. stipularis is a lovely small tree from the northern Andes, where it grows on the edges of the forest. The leaves are variable in shape, but mainly heart-shaped, with a curious kidney-shaped stipule (hence the name) at the leaf base. The attractive, deep pink flowers appear in bunches in early summer under the branches. It is inclined to get leggy in shady spots, but does respond well to the shortening of any branches. There is a large specimen in an open situation close to the house at Pine Lodge Gardens, east of St Austell.

Vallea stipularis.

The plants listed below are for the speculative plant addict. They are of borderline hardiness in milder counties or, having been brought recently to the attention of botanical scientists, deserve a quick reference for being completely 'on the edge':

Aesculus wangii (Hippocastanaceae):
 south-east Asia
Aleurites fordii (Euphorbiaceae):
 south-east Asia
Brachyoton sp. (Melastomataceae): Bolivia
Bretschneidera sinensis (Bretschneideraceae):
 China
Cavendishia spp. (Ericaceae): South America
Drimys granadensis (Winteraceae):
 South America
Engelhardtia spp. (Juglandaceae):
 south-east Asia
Hagenia abyssinica (Rosaceae): East Africa
Illicium mexicanum (Illiciaceae): Mexico
Meryta sinclairii (Araliaceae): New Zealand
Nyssa leptophylla (Cornaceae): China
Rhodoleia sp. (Hamamelidaceae): Vietnam
Rhoiptelea chiliantha (Rhoipteleaceae):
 south-east Asia
Styrax glabrescens (Styracaceae): Mexico
Tapiscia sinensis (Staphyleaceae): China
Ungnadia speciosa (Sapindaceae): USA

***

Since the late twentieth century, there has been much talk of global warming, and the potential of gardens in the milder parts of the British Isles to become subtropical. Whether or not this happens, there is no doubt that cold winters have not suddenly disappeared as a hazard, and certainly other problems may well emerge with a weather pattern that seems to swing from one extreme to another. But in the intervening years between cold spells, the curious gardener will have a wider selection of plant material to grow than ever before. Modern transport and technology make it much easier to replace lost plants.

The plants discussed above are necessarily just a personal selection, for this short chapter could easily have been a whole book on its own. It has been a brain-twisting exercise to shoehorn in some plants rather than other deserving candidates. But hopefully the selection will provide

stimulus for gardeners to try something new and unknown, just as the first woodland owners did so successfully in the 'milder counties'.

3 Conifers

Chris Page

This chapter is dedicated to the memory of the late Alan Mitchell, who first sparked my enthusiasm for conifers in the British Isles, and of the late Major W.M. Magor, who introduced me to the trees and gardens of Devon and Cornwall.

Mention of the word 'conifers' to most gardeners immediately conjures up images of dark, lowering forests, of overgrown cypress hedges, and endless arrays of dwarf garden cultivars. This chapter is not about these: it is about the value of species conifers as verdant, individual arboricultural subjects. Often these conifers are of unusual genera, from the mountains of exotic places. All are primitive plants. They form trees that achieve a grandeur with maturity; many are of a size and form specifically appropriate to attractive, evergreen landscape use in the present – and likely future – climate of south-west England.

Left: A grove of wild *Sequoia sempervirens* in California, forming one of nature's great cathedrals. (See page 69.)

Background to the cultivation of conifers

Conifers include the world's biggest, tallest, and most ancient living things. They are the reptiles of the plant world, and have existed on Earth since long before the dinosaurs. Indeed, some still show adaptations, or evolutionary scars, that originally developed to prevent dinosaurs from eating them. That these magnificent trees have survived and continue to flourish in so many parts of the world is a tribute to their tenacity.

Today, there are some 620 species of conifers world-wide, which are members of one-third of the world's forests. At least half of these species are likely to be hardy somewhere within the British Isles, with increasing numbers of unusual and exotic genera appropriate for cultivation in the south-west. These are species especially from the world's temperate rain forests and from the cool, cloud-wrapped flanks of isolated tropical mountains, usually from many of the islands of the world. For only under such mild, moist conditions are many of the tender, Southern-hemisphere conifers, and those from the oceanic, high-rainfall fringes of the mountains of the Pacific – where natural generic diversity of conifers is at its highest – likely to become increasingly hardy outdoors. Apart from the south-west of England and Ireland, other places where such tender species might be tried include the coastal fringes of France and the Iberian peninsula (especially Portugal).

This chapter concentrates on these wild species conifers (rather than cultivated varieties), for we can learn much of value to their cultivation and climatic appropriateness from a knowledge of the ecology and habitats of the species in the wild, and the likely genetic diversity that may be present. We shall look at conifer species worthy of cultivation, which either have a proven track-record of hardiness appropriate to south-west Britain, or are clearly 'on the edge' of hardiness. These are relatively 'exotic' species – we shall not be con-

Conifers in cultivation. Above: *Podocarpus andinus*, male cone detail. Above right: *Larix occidentalis*, foliar and female cone detail. Right: *Taxus baccata*, female cone detail.

The tradition of landscape use of conifers, a quintessentially British scene: *Cedrus libani* in central England.

cerned with the many other species which could be grown, but which are also widely hardy elsewhere. The conifers are presented here by natural region of origin in the wild.

The importance and diversity of landscape uses of conifers

Conifers have a diversity of traditional landscape uses in cultivation, which have developed through time with the planted landscape:

- As arboretum specimens, they are pre-eminent, through their size and diversity of form. Variations in tree habit and colour of greens, and diversity of bark types and cones have all contributed to sustained interest in conifers as arboretum specimens. Most thrive in the majority of loam soils, and the tendency of many species to thrive particularly well in poorer, sandier soils provides a special potential for their use on many sites where such soils are less suited to other purposes.

- As feature trees in other landscapes, the distinctive crown forms and (mostly) evergreen habits of conifers provide valuable contrasts to areas of broad-leaved trees. The sheer longevity of individuals, and the continuing improvement and individualization of crown forms with age, are great advantages for this purpose. As backdrops for other, more floriferous planting schemes, the evergreen nature of conifers can be a particularly useful foil.

- As avenue trees, conifers maintain long traditions of use. Avenues of conifers, such as the famous monkey-puzzle (*Araucaria araucana*) avenues at Bicton (Devon) and Pencarrow (Cornwall) make spectacular landscape statements. Irish yew (*Taxus baccata* 'fastigiata') is widely used along churchyard paths, and thrives in the climate of the south-west. Italian cypress (*Cupressus sempervirens* 'stricta'), which also thrives in west Cornwall, adds a touch of the Mediterranean.

- As windbreaks, conifers are valuable because of their longevity; their evergreen habit, and the salt-tolerance of certain species. Widely used are Radiata pine (*Pinus radiata*) and Monterey cypress (*Cupressus macrocarpa*). These are perhaps at their most effective when intermixed with other, broadleaf windbreak species such as Holm oak (*Quercus ilex*). To maximize their effectiveness, such windbreaks need to be adequately profile-structured, and to have new tree generations interplanted about every 50 years.

- As markers of specific memorable occasions, conifers have the advantage of being evergreen, reliable, and long-lived. For these reasons, many individual specimens have been planted, with varying degrees of ceremony, both by individual families, and in wider national life. Conifer plantings were used to mark the ends of the First and Second World Wars and, more recently, the millennium (yews are special favourites here). One cannot help comparing the cost-effectiveness and appropriateness of hope, growth, and future longevity achieved by such plantings, with some of the less durable achievements with which such events have been more expensively marked!

- Additionally, conifers have many minor uses. For example, certain species respond to trimming, and can be used to form evergreen hedges. The most widely used and successful of these in Cornwall is always English yew (*Taxus baccata*). Its great predictability in response to trimming, and generally slow growth rates, also makes it suited to topiary. The Southern hemisphere Andean podocarp (*Podocarpus andinus*) also makes a useful and attractive hedge. Of course, conifers also have great bonsai potential, with species such as Japanese red pine (*Pinus densiflora*) being among traditional favourites, due to their natural tendency to grow on rocky bluffs into a wide, multi-layered crown form, with craggy habit. Such 'Willow pattern' trees, in a variety of sizes, have distinctive places in garden design, and can look well as centre-pieces in man-made rock-gardens.

- As future revegetation materials, and as 'green-banks' – both vitally important potential future uses of selected conifer species, especially in west Cornwall. Selected conifers have a role in the managed revegetation of metalliferous mine-spoil sites, and the development of Cornish gardens as future 'green-banks' for rare and threatened tree species. (Aspects of these future roles are outlined at the end of this chapter.)

Britain and Ireland both have long traditions of cultivating coniferous trees, and quite detailed records of their progress in cultivation have been kept (and continue to be updated) for well over a century.

Conifers from temperate South America

The conifers of temperate South America include the species of southern Chile – some of which cross the border into southern Argentina – but not the more montane species of central and

Saxegothaea conspicua: tree in cultivation in west Cornwall – the largest known to me outside the wild.

Temperate rain forest in southern Chile, showing the wide mix of trees typically present.

co-associate as the dominants of Chile's mossy, temperate rain forest ecosystems, with, for example, Southern beech (*Nothofagus*), and understorey *Drimys*, *Eucryphia*, *Embothrium*, *Chusquea* bamboo, and *Blechnum* ferns.

Saxegothaea conspicua (Prince Albert's yew) is a tall, slender, but bushy-crowned evergreen tree, resembling a large and more open-crowned yew with brighter, grey-green foliage, and usually curved leaves. In the wild it develops a tall, shaft-like trunk, characterized by a thin, smooth bark, which sheds in large, jigsaw-like plates, leaving irregular patches of grey, purple, and red-brown. It requires shelter, but is shade-tolerant. It has proved slow-growing in cultivation, with established trees in the south-west achieving scarcely more than 7.5–11m in about 50 years, making it appropriate for smaller sites. It may well prove to grow faster under modestly warmer and wetter conditions.

northern parts of America. The latter have hardly, if at all, been introduced anywhere, although they might make cool greenhouse or conservatory specimens, or are other species for the future.

Today, the climate of Cornwall matches closely that of the Pacific oceanic margins of southern Chile, approximately south of the latitude of Valdivia. There is a long history of interest in Britain in the introduction of species from this region, begun by the pioneering introduction of the monkey-puzzle tree (*Araucaria araucana*) by Archibald Menzies in the late eighteenth century, and continued by the Cornishman William Lobb, who collected more widely, and brought home many woody species from this region, many of which still thrive in Cornish gardens.

The wet, coastal forests of Chile (above) are home to a number of conifer species with particular potential for wider cultivation in Cornwall. So far, only a few specimens of most of these have been available for long-term trials, but virtually all have succeeded, suggesting that wider introductions, representing much more of a genetic array of provenance sources, should further expand their potential. Species particularly appropriate to the south-west include *Saxegothaea conspicua* (Prince Albert's yew); *Podocarpus salignus* (Willowleaf podocarp); *Podocarpus nubigenus* (Cloud podocarp), and *Fitzroya cupressoides* (Patagonian cypress). All of these form tall (30m plus) trees in the wild, with *Fitzroya* having the largest stem diameter (*c.*7.6m) of any conifer I have seen. In the wild, they often

Saxegothaea conspicua: wild tree habit in temperate rain forest, southern Chile.

Podocarpus salignus: foliar and female cone detail in cultivation.

Fitzroya cupressoides showing spire-like crown shape in temperate rain forest, southern Chile.

Podocarpus salignus (Willowleaf podocarp) is a broadly open-crowned tree, much resembling a large willow, but evergreen in its foliage. It is the strongest-growing of all species of *Podocarpus* in the climate of south-western Britain, especially west Cornwall, and was first introduced from Chile in 1849. In the wild it forms tall trees in excess of 30m, but is now extremely rare due to demand for its high-quality, fine-grained timber. Specimens in cultivation in the south-west have made 14–18m growth in about 50 years. Existing groups of *P. salignus* that have matured now self-seed in older Cornish estate gardens – for example, Trengwainton, Tregrehan, and Caerhayes – attesting to the special climatic appropriateness of this species when introduced into our climate.

Fitzroya cupressoides 'Alerce' is a magnificent, cypress-like tree in the wild, with billowing masses of bright green foliage, and a deep rust-red trunk. It was introduced to Britain by William Lobb in 1849. The genus was named after Captain Fitzroy who commanded the *Beagle*, on which Charles Darwin sailed, and who made landfall in Falmouth on the return voyage. It is a slow-growing, but eventually massive tree in the wild, and very long-lived – some specimens are known to be more than 3,000 years old. It makes similarly slow, but steady growth in cultivation in Cornwall, where the very few specimens as yet planted have made 11–15m in a century. It does best on moist, acidic soils, in relatively sheltered sites.

Araucaria araucana, the monkey-puzzle or Chile pine, occurs as groves or more extensive pure forests, mainly on mountain flanks and ridges, both in the coastal range of Chile and the high Andes. Most early introductions to Britain probably came from the more accessible coastal range. In the wild, the monkey-puzzle grows in winter-cool (often snowy) altitudes, which nevertheless receive high light, especially in the summer months; some are in granitic, rocky terrains. In cultivation, the species thrives very well in south-west England, maturing in the course of a century or so: there is a particularly fine avenue at Bicton, Devon. The

Araucaria araucana: wild forest habitat in temperate rain forest, southern Chile, growing on granite in the coastal range.

species reproduces especially well from cultivated seed, and self-sets are occasionally found in the vicinity of parents, especially in disturbed ground. William Lobb made many of the early introductions to Cornwall, and it was during the planting of specimens at one Cornish estate – Pencarrow – that a visitor remarked that it would puzzle a monkey to climb it – hence the name 'monkey-puzzle tree'. Indeed, a local tree surgeon described graphically to me what a nightmare it was for a professional, armed with a chainsaw and protective gear, to climb among the sharp leaves. These adaptations to the tree evolved in order that it would not to be eaten by herbivorous dinosaurs, for the genus *Araucaria* originated in the Jurassic period, and has changed remarkably little since.

Pilgerodendron uviferum (Chilean bog cypress) is a small, slender tree, adapted to survival in wet, acidic soils, usually around the margins of montane bogs and riverine swamps. As a wild plant, it is probably the southernmost conifer in the Western hemisphere. In cultivation in west Cornwall, I have found it to make steady, if slow, growth, similar to that in the wild. Specimens retain their characteristic wild, spire-like habit, and are especially successful in moist, acidic soils.

Pilgerodendron uviferum: trees skirting cushion bog in temperate rain forest, southern Chile.

Austrocedrus chilensis: wild forest habitat in temperate rain forest, southern Chile.

Many of the species from southern Alaska and Vancouver Island, through the Olympic Peninsula, Oregon, to coastal California, thrive in the damp, oceanic climates of these regions. Those of the Olympics and further north are often most suited to cultivation conditions in the west of Scotland; those from the Olympics and further south are more appropriate to Wales and especially Cornwall.

Thuja plicata (Western red cedar) and *Xanthocyparis (Cupressus) nootkatensis* (Nootka cypress and, before DNA analysis, considered to be a species of *Chamaecyparis*) are two cypresses whose hardiness spans this north-south divide, coming, as they do, from oceanic coastal climates. The former stretches from Alaska, south to mid-California; the latter from Alaska to northern Oregon. Both, in the wild, are magnificent forest dominants, with *T. plicata* in particular forming the second-largest trunk diameters of any wild conifer I have encountered. As a measure of the extraordinary growth rates of conifers from this region, many existing specimens of *T. plicata* are recorded in cultivation to be some 37–40m and more in height; those of cultivated *X. nootkatensis* over 26–27m. In the wild, even modest-aged specimens of *T. plicata* often become senescent (dying) at their tops – a phenomenon that they also tend to exhibit in cultivation, often to the concern of their

Lepidothamnus fonkii (Chilean rimu) – a species of spring-fed marshes in the wild – is of potential value in cultivation mostly as a curiosity, since it is one of the few wild conifers in the world that has a small, shrubby, somewhat hebe-like habit. So far as I know, it has yet to be successfully introduced to Britain.

Austrocedrus chilensis (Chilean cedar) exists as a very few introductions, but in contrast to all of the above-mentioned species, is a plant of drier soils in the sunnier, more Mediterranean climates of Chile. In the wild, it appears to be in steep decline, and although it seeds well, the seed is subject to extensive insect-attack, and can be ungerminable. It is a potential subject for plantings in similar warm, sunny sites in south-west England, and should be tried from cutting-grown material.

Of all the southern South American conifers, the small, slender, evergreen *Pilgerodendron uviferum* is my favourite.

Conifers from the Pacific western USA

Many of the numerous species of conifers from western North America have a long history of introduction into the British Isles, stretching back to those of Archibald Menzies, after whom the *Pseudotsuga menziesii* (Douglas fir – which thrives especially well in Scotland) is named.

Thuja plicata: wild forest habitat in temperate rain forest, showing the enormous bole size of an ancient tree, in western Washington State, USA.

owners. At this stage, however, they are likely to produce new rings of healthy trees around them, through layering of the large lower sweeping limbs, which root into the ground.

Sequoia sempervirens (Coast redwood) is the dominant species of the coastal fog-belt of California, and the world's tallest tree. Mature wild specimens are regularly 58–85m tall, with exceptional individuals reaching 99–107m. They have shaft-like trunks, 2.4–4.6m in diameter, and clear of branches for the first 24–30m. Walking in mist-shrouded forests of these trees is like walking in

Sequoia sempervirens: tree growth in cultivation in west Cornwall, after about 100 years.

nature's greatest cathedral (see page 60)! The cool, maritime climate in which Coast redwoods thrive in the wild is not dissimilar to that in parts of Devon and Cornwall, and many of the best cultivated specimens of this species have long thrived in south-western gardens. In north Devon, trees have been recorded making some 35–45m in 120 years, and others approaching this size occur in west Cornwall. *Sequoia sempervirens* should certainly

be planted even more widely. To imitate the habitats of the plant in the wild, trees should be set as pure small groves beside streams in sheltered valley-sides, where they have plenty of room to achieve unhindered progress, and constant access to good ground moisture. A special feature of this species is its ability to regenerate from stumps, and sometimes even from small wood fragments (sold as 'redwood burrs' in the western USA). An outcome of this regenerative ability that I have observed in cultivation is lines of new trees arising from a series of vertical sprouts rooted along old fallen trunks!

Cupressus macrocarpa (Monterey cypress) and *Pinus radiata* (Radiata pine) both hail from the very limited area of the Monterey Peninsula of California. Both are highly salt-tolerant, with good rates of growth on poor soils, in windy, salt-laden conditions, where each grows readily, often to well over 30m in south Devon and Cornwall. Both have been planted widely as windbreak species. *Pinus radiata* reproduces particularly well from cultivated seed, and self-sets especially in disturbed ground. Both thrive in coastal south-west England (though are hardly seen elsewhere), and can form virtual bonsai plants in the most windswept sites in salt-laden conditions. They provide good windbreak species on the Isles of Scilly, for example, where, due to close planting, several eventually became top-heavy, and were finally blown over in the 1990 hurricane. Wide initial spacing and additional renewal every 50 years is a good policy. In many sites in the south-west of England, one feels that both species, and especially *P. radiata*, evolved for our climate. There are some particularly attractive and characteristic tree groups of *P. radiata*, absolutely 'at their best', clinging tenaciously, and flourishing in the face of all the elements, on the craggy seaward bluffs of St Michael's Mount in Penzance Bay. Other good examples are those at Fowey in south Cornwall. A returning Devon or Cornish resident knows that he is truly back in the West Country when he starts encountering these trees in successful semi-natural cultivation.

Abies bracteata (Bristlecone or Santa Lucia fir) is a spectacular fir of the flanks of the Santa Lucia mountains, a little south of the Monterey Peninsula. It is so-called because its cones possess long, spine-tipped bracts that emerge from between the scales, forming 'whiskery' cones. Its shoots are

Abies bracteata: foliar detail showing acutely pointed buds.

also unusual for a conifer, having slender, acute buds like a beech (*Fagus*). As a young tree, the Bristlecone fir is said to be susceptible to frost damage. In western Britain, however, it makes particularly successful growth, achieving 15–34m in about 60 years. Several splendid and well-set specimens can be admired on the campus of the University of Exeter, in Devon. Yet the species is surprisingly under-used.

Torreya californica (Californian nutmeg tree) is a small, wide, yew-like tree, with spine-tipped leaves of a vivid grass-green colour, native to the California coast range and the lower western slopes of the Sierra Nevada. It has separate male and female trees. In the wild it grows as scattered plants along steep, narrow stream valleys, which become dry in summer. *Torreya californica* was introduced to Britain by William Lobb, but remarkably few trees exist in cultivation in the British Isles. In Cornwall its growth is some of the best anywhere, having been recorded to make over 12–15m on several sites in 70 years. It should certainly be more widely planted as small groves in steep, moist, rocky valley sites.

Several other western North American pines have important places in cultivation. Although widely hardy elsewhere, *Pinus contorta* (Lodgepole pine), for example, also has some provenances that are highly salt-tolerant, making it a valuable element in compound windbreaks in south-west England, since it does not grow as large as *P. radiata*. *Pinus muricata* (Bishop pine) also has provenances that are reputedly very salt-tolerant, and deserves trialling here. *Pinus ponderosa* (Ponderosa pine) forms a magnificent tree in the wild, making well over 30m in dry, sunny, slightly inland sites in the Pacific north-west, as do several other related species. It surely has great potential for experimentation in sufficiently well-drained sites in south-west England. Among other western North American pines worthy of more trialling here is *P. coulteri* (Big-cone pine), which, as its name implies, is notorious for bearing the world's heaviest (rugby-ball sized!) woody cone.

Of all these species, the little-cultivated *Torreya californica* is my special favourite.

Conifers from the south-eastern USA

Conifers from the south-eastern USA – especially from Florida – have received remarkably little general experimentation in cultivation in Britain, although many are unusual. For example, in limestone river valleys, Florida has one yew (*Taxus floridiana*) and one nutmeg (*Torreya taxifolia*). Both are rare and threatened in the wild, and for this reason deserve careful experimentation in cultivation, where they would be appropriate for planting in sheltered, sunny, rocky sites, perhaps with limestone added.

The south-eastern portion of the USA has a large number of pine species adapted to hot summers, cool winters, and for the most part, very poor, sandy soils: *Pinus taeda* (Loblolly pine) is a good example. In the wild, one species that has struck me as being particularly beautiful and worthy of trial introduction is *P. palustris* (Longleaf pine). This has long, graceful, grass-green foliage. As a lowland species in Florida, it may be too tender for all but the mildest spots, and like most Florida trees it is probably strongly light-demanding. Yet it could be a particular future tree candidate here, especially in sunnier sites.

Taxodium (the Swamp cypresses), represented by *T. distichum* and *T. ascendens*, occur in the wild from New Jersey and Virginia, south to Alabama

Torreya taxifolia: tree habit in the wild in northern Florida.

and coastal Texas. They are characteristic of the margins of the Everglades freshwater swamp forests of Florida. Unusually, for conifers, they are deciduous. Despite their natural habitat, they thrive when planted in ordinary, moist garden soils in southern England, and are particularly appropriate for planting around the margins of clear lakes. There are one or two particularly fine specimens in parks and gardens in south-west England – for example, in parkland on the edge of the Fal estuary in Truro, and in the Fox Rosehill Gardens in Falmouth.

Conifers from montane Central America and Mexico

The mountains of Mexico contain an extraordinary array of native conifers, especially of the genus *Pinus*, of which there are 47 species within the region. The region also represents the southernmost New World limits for several other northern genera – *Taxodium*, *Picea*, *Pseudotsuga*, and *Abies* (of which some species, such as *A. guatmalensis*, may prove appropriate here, and is so far showing good growth rates in both Cornwall and south Wales). These are some of the trees on which the migratory Monarch butterflies famously roost in

Taxodium distichum: wild forest habitat in northern Florida.

great numbers. Most exist in the wild in mountain valleys, and on cloud-wrapped mountainsides, often in conditions slightly milder than those in Britain. However, many must have substantial areas of climatic overlap, and it is remarkable how few of these species have been tried experimentally in cultivation in south-west England.

Indeed, in Britain, only a very few pines of these origins are usually present in cultivation, with most of these being in the south. These include *Pinus ayacahuite* (Mexican white pine), from Mexico and Guatemala, which is grown for its fine, graceful foliage habit, and very long, soft cones; and *P. patula* (Weeping Ocote pine), from central and eastern Mexico, which has graceful, drooping, slender, grass-green needles. Both attain about 30m in height in the wild, and have been recorded as reaching over 21m and 27m respectively in cultivation in south-west England. Although both were introduced to Britain *c.*1837–40, they remain relatively scarce – mainly in a few estates, collections, and parks – and deserve wider planting. Hillier also recommends *P. leiophylla* (Chihuahana pine), *P. montezumae* var. *lindleyi* (Montezuma pine), and *P. pseudostrobus* (Smooth-bark Mexican pine) – the latter has reached almost 20m in Cornwall. *P. duragensis* (Pino blanco) and *P. engelmannii* (Apache pine) also appear to be likely good candidates for future use in Cornwall.

We can only anticipate that – especially in the event of climatic warming – more of the enormous conifer diversity of this origin could find success in cultivation in south-west England.

Conifers from the mountains of the Mediterranean and North Atlantic islands

Collectively, the mountains of the Mediterranean and North Atlantic islands contain an array of conifers that show success when planted in Britain. These are characterized most impressively by the cedars – *Cedrus atlantica* (Atlas cedar, from the Atlas Mountains of Algeria and Morocco); *C. libani* (Lebanon cedar, from the Taurus Mountains of Syria, Lebanon, and adjacent south-east Turkey), and *C. brevifolia* (Cyprus cedar, from the Paphos Forests of Cyprus). All come from limestone areas, and relatively dry, sunny climates, often with heavy winter snow. These cedars are particularly striking feature trees, with spaced, layered crowns – of considerable beauty when well-

spaced in open park-like landscapes – borne from stocky trunks with scaly bark, often reminiscent of some magnificent lizard. All have much provenance variation in the wild, and some have succeeded to maturity in well-drained sunnier enclaves in south-west England. But each of these species is at its very best in Britain in the mid-English shire counties, where there are magnificent specimens as far apart as Malvern, Cheltenham, Bath, and Bury St Edmunds. (*Cedrus deodara*, which, by contrast, comes from the Himalayas and succeeds well in the south-west of England, is described below – see 'Conifers from China and the wider Sino-Himalayan region'.)

Some *Cupressus* may be worthy of experiment here, in drier and sunnier sites. These include *C. dupreziana* from Algeria, and especially *C. atlantica* from the mountains of Morocco. The latter has been successfully established in Cornwall, and shows great promise with respect to winter hardiness. *Tetraclinis articulata* is also now thriving in one or two Cornish sites, with plants in Falmouth making over 2.5m in a little over ten years.

Pinus pinaster (Maritime pine) is surprisingly hardy in Britain, and succeeds sufficiently well in Cornwall to be not only a garden tree, but also one of the few tree species to grow on local metalliferous mine-spoil sites, where it forms low-growing, open communities, with a semi-natural character all of their own (see also 'Managed revegetation of metalliferous mine-spoil sites', below). Another pine from the Mediterranean, *P. pinea* (Stone pine) is also successfully hardy, and has been widely planted on Tresco, Isles of Scilly, subsequent to the 1990 hurricane. From a little further north, but appropriate to group here, is *P. mugo* (Dwarf mountain pine), with upward-curving, sparsely branched stems, the slow growth and small size of which can be useful in some garden settings.

Also experimental, but appropriate for consideration here, are the species from the wetter climates of the Canary Island mountains. Of these, I have tried the beautiful *Juniperus cedrus* (Cedar juniper), recently introduced to four sites in west Cornwall and growing well. Apparently there were no older introductions of it in south-west England (it is not mentioned among suitable junipers for milder counties by Arnold-Forster) – presumably because no one expected it to be hardy here. Similarly, there is probably great potential, especially in the event of climate warming, for the beautiful Canary Island pine (*Pinus canariensis*). Older specimens in Cornwall have been recorded to make almost 8m in 15 years, and to have achieved heights of 17m. Very few of these conifers have been tried, and experimentation with new provenances is currently in progress.

Pinus canariensis: bark and foliage in wild environment.

Conifers from Japan

The Japanese islands offer a wide range of climates – from those of chilling winters, with winds directly from Siberia in Hokkaido Island in the north, to those of humid, subtropical, oceanic conditions in Yakushima Island off southern Kyushu in the south. There is a high, mountainous backbone, with rugged topography and a great variety of (mostly sedimentary and volcanic) rock types. Most of the surface of these islands was originally clothed with dense forest, from subalpine to warm temperate, containing a rich mixture of coniferous and broadleaf trees, and much of this still exists. It was here that I first fully appreciated that the majority of conifer species in the wild grow either as small, pure patches forming a mosaic within wider mixed forests, or as ones of even more intimately mixed composition with broadleaves – for example, of *Betula*, *Acer*, *Ulmus*, *Fagus*, *Quercus*, *Aesculus*, *Fraxinus*, *Castanopsis*, *Cercidiphyllum*, *Zelkova*, and *Pterocarya* – forming the 'pan-mixed forest' of Japanese literature. In fact, Japan has over 45 native species of conifer, mostly of limited range. The forests – espe-

cially the warm temperate – can have a rich and diverse shrubby undergrowth, including bamboo (for example, *Sasa*, *Phyllostachys*); rhododendron (for example, *Rhododendron fauriei* on Mount Fuji; *R. yakushimanum* on Yakushima); exotics such as *Camellia*, *Photinia*, *Osmanthus*, and *Gardenia*, and a great diversity of ferns (especially of *Dryopteris*, *Polystichum*, *Arachnioides*, and *Athyrium* species).

The importance of the Japanese tree flora is that, since Japan was not glaciated, the diversity of its genera and species represents more closely, in island form, that which was present during the late Tertiary period. It is therefore the nearest living equivalent to the flora in Britain and Ireland before the glaciations decimated them. By re-introducing species from Japan (as well as some from China), we are effectively returning the nearest living equivalents of what we would have had, had the glaciations not destroyed these original species here.

Of the more widespread, northern piniferous genera, Japan has a diverse array of *Pinus*, *Abies*, *Picea*, *Larix*, *Pseudotsuga*, and *Tsuga* species. Of these, the main species relevant to our cultivated area might well be *Abies firma* (Momi fir) and *Tsuga sieboldii* (Southern Japanese hemlock). These two species co-associate to form some of the main southernmost conifer and conifer-broadleaf forests (such as on Yakushima Island), and might well be planted in such association in cultivation. Confined to small, southern enclaves, usually as

Tsuga sieboldii: wild forest habitat in temperate rain forest, Yakushima Island, southern Japan.

scattered trees on rocky knolls in broad-leaved forest, is *Pseudotsuga wilsonii*, which appears more slow-growing than its American counterpart, but forms a massive tree with spreading crown as it ages. However, from its near-coastal locations, we might infer that it is probably extremely tender.

A further pinaceous element with a potentially different purpose in cultivation is *Pinus thunbergii* (Japanese black pine) – a remarkably sturdy tree in the wild, which is encountered in Japan only immediately adjacent to coasts, often growing on beach-heads, apparently in sand or among rocks. A few older specimens in the south-west have made nearly 24.5m in height. It therefore seems a likely candidate for wider experiment in salty, coastal areas of Cornwall.

Thujopsis dolobrata (Hiba Arbor-vitae) is a Japanese endemic species and genus, and is an important forest tree in Japan. It occurs from southern Hokkaido and Aomori Prefecture in northern Honshu to southern Kyushu, where it grows either as pure forests (mainly in the north), or in mixed association with broadleaves (especially in the south). Within this range, the Japanese recognize at least two wild varieties: var. *hondai* in the north, and var. *dolobrata* in the south. Across its entire range, however, it is a considerably diversified species in the wild, and there is even further variation with source. All have leafy shoots, which have been described appropriately as having the appearance of stout, glossy, reptilian scales. It makes large trees of over 30m and 200–300 years of age in the wild, usually on rich volcanic soils, where there are clearly many different forms. It is reputed to grow only slowly in cultivation, especially at first, and this may be due in part to the

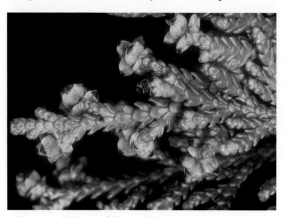

Thujopsis dolobrata: foliar and female cone detail in cultivation.

use of unsuitable provenance sources, for it is clearly vigorous even at a young stage in the wild. By contrast, some trees have been very successful in cultivation in south-west Britain, making more than 15–18m in 100 years in east Devon and west Cornwall. The finest specimen I knew, in the upper garden at Penjerrick, west Cornwall, had a bole diameter of over 1m when it was blown down in the 1990 hurricane. More specimens, and especially more varying provenance sources, of this fine tree should be planted: especially on well-drained sites on better soils.

Cryptomeria japonica (Sugi) is a widespread and extraordinarily diversified single species within Japan, with contrasting natural provenances. It grows at many different altitudes, on different rock types, in different winter climates, and with different lengths of growing season. *Cryptomeria* forms light, open, natural forests of great beauty, containing a diversity of life – in one natural forest, for example, some 300 species of ferns have been recorded. It thrives in rich, moist soils, which can include granitic ones. Of the many different forms, the Pacific coast Dai-Sugi, with long-persistent lower branches that readily layer, and the lower-growing, broad-crowned Yaku-Sugi Yakushima Island form, would seem to offer the most likely stocks for further experiment in cultivation in the Cornish climate. Trees reach heights of 37–49m in the wild, over more than 250 years, and may live very much longer than this. In Britain, trees make best growth in the climates of the west. In south-west England, on good, moist soils, trees have achieved well over 21–24m in 120 years, with tall crowns composed of successive masses of bright green, billowing foliage, borne on upsweeping orange-brown branches.

Sciadopitys verticillata (Japanese umbrella pine) – a conifer genus endemic to Japan – occurs on steep, well-drained, granitic mountain valley-sides in the southern Japanese Alps. Wild trees reach 18–24m in height at well over 250 years of age. This slow-growing species of curious appearance, forming a narrow-spired crown, is occasional in cultivation, although it clearly thrives in mild, moist, cloudy climates. Trees are recorded to make some 11–14m in height in about 70 years in south-west England; and, in time, the species can make a spectacular, beautiful, and unusual evergreen specimen tree or small group. Trees of known wild origin are, however, rare. It is interesting to note that *Sciadopitys*

Sciadopitys verticillata: foliar habit in cultivation.

was a conspicuous member of the mid-latitude, pre-glacial flora of Europe.

Torreya nucifera (Kaya) of central and southern Japan – a narrow, yew-like tree – is a species of damp, stream-fed, valley bottoms in the wild. It is of proven hardiness in Britain, and worthy of wider cultivation on moist soils in sheltered valley sites in the south-west.

Podocarpus macrophyllus and *Nageia* (formerly *Podocarpus*) *nagi* are both species of particularly southern latitudes in the forests of south-western Honshu, where they occur at the northern edge of the east Pacific-fringe range of their respective genera. The former has typical podocarp, willow-like (but evergreen) foliage; the latter has broad, glossy, unusually multiveined leaves, which are boat-shaped. Both can form large trees, and planted trees of *N. nagi* in Japanese temple grounds are said to be over 1,000 years in age. Both should certainly be subject to more, and wider, experimental cultivation in milder, sheltered pockets in the south-west of England.

Of all the Japanese conifers, the slow-growing *Sciadopitys verticillata* is my special favourite, although, where space allows, the faster-growing *Cryptomeria japonica* can be particularly beautiful, and deserves far wider planting as small, well-spaced groups.

Conifers from China and the wider Sino-Himalayan region

The enormous region stretching from the South China Sea and Taiwan, to Vietnam and across the Himalayas, incorporates a vast range of climates and plant habitats. Overall, the geographical position of China, on the eastern side of the Asiatic landmass, ensures that at every altitude climates are more continental than in Europe. Extremes are perhaps least apparent in the more southerly latitudes of mainland China, and in the insular position of Taiwan, whose species thus rank high in importance in this list.

Like Japan, the whole of the area of China was unglaciated during the Pleistocene period, and consequently much of the pre-glacial flora survives. The combination of climatic and habitat diversity, and lack of glaciation, combine to ensure that this vast region harbours the largest, richest, and most diverse conifer flora in the Northern hemisphere. Its conifers include many endemic species, and some restricted and endemic genera.

We shall look at a small selection of examples of conifers, mainly from the more southerly latitudes of this region. For convenience, these are grouped here under families, as a list. Some have been tried in cultivation and found successful. However, even for these, a very limited number of introductions suggests that the cultivated genetic base is probably highly limited, and that much of the wider provenance variation that is likely to be present in the wild has yet to be sampled. For many other taxa, which are virtually untried in total (many yet un-introduced), the suggested array of taxa is particularly highly experimental.

Chinese Taxaceae

Candidate species include: *Amentotaxus* spp. (notably *argotaenia, assamica, yunnanensis*); *Cephalotaxus fortunei; Pseudotaxus chinensis; Torreya* spp. (notably *grandis, jackii*). Of those for which there is already some cultivated experience in Cornwall, *Amentotaxus* has proved hardy as a cool greenhouse plant, and is particularly beautiful, and *Pseudotaxus* has proved hardy out of doors in both east and west Cornwall.

Cepahalotaxus fortunei: detail of foliar habit in cultivation.

Amentotaxus formosana: foliar and female cone detail in cultivation.

Fokienia hodginsii: foliar detail in cultivation.

Chinese Cupressaceae

Candidate species include: *Cupressus* spp. (for example, *duclouxiana, gigantea, funebris, torulosa, cashmeriana*); *Chamaecyparis formosensis; Calocedrus formosana; Calocedrus macrolepis; Fokienia hodginsii; Juniperus indica,* and *J. recurva.* Of those for which there is already some cultivated experience in Cornwall,

Juniperus indica thrives well, forming a bush with drooping foliage, and the particularly beautiful *Cupressus cashmeriana* has proved hardy and successful in at least two west Cornwall valley-garden sites. Of these Chinese conifers, *Cupressus cashmeriana* is, in my view, one of the most successful, and well deserves far wider cultivation in west Cornwall gardens.

Chinese Taxodiaceae

Candidate species include: *Metasequoia glyptostroboides; Glyptostrobus pensilis; Cunninghamia sinensis,* and *C. konishii; Taiwania cryptomerioides,* and *T. flousiana.* Of those for which there is already some cultivated experience in Cornwall, *Metasequoia glyptostroboides* (Dawn redwood) grows particularly rapidly and successfully in inland Devon and Cornwall, and is best in moist, but well-illuminated sites. This also applies to *Cunninghamia sinensis* (China fir), of which some provenances perform well (with a few trees planted post-1844 achieving over 21–24m in well-drained soils in Cornwall, including a blue-foliage form believed to be an introduction from northern Hupeh. *Glyptostrobus* and *Taiwania* are, so far as I am aware, as yet untried over any prolonged period. However, young trees of *Taiwania,* of known wild origin and tried for over ten years, have proved hardy in many parts of Britain and Ireland, and have made some 3m in ten years in Cornwall. They have, however, proved susceptible to slug damage wherever planted. It is interesting to note that both *Glyptostrobus* and *Taiwania* were members of the pre-glacial flora of southern Europe.

Chinese Pinaceae

Candidate species include: *Abies chensiensis, densa, forrestii,* and *delavayi; Picea* spp. (for example, *spinulosa, farreri, likiangensis, brachytyla,* and *morrisonicola*); *Tsuga dumosa; Pinus* spp. (including *gerardiana, armandii, roxburghii, bhutanica,* and *krempfii*); *Larix griffithii; Cedrus deodara; Pseudolarix amabilis; Nothotsuga longibracteata; Cathaya argyrophylla; Keteleeria* spp. (for example, *formosana,* and *fortunei*). Of those for which there is already some cultivated experience in Cornwall, there are several very successful trees. These include *Abies densa; Pinus armandii* (Armand's pine), and *Pinus bhutanica; Larix griffithii,* and *Pseudolarix amabilis* (Golden larch). Of these, on grounds of horticultural attractiveness, *Abies densa,* with sweeping, pagoda-like branch form;

Pinus bhutanica, with long, graceful, drooping foliage, and *Pseudolarix amabilis*, with bright green spring leaves and golden autumn foliage, deserve especially wider planting. Although relatively recent introductions (late 1980s), *A. densa* has made about 5m in height in ten years, and *P. bhutanica* about 6m in the same period, in well-drained, sheltered sites in west Cornwall. Older specimens of *Pseudolarix* have achieved heights of 18–20m in west Cornwall, although remarkably few have been planted. *Cedrus deodara*, introduced as early as 1831, is the only true cedar to perform well in our wet climate (which is much closer to that of its Himalayan home than it is to that of the other true cedars), though reasonable shelter and freedom from salt winds, perhaps on more inland sites, are desirable for it. In good sites, specimens regularly make fine trees of about 26–29m in height in a century. *Pinus gerardiana*, *krempfii*, *Nothotsuga longibracteata*, *Cathaya argyrophylla*, and the species of *Keteleeria* are all particularly exciting, but rare, wild taxa deserving careful and sensitive experimentation in cultivation conditions.

It is interesting to note that *Nothotsuga*, *Cathaya*, and *Keteleeria* were widely present in the pre-glacial flora of northern Europe, when they grew in association with numerous pines, as well as *Cunninghamia*, *Taiwania*, *Sequoia*, and *Sciadopitys*.

Cunninghamia konishii: tree habit in cultivation: Glendurgan, Cornwall. The tree is probably at least 80 years old.

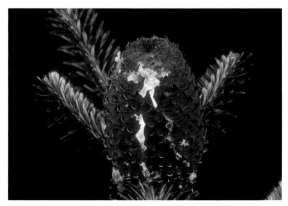

Abies forrestii (named after the plant collector, George Forrest): detail of female cone habit in cultivation, autumn.

Picea likiangensis: foliar and female cone detail in cultivation.

Ginkgo biloba. Above: ancient cultivated tree surviving in Japanese Temple ground, Kyoto, Japan. Below: foliar detail in cultivation, spring.

Chinese Ginkgoaceae

Although not strictly a conifer, but a more primitive conifer-relative, *Ginkgo biloba* (the Maidenhair tree) is conveniently included here. The tree is curious in many ways. It is the world's only tree species that has motile sperm, while the species also has separate male and female trees. As mature trees, some specimens produce curious, pointed outgrowths from high on the trunks and branches. Plants are characterised by their beautiful, fine-veined, fan-shaped cleft leaves, which turn a beautiful amber-yellow in autumn and are deciduous in winter, and there is much variation in leaf-form, especially between young and old trees. Plants are highly light-demanding; they usually grow only slowly at first, and thereafter somewhat unpredictably! However, specimens in Devon and Cornwall – planted in good soils on well-drained

sites – grow at rates of around 15m in 50–60 years, and have so far achieved heights of over 26m, and trunk girth of about 1m. Despite its slow initial growth, this tree deserves wider planting in sites where there is adequate space for it to reach eventual maturity.

This magnificent tree belongs to a botanical family 200 million years old. It survived through history only in China, where it was planted as a sacred tree in monastery gardens, which are the origin of all of our modern cultivated trees – the first was planted at Kew in 1760. It thrives in Japan, where specimens survived the Second World War even in Hiroshima, and today is virtually the only street tree that unhesitatingly tolerates Tokyo car exhaust fumes! Primitive and curious it may be, but ginkgo is clearly one of nature's great survivors.

Ginkgo was also a member of the pre-glacial European flora, when this was represented by what are probably several species.

Conifers from the Australian, Tasmanian, and New Zealand region

There are a large number of conifers throughout the Australian, Tasmanian, and New Zealand region, making it – together with the adjacent south-west Pacific islands – the richest conifer centre in the Southern hemisphere. Most are insular species, endemic to their respective island areas. In the wild, they are chiefly characteristic of Southern temperate rain forest communities, often forming tall and vegetationally dominant trees. Most belong to the families Podocarpaceae and Araucariaceae, with a few in other families. All are evergreen, and often they are of particularly unusual and of relatively exotic horticultural appearance by Northern-hemisphere standards.

In their wild habitats, most of these conifers are closely adapted to oceanic conditions, with moist climates, cloudy skies, and frequent light rain, often interspersed with intermittent periods of particularly bright illumination and higher than average temperatures. However, there is wide provenance variation in most of the spe-

Athrotaxis selaginoides: female cone habit in detail, in cultivation, autumn.

in the Cornish climate, where they make better growth than elsewhere except for south-west Ireland. Despite this potential, there are only scattered records of *A. cupressoides* (Pencil pine) and *A. laxifolia* (Summit cedar) seen in a few Cornish gardens. These are slow-growing, but records show their eventually making nearly 9m, and 12–17m respectively. *Athrotaxis selaginoides* (King Billy pine) is faster growing, and somewhat more widely planted, possibly on account of its ready ability to strike from cuttings, and for these to form plants with good leaders. These can grow into handsome trees with upsweeping branches, and specimens I have planted of several provenances have grown almost 5m in ten years in the Cornish climate, on a moist, well-drained slope.

cies (by habitat, latitude, or altitude in their native habitats), hence several of the coniferous species of these regions are likely to have provenances that have sufficient cool-climate tolerance to be valuable horticultural subjects today in the far south-west of our region.

An overall list of such species includes: *Athrotaxis cupressoides, A. selaginoides* and *A. laxifolia; Libocedrus bidwillii* and *L. plumosa; Phyllocladus aspleniifolius, P. glaucus,* and *P. trichomanoides; Lagarostrobus franklinii; Dacrydium cupressinum; Dacrycarpus dacrydioides; Prumnopitys ferruginea; Lepidothamnus laxifolius; Diselma archeri; Podocarpus totara; Wollemia nobilis; Araucaria bidwillii; Agathis australis;* and *Manoao colensoi.*

Of those for which there is already useful cultivated experience in Cornwall, *Lagarostrobus franklinii* (Huon pine) performs well, especially beside water, in several west Cornwall gardens, but makes only slow growth here, seldom exceeding 5–9m in height, and often adopting a weeping habit characteristic of the branches of this species in the wild, without an obvious leader. This may be the result of the trees having been initially cutting-propagated: introduction of new, seed-grown material from a variety of wild parent sources is much to be desired.

Also from Tasmania, the genus *Athrotaxis* is seen surprisingly rarely in Cornwall, its few specimens perhaps reflecting a scarcity of available material, and possibly, a false presumption of tenderness. All, however, make fairly small trees, which are entirely hardy

Agathis australis: wild forest habitat in temperate rain forest, northern New Zealand, probably at least 800 years of age.

Several *Libocedrus*, such as *L. bidwillii*, seem hardy here, though all remain rare in cultivation. All have the potential to make particularly beautiful small trees of bushy, billowing crown form, composed of fern-like foliar sprays, often of bright, grass-green colour. So far, *Libocedrus plumosus* is proving to be a very worthwhile hardy conifer in cultivation, and is now established in several Cornish gardens.

All *Phyllocladus* – for example, *P. asplenifolius* (Celery-top pine) – are also rare in cultivation, and deserving of wider future experimentation. Slender, rather slow-growing specimens of *Podocarpus totara* have made good progress where planted in the past, while older, nineteenth-century records suggest that species such as *Araucaria bidwillii* had already survived over 50 years in a sheltered valley site in west Cornwall. Again, the number of provenance introductions would appear to be highly limited, and wider and more systematic experimentation with these genera might well bring forth desirable cultivated trees. Similarly, *Araucaria heterophylla* (Norfolk Island pine); *A. angustifolia*

Phyllocladus aspleniifloius: foliar detail in the wild.

(Parana pine), and *Agathis australis* (New Zealand Kauri) all appear to be on the very margins of hardiness in mainland west Cornwall today (although there are records of *A. heterophylla* having grown to 27m on Tresco, in the Isles of Scilly). All are clearly subjects for careful experimentation for the future in milder, mainland enclaves.

Probably the most beautiful of all of the coniferous trees from this region is *Dacrydium cupressinum* (Rimu), from New Zealand, which has slender, gracefully drooping, long, pendulous trains of bright, sea-green foliage, forming billowing masses with age. A few specimens exist in southern Ireland, so it is surprising to see so few established individuals in Cornwall (though there is a record of one having once grown to 10m on Tresco). New Zealand represents the southernmost extent of the whole genus, however, which is essentially tropical montane in locations such as New Guinea, New Caledonia, and Malaysia, from which sources the New Zealand member is thus an evolutionary outlier. Clearly, it is tender for these reasons, enjoying high oceanicity of climate without cold extremes. Its long-term hardiness in Cornwall is therefore questionable, and it thus truly represents a species closely 'on the edge' in this respect. However, Rimu is wide-ranging in its New Zealand home – where it forms one of the most magnificent of native trees, reaching 50m in height – and extends to Southland, often co-associated in the wild with Kamahi (*Weinmannia racemosa*). Today, there is a 3m specimen at Trengwainton, and more recently introductions have been made to Tregrehan. My own single specimen – tried experimentally in inland west Cornwall at 100+m altitude – has so far made unhesitating progress over ten years, despite suffering

Phyllocladus aspleniifloius: tree habit in temperate rain forest, Tasmania.

the handicap of having a mature oak tree fall on it! There is considerable scope for wider experimentation with introductions of this species.

Of all of these Australian conifers, *Athrotaxis selaginoides*, from Tasmania, and *Dacrydium cupressinum*, from New Zealand, are my favourites.

Conifers from other potential tropical montane sources

This sparsely-distributed, scattered, and horticulturally little-known eclectic assembly includes a diversity of hardly-tried conifers, especially from African and south-west Asian/Pacific montane sources. These are species with a future that would be best assured under cool, but well-illuminated glass, but which may, especially in future, have possibilities outside. My highly conservative list thus includes:

Afrocarpus (formerly *Podocarpus*) *falcatus* (south and south-east Africa); *Podocarpus* spp. – for example, *P. henkelii* and *P. latifolius* (South Africa: Cape Province, etc.); *Widdringtonia* spp., possibly *W. whytei* (Malawi, Mt Mulanje); *W. cedarbergensis* (Cape Province, Cedarberg Mountains); *Dacrycarpus* spp., including *cinctus* from the Moluccas (Ceram), Sulawesi, and New Guinea; further species of *Nageia* from the west Pacific basin, and *Papuacedrus* species – for example, *P. papuana* – from the New Guinea mountains. And, especially as cool greenhouse subjects: *Acmopyle pancheri*, *Dacrydium araucarioides*, *Neocallitropsis araucarioides*, *Parasitaxus ustus*, *Falcatifolim taxoides*, *Agathis ovata*, and *Sundacarpus amarus*. All but the first and last of these are from New Caledonia.

I have grown most of these as cool (frost-free) greenhouse subjects, and confirm that under such conditions they (and very many others) have performed surprisingly well. This evidence suggests that day-length and illumination factors are not limiting, and that it is likely to be mainly temperature regimes that will control the success of these taxa as horticultural specimens for the future.

Of these potential future trees, it is those from the Pacific island of New Caledonia which are some of the most diverse and most fascinating in appearance of those found in the wild, and which include some of the world's most threatened species. Of these particularly, *Neocallitropsis araucarioides* is, in my view, the most beautiful conifer in the world.

Acmopyle pancheri: the curious female cone, detail in cultivation, from the mountains of New Caledonia.

The present and future of conifer cultivation 'on the edge'

In the wild, most of the conifer species discussed in this chapter grow to form individuals of magnificent stature, and are usually natural forest dominants or co-dominants. Indeed, the species discussed here include the world's tallest, and some of its most long-lived, trees. As either wild or cultivated specimens, most improve in majesty and grandeur of form with age. The majority reach such maturity only after a century or more, sometimes many centuries. By this time, most will have become highly individualistic in form, and aged conifer citizens wear such cragginess well.

Planting in garden landscapes

In cultivation, the majority of conifers demand large and long-term planting spaces to achieve the full benefit of their ultimate grandeur. So wherever possible, they should be treated as specimen trees – either as individuals or as groups – and planted with centres normally spaced at least 10m apart. Although as young trees they may initially look somewhat 'lost' at such spacings, they will be able to develop their maximum form unhindered, usually retaining branches to near ground-level, which can be pruned back later as required. Other, shorter-lived trees can be planted in between: most conifers mix well with broadleaves. Such planting formulae have long had a place in the traditional setting of the grand estate, where conifers have been used extensively and to great effect by landscape designers such as 'Capability' Brown. It is a mistake to believe that all such planting should be done at once. In the managed landscape, there needs to be opportunity for new generations of trees (both broadleaf and coniferous) to be added in the future, and it will be subsequent generations of our children who plant these. Our plantings today are a bequest, and a positive symbol to the future, and should always be perceived in this perspective.

Managed revegetation of metalliferous mine-spoil sites

Conifers have considerable future roles to play in the managed revegetation of a variety of former industrial sites, especially metalliferous mine-spoil sites. These areas are typically dominated by poor, siliceous rocks, which still contain appreciable residues of tin, often copper, and sometimes other metals, and arsenic and acidic sulphides. Pines in particular have been tried successfully on some of these sites in west Cornwall – but only a very few species.

It is also important to note that many abandoned mine-spoil sites are now developing their own specific and distinctive floras and faunas, which are often different from those of undisturbed terrains in Cornwall. These have unique and evolving biodiversity value in their own right, which it is also important to conserve.

Nevertheless, pine woodlands on some old mine-spoil sites are developing into new and quite distinctive habitat types in their own right. These are also different from existing native areas, and the biodiversity value to be achieved by these sites should not be overlooked. The best are where trees are planted widely, to allow light to penetrate between mature canopies, forming naturally open, well-illuminated, park-like, semi-natural landscapes, within the shelter of which develops an associated diversity of flora and fauna.

In such future developments, great sensitivity and close collaboration are needed, with biodiversity surveys of the sites themselves, in order to identify those that may or may not be appropriately planted with tree species. The motto must be one of 'horses for courses', for together, both routes can lead to considerable landscape and biodiversity enhancement. Both have their place, provided that they are achieved sensitively, co-operatively, and in appropriate settings.

As future 'green banks'

The history of conifer introductions into these islands has shown that a very great number of species not only survive if sited appropriately within our many different climates, but often grow well, especially under conditions of British rainfall! In terms of temperature extremes, these climates vary from relatively continental in northeast Scotland, to relatively mild and oceanic in south-west England. Experience has shown that there are conifer species from many parts of the world which are particularly appropriate to each of these extremes, and to virtually all climatic intermediates, and that matching of the climate in cultivation to that of the wild source of the material is especially important with conifers if greatest success of individual species is to be achieved.

Cunninghamia konishii: young plant from seed of known wild origin, under propagation.

Araucaria araucana: wild tree habit with characteristic parasol-like crowns, southern Chile.

tant. We can predict that such issues will become even more important in future, especially as the world's wild forests continue to diminish.

It was with the plight of so many of the world's rarest conifer species' safe future in mind that, in 1976, I was fortunate to have the opportunity to establish Edinburgh Royal Botanic Garden's *Conifer Conservation Programme* (now continuing as the *International Conifer Conservation Programme*). This Programme is dedicated to bringing together the roles of science, horticulture, and conservation to focus directly on the many scores of indigenous conifer species whose wild numbers have already critically declined. The Programme has aimed to establish cultivated populations containing as wide an array of available genetic diversity of individuals of these species as possible, and to set these in permanent 'safe-haven' sites in cultivation in the British Isles, where they can be well tended, and their onward growth and progress carefully observed, monitored, and recorded.

The original stimulus for this was a lengthy trip I made to the wild mountain forests of Japan, Taiwan, and Tasmania, where I saw for myself some of the world's most unusual conifer species, and the fragility of their wild survival, but from which I was still able to collect good seed. As a result, the taxonomically distinctive *Sciadopitys verticillata* became the species I used to pilot the Programme. Since then,

History has also shown from early introductions such as that of the monkey-puzzle (*Araucaria araucana*), from the coastal ranges of southern Chile, and the southern Chinese Silver fir (*Abies delavayi*), that since their introduction, populations have declined in abundance in the wild, sometimes greatly. Yet those that were planted in cultivation, such as the monkey-puzzle, are now, a century and more later, producing good home-grown seed. From this, new plants can often be reared successfully – especially from tree individuals planted originally as groups (including avenues), allowing inter-pollination between individuals to take place. That this has happened already is, in a way, an accident of history, but it is one from which we can learn much today, when species are becoming rare in the wild, and issues of species conservation are impor-

Araucaria araucana: developing female cones in cultivation.

Abies delavayi: tree habitat in the wild, in an increasingly deforested landscape in western China.

a great number of threatened species have been introduced successfully into well-managed, long-term, climate-matched sites in the British Isles, resulting in the successful outdoor establishment of whole populations of many. It was important that the Programme itself had a long-term future, and since I retired in 1996, this work has been ably taken forward by my former deputy, Martin Gardner. With progress recorded, and success between different sites compared, these 'green-banks' are already providing valuable information on the requirements for best success of individual species under study; their surviving genetic diversity, and conditions for their ultimate seed-pro-

Abies delavayii: male cone habit at pollen-shed stage in cultivation, spring.

Abies delavayii: female cone habit at pollination stage in cultivation, spring.

Future hope: *Araucaria araucana.* Seed germination from home-produced seed in experimental cultivation in Britain.

Araucaria araucana: seedlings from home-produced seed in experimental cultivation in Britain. These will be trees in our grandchildren's generation.

duction behaviour. Meanwhile, the populations themselves are growing into seed resources for potential wild re-establishment of species in the future, which will be achieved within our grandchildren's generation. Growing trees is always a long-term business!

During the whole of the twentieth century, and especially during the latter half of it, there was a dramatic increase in the exploitation of timber resources on every continent where conifer forests occur. In particular, primary 'old growth' (i.e., original) forests are being lost virtually wherever they occur. This is a loss not only of species and of ancient trees, but so often too, a loss of the whole ecosystem of which these trees are the dominant elements. Aware of this, my colleague Aljos Farjon and I undertook the compilation of an end-of-the-century global assessment of conifer diversity and threats to the world's coniferous trees, to bring these issues more specifically to international attention (Farjon & Page, 1999). The most threatened species and the world's conifer 'hot spots' of high numbers of threatened species were particularly identified. Conservation of all of these species in the wild is the primary objective, but conserving species in cultivation in multiple locations provides an additional safeguard, should loss of entire species in the wild eventually occur.

As far as the south-west is concerned, there is a particularly important present and future role to be played here. For many of the conifer species considered in this chapter (for which further details may be found in some of the works mentioned in 'Further Reading') originate from the world's temperate rain forests and tropical mountain forests, where the often isolated and ancient tree species are especially under constant threat from logging.

With likely further climatic amelioration enhancing the 'warm and wet' image of the far south-west of England in the future, additional conifer species, especially of these origins, may well come into the range of even stronger candidates for outdoor cultivation. In this sense, Cornwall in particular provides a valuable 'trial ground' on the rather rapid learning curve of cultivated information on species for which there is, as yet, only minimal historic experience, but on which we can build scientifically from knowledge of the ecology of these species in the wild. In cultivation, such conditions are more likely to be matched if future temperatures take the form of especially milder winter minima, with adequately dispersed and continuingly gentle and steady rainfall.

In this event, our role in the far south-west in pioneering the study of plant adaptations to such changes would become an important one, both in the wild and in our cultivated environments, with increasingly wider application of the data and of the horticultural experience-base elsewhere – and perhaps quite widely – in future years.

4 Palms

Mark Brent

The majority of palms exist within a band of 40°N and 40°S, with only a few species crossing this threshold. The number of genera within the family Palmae – or Arecaceae – is currently around 192; species number some 2,500: as with all plant families, there is constant taxonomic revision. The taxonomy of palms has occasionally been a source of controversy, and in this chapter Henderson *et al.* (1995) and Gibbons (1993) have been used. A more complex reference to both nomenclature and botany may be found in *Genera Palmarum* (Uhl & Dransfield, 1987).

Left: *Trachycarpus fortunei* – Chusan palms – in the valley at Trebah, Cornwall. (See page 88.)

Phoenix canariensis, Tresco Abbey Garden, Isles of Scilly.

Introduction

Seldom does an introduction to palms fail to mention their unquestionable regal appearance: the palm authority E.J.H. Corner (1966) eulogizes that of all land plants the palm is the most distinguished, 'the perfect idea, popular or philosophic of what a plant should be' – and the connotation – a delight to the promotion of tourism – that their presence is an indication of a benign, mild climate. These notions are further attested by the dramatic impact of palms in many familiar gardens: the majestic *Trachycarpus fortunei* in the valley at Trebah (photo page 86), which surely persuade visitors to forget any lingering doubts that they are truly glimpsing a small piece of the Himalayas relocated in Cornwall; the irrepressible *Phoenix canariensis* withstanding the Atlantic gales in the island garden of Tresco Abbey; and the grove of *Trachycarpus* that adds to the serenity of the churchyard at St Just-in-Roseland.

However, there is a conundrum in Cornwall in that, despite the renowned qualities of the climate, there is a limited diversity of mature palm species in the county, and certainly not a stock that could be compared with, say, the south of France. Closer to home, the Isles of Scilly sustain mature palms of several descriptions – *Phoenix*, *Jubaea*, and *Livistona*. In Torquay, south Devon, and further south, in Brittany, are *Phoenix* and *Jubaea* of an impressive size. Mature specimens of *Butia capitata* are seen occasionally in Cornwall, perhaps the finest example being in the village of Flushing. *Chamaerops humilis* has long stood the test of time in many parks, and *Trachycarpus fortunei* has indeed naturalized in several gardens.

Yet one has to ask why, in a county so famed for an interest in tender plants, there are no large *Phoenix canariensis*, or indeed *Jubaea chilensis*? The lack of the latter is particularly puzzling in view of the fact that the famed Chilean plant collector, William Lobb, was a Cornishman. References to palms in the seminal works of Thurston and Arnold-Forster are sparse; indeed Arnold-Forster

Trachycarpus fortunei, St Just-in-Roseland churchyard.

devotes as much space to *Paulownia tomentosa* as he does to the entire subject of palms. Conjecture from an older generation of gardeners is that the architectural qualities that appeal to present-day garden designers and plant enthusiasts were seen by some as too stark, and therefore not suited to the Cornish environment.

However, research in journals and in the archives of Treseder's Nurseries confirms an active interest in the cultivation of palms in early twentieth-century Cornwall, notably in locations such as Falmouth. One reason for the demise of cultivation here may have been urbanization, and the loss of some fine gardens. Tom Hudson of Tregrehan is more prosaic in his suggestion that many individuals and estates may have been guarded about particularly treasured species, the cultivation and loss of which may have gone unreported.

Verbal evidence by the Cornish garden historian, Douglas Ellory Pett points to climate as being responsible for the present lack of large specimens of certain species in the county. Pett reports witnessing several fine, trunk-forming *Phoenix canariensis* in the environs of Penzance succumb to enduring catastrophic cold spells in the early 1960s. Indeed, such were conditions at this time that the Royal Horticultural Society commissioned a cold report, in which damage is recorded as afflicting the health of sizeable palms in Torquay and elsewhere.

But the question remains: why did the Torquay and Tresco specimens survive, when Cornish trees died? Pett alludes to the fact that the ground froze considerably – a rare occurrence in coastal Cornwall – which may have crippled the vulnerable surface roots. Another factor is the relative humidity of the regions: Tresco has lower rainfall than the mainland, and compared with locations in west Cornwall, Torquay hides in something of a rain shadow, and so receives less inundation than similar locations in Cornwall. Luck, in the form of snowfall patterns and weather fronts, has also been a significant factor.

Apart from Trebah and Tresco, there are very few instances in Cornwall of palms being used deliberately as a dominant element in a landscape. Lamorran House Gardens in St Mawes, created since 1982 by Robert Dudley-Cooke, is perhaps the sole example of an 'intended vernacular' or style being enhanced by the use of palms. In Falmouth – inspired by the brothers Simon and Tim Miles – a conscientious and deliberate effort to utilize palms in municipal areas has been made with great success. Slowly, a greater diversity of species is filtering into public gardens as part of their regeneration. Hopefully, the foresight of those who have contributed to the planting of palms in the valley at Glendurgan, for instance, will be rewarded in time. Apart from these examples, it is quite often private individuals who have been the most intrepid in recent times, and they should not be forgotten.

Such is the new-found enthusiasm for cultivating palms – brought on by factors as diverse as the availability of material, through the efforts of individuals such as Martin Gibbons at the Palm Centre in London; increased foreign travel, and changing tastes in garden design – that it is to be hoped that a more lasting and diverse legacy of palms will be established in Cornwall.

This chapter discusses palms as they relate to warm temperate zones, in the form of a geographical journey. It aims to bring to light current efforts to cultivate those palms which, more often than not, exist 'on the edge', and which could be further exploited on the Cornish mainland. Minimum temperatures are given where possible.

South America

South America has long been recognized by Cornish gardeners as having a tremendous wealth of botanical treasure of great potential for our gardens. It is quite surprising, given their distribution around the margins of the more temperate regions of the continent, that many more palm species than were previously considered for cultivation have not been utilized in our gardens. Of those species that display fundamental levels of hardiness, only *Butia capitata*, the Jelly palm from

Butia capitata.

Butia yatay.

Syagrus romanzoffianum at La Mortola, Italy.

southern Brazil and Uruguay, can be seen to have reached any significant size in Cornwall. Three mature examples may be observed flowering on a regular basis around the county – two in Penzance, the most accessible, but alas in some state of decay, at Trewidden; the third, and perhaps the finest, in a private garden in Flushing. Many more specimens have been planted in recent years, and some are achieving impressive proportions, notably at Lamorran and Fox Rosehill. Recently, the availability of this blue-grey, feathery palm, with distinctive shoehorn leaf bases left behind on the trunk after pruning, has become much more widespread within the nursery trade. European imports are being supplemented with semi-mature specimens, shipped directly to the UK from South America. Additionally, several other species of *Butia* may be considered for cultivation: *B. yatay*, of which there is a fine example at Lamorran, makes a particularly beautiful specimen, its feathery appearance being much more refined than that of its cousin *B. capitata*. Other species will no doubt present

themselves in the near future, particularly a third species, *B. archeri*, and *B. eriospatha*, which shares a similar range to the southernmost distribution of *B. capitata*.

Reaching one of the southernmost latitudes in the Americas – equal to that of the genus *Jubaea* – is the Queen palm, *Syagrus romanzoffianum*. Genetically close to the true coconut, the Queen palm has on occasion been grown in Cornish gardens. While exhibiting graceful disposition to growth in the more sheltered parts of the Mediterranean region, its drawbacks – as far as cultivation in Cornwall is concerned – are its dislike of salt-laden gales and, more pressingly, its need for far more summer heat than our climate provides. However, an example grows in the gardens of Lamorran, having 'existed' for a number of years, and fended off a frost of -4°C, albeit in a dry cold spell. Other species, given *Syagrus*' distribution in Brazil, could be worth trialing in the future. A bi-generic, but self-sterile *Butia* × *Syagrus* hybrid – × *Butiagrus narbonndii* – evidently originating in North American cultivation, could well provide ornamental zest, underpinned with inherent robustness from the *Butia*. Robert Lee Riffle (Riffle, *et al*, 2003) considers this hybrid (or 'mule' palm) to be the best tropical-looking palm for non-tropical locations.

Considerably more sturdy, and hailing from the homelands of the monkey-puzzle (*Araucaria araucana*), is *Jubaea chilensis*, the Chilean wine palm, which is perhaps at its best before the foliage is raised too high on a steely trunk of some girth. It is surprising that there are no mature specimens in Cornwall, especially since there are sizeable trees in Torquay; three were planted in a private residence in 1900 (Bean, 1937), and another in Tresco Abbey Garden in 1914 (King, 1985). Given the Cornish passion for Chilean plants, this defies logic! Bean reports the 1879 experiment to grow this palm outside at Kew, which clearly indicates that the notion of its potential hardiness has been with us for some time. Several decent plants are being established at Lamorran; at the wonderful garden at The Old Rectory, Marazion (seed obtained from Tresco, *c.*1970), and in the public

Jubaea chilensis at Lamorran House Gardens, Cornwall.

parks in Falmouth. With the availability of more sizeable stock, others are being introduced to gardens like Heligan. *Jubaea chilensis* is likely to withstand temperatures of -8°C, and although slow to establish, surely lends itself to wider cultivation. It is definitely an investment for the dedicated. Don Tollefson (1997a) wisely regards this palm as being a behemoth, not to be planted in restrictive positions.

A rather more fierce genus from South America, introduced to Cornwall more recently, is *Trithrinax*, whose name derives from a Greek word meaning trident, or three-pronged fork; thus *Trithrinax* relates to three tridents. Few plants, let alone palms, could compare with the armoury presented by this genus. The corrugated, blueygreen fronds of *T. campestris*, tipped with spines, provide at least one defence option to the plant, but the spines covering the trunk warn of the palm's hostile intent long before the foliage is encountered. Although not for the faint-hearted, the colour of its fronds, its sturdiness, and the fact that it is considered one of the most cold-tolerant palms in South America, ought to be of interest to those seeking a challenge. Perhaps a slightly more aggressive alternative to *Brahea armata*, its seasonally dry habitat does dictate a fair degree of drainage, and the need for summer warmth. American experiences suggest a minimum of -12°C!

Slightly more friendly is the species *Trithrinax brasiliensis* (syn. *T. acanthacoma*). Softer in leaf, and with a frond more reminiscent of genera such as *Trachycarpus*, this has been nurtured steadily for some time at Lamorran, and imported specimens are becoming increasingly common. A key element of its appeal, especially in a good example, is the ability of the narrow, brown needles surrounding the apex of the trunk to form a webbed pattern. *Trithrinax brasiliensis* should be hardy to about -5°C, although humidity at this temperature would pose a problem, especially given the palm's normal dry forest habitat.

Leaving the wildest member of the pack to last, *Trithrinax schizophylla* (syn. *T. biflabellata*), hailing from western Paraguay and northern Argentina, is found occasionally in specialist nurseries. Its trunk, encased in persistent needles not unlike knitting needles, ought to appeal to the masochistic palm grower. It is well worth experimenting with, but should not be planted close to the edge of a path: I speak from experience!

Juania australis is a solitary species originating from the Juan Fernández Islands (of Selkirk's Island fame) off the coast of Chile. Described in some quarters as practically 'ungrowable', its needs are often considered to be fussy in the extreme: few palms will sulk if night-time temperatures exceed 15°C. Several individual plants were distributed in the early 1990s, and perhaps the best example I have seen is in the garden at Earlscliffe, Dublin – home of the Irish horticulturist, David Robinson. In this situation it encountered particularly harsh conditions in the winter of 2001, when a fall in temperature to -7.5°C, and snow, put it to the test. In Cornwall, other examples, less severely

Juania australis at Earlscliffe, Dublin, Ireland.

tested, can be seen flourishing in the sheltered valley of Glendurgan. Regrettably, its isolated habitat and protection by the Chilean government have limited the availability of *J. australis* to only the fortunate few. An Andean relative of spectacular habit – but alas, of only limited trial at Lamorran – is the genus *Ceroxylon*, the Andean wax palm, some species of which reach heights of 60m in their mountain haunts. Henderson *et al.* (1995) regard the remaining stands of these palms as one of the botanical wonders of the world. *Ceroxylon ventricosum*, which grows at altitudes of 2,000–3,000m in montane rain forest, has been quietly located at

Lamorran: whether the slightly less giddy coastal elevations of the Bay of Falmouth are to its liking remains to be seen.

Among British palm enthusiasts, there has recently been considerable interest in the genus *Parajubaea*, which takes its name from a resemblance to *Jubaea*. Awkward to germinate, as is its cousin *Butia*, two species are known, although only one, *P. torallyi*, is known in the wild. *P. cocoides* – and possibly a form called *P. sunka* – is known only from cultivated plants in Andean towns at high elevations in southern Colombia and Ecuador. Henderson (Henderson, *et al*, 1995) suspects that the two species are so close that *P. cocoides* probably originated from the wild *P. torallyi*: given that palms are among the most important economic plants on the planet, conjecture often points to the occurrence and distribution of similar and very close species being down to indigenous peoples. Enthusiastically acclaimed in northern California, *P. cocoides* will be experimented with at Lamorran once material has reached an appropriate size. North American experience suggests that it thrives in a temperature comfort zone of 16–24°C in the daytime, and 7–13°C at night, doing particularly well in the cool, humid conditions with a marine influence around San Francisco.

North America

In the continent of North America, interest in palms is weighted more heavily towards experience gained from the cultivation of palms, than to the endemic palm species themselves. However, this is not to say that habitats in the USA and Mexico do not possess admirable plants that could be grown in Cornwall.

Palms such as *Washingtonia* will be immediately familiar to anyone with a passing knowledge of the environs of California, even if gained from a movie background. The crux comes with the fact that although many species in this region are able to withstand severe cold – *W. filifera* reputedly fends off -28°C (Henderson, *et al*, 1995) – other continental factors enter the equation: notably higher, prolonged summer temperatures; fast daytime temperature recovery after a frost incident and, perhaps more crucially, relatively lower levels of humidity than would be experienced in Cornwall during a cold spell. Translating this to the selection of palm species is neither easy, nor entirely predictable.

Avenue of *Washingtonia filifera*, Lisbon, Portugal.

Certain species of *Sabal*, for instance, with a little coaxing, can exist quite happily in the Cornish environment, although growth rates can be frustratingly slow. *Sabal minor* is often the most widely available in the nursery trade, originating anywhere from Florida northwards to the Carolinas, and growing as an understorey plant in semi-deciduous woods. Many growers of this palm have experienced its ability to 'shrink', as a size-able bought specimen responds to the cool Cornish summers. Slightly better success has been achieved with an offshore cousin, *S. bermudana*, the Bermudan palmetto, which has grown unhindered for 13 years in the garden of Robert Dudley-Cooke at Lamorran, not unduly rushed in its growth, yet seemingly suited in its island origins to an equally maritime location across the Atlantic. Perhaps the best option for this genus would be to grow it in free-draining, raised beds in full sun. The Old Rectory, Marazion, has perhaps the finest example of *S. palmetto* in the county (possibly *S. dominguensis*), planted in 1988, using this situation and taking additional advantage of the thermal effect of surrounding walls to prolong

the daytime warmth. Tollefson, an extremely experimental palm grower in California, has the adage that 'Sabals grow slowly, but time passes quickly' (Tollefson, 1997a).

Closely allied to the genus *Sabal* is the small, clump-forming Saw Palmetto, *Serenoa repens*, – selected forms – whose fronds are enhanced by a silver-blue hue. It seems to originate mainly from the coastal areas of Florida, and although probably not appreciated in its native habitat – it forms dense, impenetrable masses, and the fronds are extremely well armed with spines – it could be worth experimenting with in exposed coastal situations with very free-draining soils. So far, it has been frustratingly unsuccessful at Lamorran, but new material was planted in 2003.

Rapidophyllum hystrix is another sedate palm in terms of growth, but it has an almost unrivalled reputation among palms for cold-hardiness in cultivation. Not a particularly large palm, it has short, clustered stems armed with stout, needle-like leaf-sheath spines, and originates from the south-eastern USA. Perhaps useful as a ground cover and space filler, it has much to commend it, if only for a steady and reliable palm; 'meek' might be an apt description of its relative decorative attributes.

Sabal palmetto established in west Cornwall.

The genus *Washingtonia* originates from the southern states of the USA and Mexico, and comprises of only two species, which generally grow in colonies in reasonably arid areas. The first species, *W. filifera*, is often found around oases. There is debate as to its particular distribution, with ethnobotanical theories intimating that its location may be due to Cahuilla Indians selectively using the species as a food source. The second species, *W. robusta*, is distinguishable from the first by only extremely subtle differences, and in cultivation it is often difficult to differentiate between the two.

A young *Washingtonia robusta*, Lamorran House Gardens, Cornwall.

As a general rule, *W. robusta* grows far taller and on a thinner trunk; lacks the persistent cottony threads on the fronds, from which *W. filfera* earns the sobriquet 'Cotton palm'; on young fronds the petiole can be distinguished by the presence of a brown coloration, and being markedly thorny, with a bright tawny patch on the base of the lower surface of the leaf blade. *Washingtonia filifera* has a far more substantial girth, and a shorter stature. To confuse matters further, the term 'filibusta' is often used among palm growers in support of a sup-

posed amalgam of both species' traits in a 'mule' palm. In warm temperate areas of the world, both species are widely used in general landscaping and, deservedly, to create stunning avenues: several parks in the city of Lisbon have this impressive feature. Both are also presented as being cold-tolerant in our particular environment, although firm evidence relating to their hardiness in the UK is thin on the ground. There are very few consistent examples from which to draw, the most notable being in the environs of Torbay – which makes claims by nurseries irritating, especially where this genus is concerned. Based on both its apparent cold-hardiness (see Jones, 1984, and Henderson, 1995) and reduced vulnerability to the humid Cornish climate, it is likely that *W. filifera* would be far more suitable planted in Cornwall and western districts of the British Isles. However, this is not to say both species are not open to experimentation: Charlie Pridham – who would freely testify to not always enjoying the most blessed of microclimates at Roseland House, Chacewater – has nurtured a handsome example of *W. robusta* through several winters, albeit with the use of winter protection, which helps to exclude direct rainfall.

A distinctive palm with stiff, blue-green, fan-shaped leaves is *Brahea armata*, the blue hesper palm, which is the most frequently encountered member of this genus in UK nurseries. Originating from Baja California in northern Mexico, it is reputed to withstand severe frosts, which, combined with an obvious beauty, is no doubt one of its chief attractions for the nursery trade. Many growers have begun to realize the importance of its natural habitat, for it is normally found growing on dry, rocky, limestone soils – which should be noted by those with acid soils in Cornwall. At Lamorran, seemingly to its benefit, it has been treated with an occasional dressing of lime, and a mulch of limestone chippings.

However, the evidence might point to this not being the whole story. Robert Read of Fairchild Gardens, Florida, recognized a notable difference between *Brahea armata* planted above Oolytic limestone in that particular garden, and those planted at the USDA plant introduction station at Chapman Field, Miami. There, in the saline marl on the bank of a drainage canal, *B. armata* were seen to flourish to a greater degree than at Fairchild, and Robert Read surmised that, as a rule, the species grew better in moist, saline soils by the coast than in the drier, non-saline limestone or sand soils of south Florida.

Brahea edulis, which hails from the island of Guadalupe off the coast of north-west Mexico, ought to be an interesting candidate, coming from a more maritime climate than its mainland cousins, and growing on rocky slopes up to 1,000m in elevation, where Henderson considers it to be threatened by extinction, due to the grazing activities of goats. A very ornamental and pleasing palm, with lush green fronds, displaying a

A young *Brahea edulis*, Lamorran House Gardens, Cornwall.

certain degree of hardiness – a short instance of -4°C at Lamorran – it is seemingly fairly resistant to salt winds. Although unlikely to reach a large size, it could be of use where *Washingtonia* is being considered as part of a collection. *Brahea dulcis* is another species that has not been widely experimented with, but Abbotsbury Gardens in Dorset have had reasonable success in establishing it. In all cases with this genus, well-drained soils and a situation not likely to suffer from stagnant, humid conditions in winter are essential.

Chamaedorea might not immediately spring to mind as a potential outdoor garden subject, especially given its traditional role as a house-

plant. However, in recent years several species have been experimented with in private gardens around Cornwall – for example, Neil Armstrong's Tremenheere near Ludgvan. Two that may be given brief mention are, first, *C. microspadix*: by no means a small palm, it can grow to 7m; Don Tollefson regards its 'delicate and tender appearance as being misleading', especially when winter lows of -16°C have been chalked up against its name. In time, *C. microspadix* can form attractive clumps of bamboo-like stalks adorned with lush foliage. Second, *C. radicalis* is a smaller palm, which again local experience – in particular at Lamorran – will confirm has an apparent ability to grow well in cool, under-storey conditions, where it can form attractive additions to the sub-planting. Not to be rushed, they have the potential to consolidate slowly and form a worthwhile addition to a collection.

Europe

Only two species of palm are truly indigenous to Europe: *Chamaerops humilis*, which is widely distributed around the Mediterranean basin, and *Phoenix theoprastii*, which has a much more confined existence, being found in any great num-

Chamaerops humilis, Lamorran House Gardens, Cornwall.

ber only in eastern Crete, and scattered elsewhere around that island.

Chamaerops humilis should need no introduction to the Cornish horticulturist, for it has long been recognized as one of the most successful plants within subtropical planting situations, and was one of the earliest palms brought to the UK – by Philip Miller in 1731. It is also one of the few palms to warrant mention by Thurston and Arnold-Forster in their respective records of early twentieth-century horticulture in these parts. This is a handsome, clump-forming palm, often producing several trunks, all of which carry fronds heavily armed with barbs on the petiole, and frequently flowers in late spring or early summer. Due to its natural cliff-side habitat in the Mediterranean, it can withstand quite significant levels of exposure.

Occasionally, tall, singular trunks are formed, and this instance is often referred to as *Chamaerops humilis* var. *elatior*. Rigorous pruning and cleaning of the trunk to a considerable height (6m) in Mediterranean areas, particularly France and Italy, almost brings about the appearance of *Trachycarpus fortunei*, to which it is related. This method of treatment ought to be considered by those who still insist, inexplicably, upon using *T. fortunei* in unsheltered situations near the coast.

The widespread distribution of this palm around the Mediterranean has resulted in several phenotypes of *Chamaerops humilis* emerging in varying habitats. A noteworthy and recent introduction is *C. humilis* 'Vulcano', which evidently originates from a small volcanic island off the coast of Sicily, close to Stromboli. It is very much more compact than the type species, and probably requires sharp drainage to succeed. Perhaps aesthetically more interesting is another cultivar, *C. humilis* var. *cerifera*. Less compact than 'Vulcano', its blue-grey hue gives it more than a passing resemblance to *Serenoa repens*. It may be a hardier alternative (Gibbons, 1993, suggests something akin to plain *C. humilis*) to both *Serenoa* and *Brahea armata*, for those seeking such a waxy frond coloration. Material in the UK has mostly been obtained from sources in the Atlas Mountains of Morocco; conjecture among palm enthusiasts is that it is very slow to establish. However, material brought to Lamorran from the island of Minorca appears to grow more quickly. Published names of this palm also include *C. humilis* 'argentea', and research conducted in the

1890s (Griessen, 1899) intimates that a form of *Chamaerops* similar in description was known as *C. humilis* 'macrocarpa'.

Phoenix theoprastii is as yet unproven in its worth, but is being experimented with conscientiously by several gardeners in sheltered locations around Cornwall. Given its natural occurrence on an island that played a strategic role in early Mediterranean sea trade, there is suggestion in some quarters that this palm derives from the true date palm, *P. dactylifera*, and is undeserving of species status. The portents for its establishment are not immediately promising, given the Arab conviction that date palms require their feet in water and their crowns 'in the fires of heaven'. Having observed this species shimmering on a hot day beside the Libyan Sea, I find it hard to imagine *P. theoprastii* enjoying Cornish mizzle! However, one successful palm grower on the edge of west London has nurtured a specimen to quite some size, which should provoke a retaliatory response from Cornish gardeners. *Phoenix theoprastii* is shorter than the true date palm, and has bristly, open fronds whose leaf bases may persist noticeably on the trunk after pruning. It should be said that *P. dac-*

Phoenix theoprastii on Crete.

Phoenix palms in Tresco Abbey Garden, Isles of Scilly.

tylifera has been established on Tresco since 1854 (King, 1985). Huge specimens – remnants from a Chelsea exhibit – have been planted at Kew (seemingly unsuccessfully), and at Paignton Zoo, Devon, where at least one tree appears to be showing signs of establishment.

Phoenix canariensis is probably one of the most instantly recognizable and widespread of all ornamental plants, let alone palms, in warm temperate regions of the world, spreading far and away from its natural base of the Canary Islands, where it is endemic. As previously discussed, this palm is somewhat perplexing, on account of its success in similar climates in immediate proximity to Cornwall. Unfortunately, it seems to have had many false dawns on the Cornish mainland, having been cut short by severe winters before it reached its prime. There have been attempts to grow it in the usual locations of Mount's Bay and the Bay of Falmouth, and there are reports of it growing to a healthy size away from the coast. For example, Hunkin (1950) mentions a large-trunked *P. canariensis* being part of the horticultural legacy of Capt. Pinwill at Trehane in mid-Cornwall. Their main undoing seems to be a combination of cold and humidity, which damages the crown, in particular the growing apex. Signs of crown damage are not unknown in other areas after a cold period – the Côte d'Azur in 1987, and closer to home, Tresco in the same year, experienced such problems. Lower levels of springtime humidity perhaps play a part in their recovery in these locations, together with more rapid improvements in seasonal temperature. The provenance of the palms involved is hard to assess, but the likely source was, and generally remains, Mediterranean regions (Griessen, 1899).

Whatever else, the potential of this palm is enormous, and there has been a renaissance in its planting in recent years, with innumerable specimens beginning to be seen in Cornish gardens. At its best it has a majestic quality, with a dense head of verdant pinnate fronds atop a considerable trunk. For this reason, adequate supportive feeding is something of a priority, as the fronds will easily turn an unhealthy yellow. Very handsome specimens in the parks of Falmouth and Penzance, and in the gardens of Lamorran and Trebah, bode well for the future. A recent unlikely source of *Phoenix canariensis*, which perhaps has a more solid provenance, is New Zealand, where it has evidently been established for some time. *Phoenix canariensis* 'Timaru' has been planted in the garden at The Old Rectory, Marazion – one interesting physical trait of these plants is the absence of sharp spines at the base of the fronds.

Intriguingly, in 1930 Thurston mentions the existence of *Phoenix reclinata*, the Senegal date palm, of some 30 years of age in a Penzance garden, well before an accession was made at Tresco Abbey Garden in 1914. Although many palm growers regard it as being extremely borderline for the UK, reports such as these do add some degree of confidence that we should at least be trying to emulate the halcyon days of Cornish horticulture at the beginning of the twentieth century. A palm more usually found in tropical and southern Africa, it is a lush, green, clump-forming species, which requires a regular supply of water during the growing season. It is one of the most impressive sights in the Palmetum at Naples Botanic Garden, where it reaches 10–15m, and forms a cascading wall of foliage. Unfortunately, most of the available stock is considered to be a hybrid form rather than the type species, but this may aid its cold-tolerance without being unduly detrimental to the aesthetics of the palm. Many palm authorities suggest that *P. reclinata* is especially good when featured next to water, but its borderline nature dictates maximum protection and warmth in Cornwall. A large specimen is currently being experimented with at Lamorran.

Trachycarpus fortunei in flower.

Asia and Australasia

Trachycarpus fortunei has been an integral part of Cornish gardens for so long that its merits are sometimes overlooked, as other species of palm are introduced and the limitations of the climate are explored. Yet it is perhaps the most handsome, cold-hardy palm that can be grown in the UK, let alone Cornwall, its versatility restricted only by extreme exposure to wind, which destroys its appearance and gives ammunition to those who distrust such plants in our landscape. Grown well, in a sheltered, humid location it has been known – from experience at Lamorran – for Mediterranean visitors to confuse it with *Washingtonia*, a familiar palm in that region. This again underlines a respect for its virtues from further afield in Europe.

Trachycarpus fortunei was first introduced to Europe in 1830 by von Siebold, who sent seed from Japan to Leiden. However, palm growers are generally more familiar with the 1849 introduction by Robert Fortune, after whom the species is named. Most examples of the species in

Cornwall no doubt originated in Fortune's later collection of seed in the Ningpo area of Chekiang, China, and the subsequent dispersal of material by Glendinnings Nursery in 1860. The vernacular 'Chusan palm' refers to the island now known as Zhoushan in the East China Sea, south of Shanghai (Gibbons, 1993), where Fortune first saw the palm in 1843. It is ideal for use in avenues or groves, and its hardiness has been exploited at Lamorran to create a reliable framework, which will resist even the wildest temperature extremes of the Cornish climate, and around which other species can be grown. The husky, fibrous trunk has also been used at Lamorran, as an ideal habitat for epiphytes, and the fibre itself is seen as a choice nest-building material by birds, especially great tits.

Trachycarpus fortunei var. *wagnerianus* is regarded as being unknown in the wild, but appears to have originated in cultivation in Japan. A German botanist, Wagner, is said to have introduced it to

Trachycarpus fortunei var. *wagnerianus*.

and occurrence in areas previously exploited for tender rhododendrons, may cause growers to be cautious. Gibbons regards *T. latisectus* as having the most beautiful leaf-shape in the entire genus. Other species include *T. oreophillus*, endemic to north-west Thailand; *T. princeps*, which comes from the monsoon rain forest of southern central China; and *T. nanus*, a dwarf member of the genus from Yunnan, China, first collected by Delavay in 1887, and now considered endangered. The latter has only recently been brought back to cultivation, and has yet to prove itself.

One species with a significant amount of mystery attached to its early introduction to Europe is *Trachycarpus takil*, which is endemic in Uttar Pradesh province, where it grows at altitudes up to 2,400m. It seems it first reached Europe via either Major Madden, or Brandis, who sent seed from Kunain to the respected palm botanist, Professor Beccari in Florence, in 1884 (Bean, 1937). According to Gibbons (1993), its subsequent distribution is unknown: there is one confirmed specimen in Rome Botanic Garden. One of its prime traits is a twisted hastula at the junction of the petiole and frond, but Gibbons does not regard this as a sure sign of identification. Other traits of the species – a bigger, more robust trunk and crown; a chestnut tomentum around the base of the leaves, and a more attractive fibrous trunk – often manifest themselves in *T. fortunei* sourced from European nurseries. The true *T. takil* could prove an impressive specimen when established, and all of the aforementioned signatures have shown themselves in one of the palms at Lamorran, which is growing at a rapid rate. This species is often confused with *T. fortunei* var. *wagnerianus* in the USA and elsewhere.

Europe. An extremely desirable form of *Trachycarpus*, it is much more compact than *T. fortunei*, particularly the fronds, which are small (45–60cm wide), a rich green, and very stiff, with a white woolly tomentum on the margins of new growth. Adequate moisture is essential, but the constitution of the fronds makes this form the most suited for more exposed locations, as well as being highly garden-worthy. It is slow to establish, but grows more quickly with age, and new sources of material should now enhance its availability.

Two palm-growing nurserymen, Tobias Spanner and Martin Gibbons have, almost single-handedly, expanded the awareness of the range of the genus *Trachycarpus* in recent years. It occurs naturally from China, through Vietnam, Thailand, Myanmar, and Nepal, to India. Within this range, several species and/or phenotypes have either been discovered or come to light again, having been previously introduced. Many have the potential to become worthy of growing in Cornwall: one such is *T. latisectus*, from Sikkim, although its altitude (1,200–2,400m)

Last, indigenous to northern India, Nepal, and northern Myanmar – where it was more than likely observed by Frank Kingdon Ward on a rhododendron collecting mission – is the species *Trachycarpus martianus*, named after another German botanist, F.P. von Martius. *Trachycarpus martianus* differs substantially from *T. fortunei*, in that it has a naturally bare trunk; white rather than yellow flowers and, most significantly, leaf petioles of exceptional length – up to 1.5m – margined with white tomentum, and of a succulent verdancy. *Trachycarpus martianus* is desirable as a solitary specimen where space can be afforded to enhance it to full effect, although the open nature of the crown demands shelter from strong wind. Hence it is probably best under a woodland canopy.

Distribution of the genus *Phoenix* spreads eastwards from the Canary Islands, and continues through the Middle East, and across Asia. Nurseries are pushing the experimentation of two Indian introductions – *P. rupicola*, the Cliff date palm, and *P. sylvestris*, the Silver date palm. The former, *P. rupicola*, is considered a slender, graceful proposition, with fine, pinnate leaves, probably requiring extreme shelter and a period of pot cultivation to assess its suitability. *Phoenix sylvestris* is similar in appearance to *P. canariensis*, but is a faster-growing palm, crowned with grey-green glaucous fronds, and is hardy in temperate parts of Australia (Jones, 1984). A sunny aspect and free-draining soil are requirements. In recent years, a few gardens in Cornwall – notably Lamorran and Tremenheere – have tested the limitations of *P. roebelinii*, the Pygmy date palm from Laos. Long used as a house-plant, it is comparatively small in stature, and has soft, feathery fronds, although these are armed with spines at the base. Its tolerance of poor light makes it ideal for indoor use. Taking an encouraging lead from warm temperate locations, such as the French Riviera, and thanks to the availability of larger specimens, it has generally been planted under a sheltering canopy of trees in very protected micro-climates. Advice for successful cultivation includes regular watering in summer; application of nitrogenous fertilizers, and the incorporation of humus into the soil, which is found to be of benefit by some Californian palm growers.

Nannorrhops ritchiana, the Mazari palm from northern India and Afgahnistan, is considered to be one of the most cold-hardy palms in cultivation. It grows in infertile, stony soils, and has a morphologically subterranean nature. The relative lack of intense summer heat in Cornwall has perhaps been the reason for its reluctance to grow successfully at Lamorran, although it 'survives'.

The Cornish climate probably precludes the growing of the true 'fish tail' palm, *Caryota*, to any great extent, although at The Old Rectory, Marazion, there has been early success with *Caryota* 'himalaya', a selection chosen by Martin Gibbons for its provenance – in this instance, Kathmandu in Nepal. But perhaps an alternative could be considered in the form of *Wallichia densiflora*, which exhibits bi-pinnate leaflets not unlike those of *Caryota* 'himalaya'. Native to the Himalayas of northern India and Assam, it grows in shady, moist conditions, and is thought of as being cold-tolerant in other warm temperate zones, partly because of its endemic occurence with *Trachycarpus*. Requiring moist, humus-rich soil, Gibbons considers that this palm should be grown much more widely. It would be a very attractive, and perhaps suitable palm for under-planting among tree ferns.

The portents for *Arenga engleri* ought to be good, since it originates from Taiwan and the Ryukyu Islands, which have served as a source of several other plant species grown in Cornwall. As yet frustratingly slow to grow in a cool summer climate, it is an attractive, clump-forming, bushy palm, with long, slightly twisted pinnate fronds, and reputed to be able to withstand light frosts (although American sources claim as low as -6°C) – hence it is suitable only for sheltered gardens.

Alone among this list is an exciting alternative to trunk-forming species, *Plectocomia himalayana* – a climbing palm endemic to the Himalayan foothills of Bengal, where it grows at an altitude of 2,300–2,500m. Its climbing nature is aided by heavily barbed stems, which can reach 27m in the wild. So far considered to be hardy to -4°C, it is regarded as the closest example of a rattan that could merit cultivation in a mild climate such as ours – if only for the specialist collector with an advantageous micro-climate. Once again, a very promising example has been established at The Old Rectory, Marazion.

The Lady palm, *Rhapis excelsa*, is another species whose wild origins are clouded in mystery: it is thought to have originated in China and Taiwan, in dry evergreen forests. Bean (1937) also regards it as having been the source of the name *Chamaerops excelsa*, which often crops up on Italian nursery stock, usually *Trachycarpus fortunei*. Extensively hybridized in Japan, where its cultivation is very popular, *R. excelsa* in its standard form has proved a worthwhile addition to the palm collection at Lamorran, where its clump-forming nature, with thin, hairy, bamboo-like stems, has been used to advantage in under-plantings in partial shade.

There have been occasional, unsatisfactory experiments with *Livistonia* – generally *L. chinensis*, the Chinese fan palm. Perhaps the sobriquet led

Plectocomia himalayana.

monly regarded as being the most cold-hardy of the two, and additionally is usually acclaimed as the palm with the most southerly habitat, apart from the variant found on the Chatham Islands. One of its last southerly outposts on New Zealand's South Island is in a reserve on Banks Peninsula, eluding herbivores in a ravine facing out over a cliff to sea (Richardson, 1996). This is one of the only palm species we could ever hope to grow in Cornwall that has a 'crow-nshaft', and has been grown on Tresco since 1864. Taking up to 30 years before it flowers and sets seed, Tresco-grown Nikaus have been very productive. Mike Nelhams of Tresco Abbey Garden testifies to the viability of the seed, which was found to germinate among the compost. Following the 1987 winter, numerous Nikaus have been planted in the garden to great decorative effect. Reputedly a number of individuals also survived for many years in a garden close to the lower River Dart in Devon, eventually succumbing to the loss of tree cover in the gales of the late 1980s as much as to the effect of frost. A protective tree canopy seems

to misleading expectations, for negative opinions have been formed about the genus. However, *L. australis*, the Australian fan palm, occurring on the east coast of Queensland, shows slightly better signs of being viable in a warm, sunny, Cornish garden, and ought to be tried more widely. Its tall, slender form, with a dense cluster of fronds atop, can be seen in Tresco Abbey Garden, where it was introduced in 1860. However, the petiole of the drooping palmate fronds is not for the faint-hearted, as it is armed with vicious teeth. The Ribbon palm, *L. decipiens*, is also endemic to Queensland, and has featured recently in local nurseries. Riffle (2003) considers it adaptable in USDA Zones 9 to 11 – sometimes 8b in drier winter climates – and to be more graceful than *L. australis*.

One of the most tropical-looking of all plants growing in Tresco Abbey Garden – and there are many to choose from – is the 'shaving brush' palm or Nikau, *Rhopalostylis sapida*, which is endemic in New Zealand. In fact, another species, *R. baurei*, occurs in New Zealand and nearby islands to the north (Kermadec), but it is the Nikau that is com-

Rhopalostylis sapida.

to be vital for their survival, given that in the wild they normally grow in dense, moist woodland or, in the case of Banks Peninsula, in a deep gully on the coast.

The epithet 'shaving brush' describes the erect nature of the feathery fronds, which have recognizable veining on the surface of the leaflets, and a noticeable crown-shaft at their base on a short (to 7m when mature), silvery-grey trunk. *Rhopalostylis sapida* has been established successfully at both Lamorran and The Old Rectory, Marazion in recent years, not only providing an attractive addition to the garden, but also displaying the progressive nature of both these relatively recent gardens and their evolving micro-climates. The form *R. sapida* 'Oceana' – also known as 'Chatham' – obtained through a palm specialist has proved to be a very adaptable palm in both these gardens, displaying evident health, and a tolerance of maritime conditions. It differs from the mainland Nikaus in its wider leaflets and pinkish-beige petioles.

Cultivation
Hardiness

The perceived hardiness of many palms is an emotive issue among many professional growers and enthusiasts, and attaining a concise assessment of the viability of particular species can be difficult. Perhaps the major issue concerns the making of assumptions about climates that are regarded as similar in nature. It is apparent and well known that the Cornish climate is diverse, and littered with micro-climates, and that exposure to the wind varies from Channel coast to the Atlantic shores.

Other parts of the world often cited for similar traits are equally subject to unique differences, but these may be overlooked by the unwary. Palm-growing areas often cited include the Côte d'Azure in France; northern Italy and the Bay of Naples, and locations in North America – for example, the Pacific north-west. Often the main benchmark quoted for a particular species in these areas is temperature hardiness – usually in terms of a minimum temperature in Celsius, or as a USDA zonal rating. But to rely on either category can lead to a false impression of the hardiness of a particular species. Temperature hardiness is only a guide: vagaries in micro-climates; age of the palm, and provenance all play a part.

Other inhibiting hardiness factors

1 *Temperature recovery:* many climates – particularly those of California and Texas in the USA – record lows similar to those experienced by even the most sheltered locations in Cornwall. The difference is that in these other climates, the temperature recovers to a respectable level on the same day. The ability of the environment to recover quickly to a tolerable level is clearly beneficial to the survival of the plant.

2 *Humidity:* a feature of the climate of the south of France is the lack of atmospheric humidity relative to that of the Cornish climate. Palms are far more tolerant of dry cold than of prolonged periods of cool, damp weather, which aids the attack of fungi to the growing apex and, if the temperature falls below freezing, can result in ice forming in the crown, with inevitable consequences.

3 *Summer temperatures:* all of the above-mentioned regions experience far greater summer heat, and for considerably more prolonged periods. This in itself is of benefit to ground-dwelling palms such as *Serenoa* and *Sabal* species from temperate climates, and also inspires the ripening of wood in the trunk-forming species such as *Washingtonia*, which require a long, active growing period to sustain the plant's viability.

4 *Winter's length:* the successful cultivation of several fringe palm species centres around the length of time that growth is impaired by prolonged periods of cool temperatures. It has been mooted by certain growers in Europe that palms such as *Howea forsteriana* – which has been tried unsuccessfully at Fox Rose-hill Gardens – are not particularly happy to assume a state of inactivity for too long. Apart from this, the clear attritional nature of a long, cool, damp winter on the constitution of a palm is self-evident.

Natural habitat

Another factor – one raised recently by collectors of rhododendrons – is altitude. Many are not convinced that the altitude at which particular palms

– notably *Caryota*, *Trachycarpus*, and the rattan relative *Plectocomia* – have been collected in the Himalayas guarantees a safe degree of cold-hardiness, particularly in view of the fact that traditional plant interests in this region have centred on collections from higher altitudes. A certain incidence of frost has often been reported as an indication of robustness of a particular species, but frequency and duration may also be limited by localized weather patterns. Provenance is extremely important, and material obtained from the very boundaries of a palm's natural range will be of fundamental benefit. As for *Caryota*, *Trachycarpus*, and *Plectocomia*, time and experience of growing them in the Cornish climate will be the ultimate proof of their viability.

Salt-tolerance

Despite frequent recommendations regarding the salt-tolerance of particular palms, bear in mind that few plants can resist a constant battering from salt-laden wind, and retain a reasonable appearance. Also, the Promenade des Anglais in Nice is a completely different proposition from the sea front in Penzance! Winter conditions in Mediterranean islands – Minorca, for example – often necessitate some level of protection for *Washingtonias*,

Lamorran House Gardens, at St Mawes, Cornwall, has a large collection of palms, which flourish in a coastal setting.

which are often cited for salt-resistance. The cliff-dwelling *Chamaerops humilis* is probably the only palm that will withstand prolonged exposure to coastal conditions; other species, such as *Phoenix canariensis*, will tolerate an amount of hardship before their beauty is degraded.

Feeding

There is often an urge among palm growers to feed the plants heavily, in order to promote rapid growth to maturity and assumed greater resilience to cold. Well-meaning as this may be, it is perhaps not in the best interests of the plant for, to quote one respected UK palm grower, ' hard and slow is the way to grow': steady progress will avoid the promotion of an excess of soft, unripened tissue, which is an open invitation to damage from both cold and salt-laden winds.

Corner (1966) also raises the issue that in their natural state palms have a cycle or rhythm of frond production, with an equal number of fronds developing in the apical bud as naturally carried in the crown – approximately 35 in *Chamaerops humilis*, and up to 200 in a mature *Phoenix canariensis*. Working with the palm's natural tendencies seems far better than forcing it.

However, high rainfall and free-draining soils in Cornwall necessitate replenishment of food.

A spring feed is applied to the palms at Lamorran House, usually in the form of top-dressing derived from Growmore or Vitax Q4 (N5.3/ P7.5/K10) – the latter has the additional advantage of supplying magnesium oxide, which can be a cause of observed deficiency in *Phoenix canariensis*. Supplemental applications may be made in summer, after which feeding is eased back to allow the hardening off of growth. This can be aided to a degree by the application of potash in late summer. A number of species – in particular *P. canariensis* – are gross feeders, and several applications of food may be required in one season. This is especially true of *Phoenix* planted in grass, which results in competition for nitrogen. Some amateur palm growers attempt to exploit lawn fertilizer as a high impact source of nitrogen, in the belief that it will boost the appearance of the foliage. However, there is a danger that this will cause a nitrogen to phosphate imbalance in the soil, with the threat of a differential leaching of phosphate. Trace minerals should not be overlooked: magnesium and boron are easily lost from soils overlying granite; potassium deficiency can manifest itself in orange spotting and a yellowing of the leaf as the palm translocates the element from old fronds to new growth. At Lamorran, foliar feeding in mid to late spring is employed as an effective way of helping the recovery of palms jaded by winter winds.

The balance of soil fertility and pH levels is perhaps a little more complex than is immediately obvious. Certain palms – notably *Brahea* – are often assumed to require a higher pH due to their origins in limestone-rich regions of Mexico, and the borders of the USA. At Lamorran, top-dressings of lime applied in the spring have benefited these species, and a mulch of limestone chippings has been laid around the species *B. armata* for assessment.

One particular asset to the feeding regime at Lamorran in recent years has been the use of dilute seaweed fertilizer, as both a root drench and a foliar feed, which can be useful in supplying micro-nutrients. Apart from being a successful feed source, seaweed appears to have other benefits, not least of which is its affect on the bioactivity of the soil in general. Research points to a constituent of seaweed called mannitol, which is believed to aid the absorption of nutrients already in the soil. Another benefit of foliage feeding is its ability to impart a waxy mucilage to the surface of the leaf. From limited experiments in California, some growers there attest to the barrier this may present against cold.

Soil mycorrihza

The importance of symbiotic fungi in the soil is another aspect of soil fertility that might benefit from further research. Individual species have often tested the patience of growers by their reluctance to grow at anything more than a pedestrian pace, despite the best of interventions. *Arenga engleri* is one such species, which might benefit from assistance of this nature: it is a very attractive species, and one evidently suitable for trialling in Cornwall. However, its ability to withstand the climate is not yet known.

Planting

The optimum size for planting palms is a moot point. Palms will exhibit as much vigour as any other tree or shrub, and they too will catch up on larger specimens if planted at a moderately small size. However, with size comes a greater resistance to cold, and if the onus is to create immediate visual impact with a planting scheme, then one must plant large. Whatever the size of the palm, the vitality and health of the root-ball is crucial. Some of the more unusual species, such as *Butia* and *Trithrinax*, have often been imported from their continent of origin in a root-balled state, and it is worth noting that up to 80 per cent of the root system may be lost during lifting, which is quite a consideration when measured against trunk size. Subsequently, establishment will be considerably slower – two to three years or more – so it is advisable to seek a supplier of larger specimens who can guarantee that the palm has been potted up for some considerable time. The practice at Lamorran is to seek root-bound stock wherever practical. The intention is that the roots should have the ability and vigour to break into the soil as quickly as possible: faster establishment relates to a reduced risk from inclement conditions. Greater success with the establishment of palms has also been seen when the base of the planting hole, and the surrounds, have been broken up to a reasonable depth, allowing not only the palm roots to tap deep down into the soil, but increasing drainage in winter, and so avoiding the occurrence of a 'sump' scenario.

What is often overlooked is watering, and the experienced will not have failed to notice the soils that are often on the root-balls of imported stock. Allowing this to dry out can be a fatal mistake, even when the palm has been planted. With larger specimens, the installation of a tree loop might be warranted, or dedicated irrigation in the form of a drip hose. Mulching wherever possible with organic material will aid water retention, and will protect surface-feeding roots from cold weather.

A slightly more radical proposal...

The pioneering Californian palm grower Don Tollefson first had the idea of 'pot-planting', or planting without removing the pot – a controversial issue around which there is much debate. The premiss was to enhance the establishment of marginal palm species, such as *Licuala*, in the Californian climate. The reasoning behind pot-planting was twofold. First, non-removal of the pot reduces the supposed trauma of traditional planting techniques, especially root disturbance; associated issues include setback, and even an evident shrinkage of the palm (see *Sabal minor*). Second, it encourages the palm to become root-bound, and thence to start sending out exploratory roots through the drainage holes into the soil in greater earnest, subsequently boosting upward momentum in the palm. It is proposed that eventually the palm will split the pot and develop in a more natural way. The counter arguments are many, and one that relates to the Cornish climate is stability in the wind. Logically, though, this system could be useful if considered as a form of semi-permanent plunging, involving borderline species such as *Howea*. It has been used with *Phoenix roebelinii* at Lamorran, which means that the plant could be extracted from the ground if extreme cold threatened.

Winter protection

In former times, Cornish gardeners collected 'furze' to protect vulnerable species from cold and wind. Reduced manpower would make this difficult now, and in any case horticultural fleeces provide an alternative. While many would question the object of growing plants that cannot stand a typical Cornish winter, protection, especially from wind, is vital in the establishment of palms. At the top end of the scale, the wigwams covered in hessian and employed by Falmouth Town Council to

Top: Root-bound *Trachycarpus fortunei*. Bottom:The planting hole and surrounds are broken up to a reasonable depth.

'Bubble wrap' provides winter protection for a tender palm
– *Syagrus romanzoffianum*.

protect *Phoenix canariensis* undoubtedly played an enormous part in their successful establishment. On a smaller scale, fleece in a tubular format pulled over individual specimens helps to create a modicum of comfort for newly planted palms that may not have lost some of their nursery foliage. Tollefson proposed the use of plastic coverings – for example, 'solar domes' – as a permanent fixture over certain species for the first year or two, to encourage more substantial growth, and no doubt in our winters this would aid species such as *Sabal*. It is an inescapable truth that palms have a single apical bud, and if this is damaged irreparably by frost, then the palm will die. Preventative measures, such as making sure the palm is not suffering from any nutrient deficiencies prior to winter, which would weaken vegetative growth, or the use of a copper fungicide wash in autumn (used in the Côte d'Azure) to combat rot-forming bacteria, will aid defence against winter cold. However, recovery from cold injury has been effected at Lamorran with the immediate

application of sulphur or copper sulphate in the crown to fight fungal rot, and the removal of seriously damaged tissue close to the apical bud.

Pests and diseases

Fortunately, palms grown outside in the UK have few problems to contend with in the way of pests and diseases. Occasionally, signs of scale and mealy-bug may occur, which can be treated with currently advised chemical or biological measures. Rust may also manifest itself, but this is easier to control, simply by removing the infected fronds. A more serious threat is posed by the palm moth, *Paysandisia archon*, which was introduced from South America on imported *Trithrinax campestris*, and/or *Butia* species. It has begun to manifest itself in landscape palms in and around the Department of Var (between Toulon and Hyères) in southern France, and in Catalonia in northern Spain (Drescher and Dufay, 2002). Described as a 'beautiful' moth, it has olive-green fore-wings and orangey-red, black and white hind-wings, and a wingspan of 9–11cm. The main problem in France is that it has been found to have a very long life-cycle, and the damage is often done long before the palm shows any signs of physical stress. In addition, presence of the moth is usually detected only when adults are seen. The moth lays eggs (white) in the crown of the palm, and the larvae bore into the stem apex (leaf bud), which is debilitating to the palm – signs of its tunnelling can be seen in the 'sawdust' around the crown of the palm. In Mediterranean Europe, the palm moth has been observed on a host of ornamental palms, including several familiar species in Cornwall – *Trachycarpus*, *Chamaerops*, and *Phoenix canariensis*. As yet, no chemical control measures have been committed in France, partly due to a poor understanding of the moth's biology, but it is certainly considered a noxious pest. Sightings by entomologists in the UK have been reported in Chichester, West Sussex, and DEFRA is monitoring the situation closely.

Landscaping potential

As we have seen, many gardens already benefit from the presence of palms. However, there is a fine line between survival, and the palm making good growth and benefiting its immediate environs. A distinct advantage of palms is that their occupancy of space in the garden is almost

Palms give a Mediterranean feel to the garden at Lamorran House, St Mawes, Cornwall.

Trachycarpus fortunei with *Yucca thompsoniana* and *Leucadendron argenteum* in a Cornish garden.

entirely predictable, due to the physical nature of monocotyledons. Apart from considered establishment and protection methods, they are very low-maintenance plants, requiring food and water like most other garden plants, and the removal of damaged or dishevelled fronds. Shelter is desirable in Cornwall, in order to achieve the most visually appealing, healthy crown of fronds.

There are relatively few palms that could be considered reliably hardy in the county: *Chamaerops humilis*, *Butia capitata*, *Trachycarpus fortunei*, and perhaps *Phoenix canariensis* and *Jubaea chilensis*, will withstand the majority of winters. As Robert Dudley-Cooke has found at Lamorran, these have the potential to form the framework of a permanent exotic planting, around which other palm species can be incorporated, emboldening the garden through plant associations.

The symmetrical nature of palms has long been recognized through the planting of avenues and boulevards in Europe, but careful choice of situation and site should be considered to avoid any scheme jarring and looking out of place. Opinions vary as to whether palms should be treated as a singular focal specimen in a scheme, or used

in a massed effect. Once a *Trachycarpus* has outgrown an intended scheme in terms of height, it can be left looking rather exposed and forlorn. However, *Phoenix canariensis* and *Jubaea chilensis* have a greater stature, which would allow them to stand alone. Generally, many of the species we can grow have the ability to create a dramatic scene of exotic lushness if placed close together in groupings, ideally in threes or fives. Some, such as *Chamaerops humilis*, have the potential to make a worthwhile informal hedge, such is the species' bushy, clump-forming nature. For more tender subjects, there ought not to be embarrassment at using them more widely as plunge specimens – a practice used in Europe, and in Victorian gardens – rather than forcing them to endure the Cornish winter. *Howea forsteriana* is a perfect choice to fill space and create a tropical illusion, in areas that require temporary, decorative, summer planting. Popularly used in cities as diverse as Hamburg, Paris, and even Nice, removable specimen palms in Versailles boxes could be an answer for street decoration in towns such as Penzance and Falmouth, which promote the Riviera message, and which desperately need something to bring dec-

oration to pedestrian areas. Perhaps the Cornish
authorities should view the summer 2003 trans-
formation of the Voie Express Rive Droite road
(running alongside the River Seine in Paris) into
Paris Plage, complete with sand and avenues of
Trachycarpus fortunei, as a source of inspiration.

Cornwall has perhaps the most versatile climate
on the British mainland: a greater manifestation
of these highly visible and aesthetically stimulating plants ought to convince visitors that our climatic advantages are not being wasted.

***

Palms at Lamorran House Gardens, St Mawes, Cornwall

Brahea armata
Brahea edulis (one semi-mature; smaller
   plants)
Butia capitata (20 young to mature plants)
Butia yatay (semi-mature specimen)
Ceroxylon ventricosum
Chamaedorea radicalis
Chamaerops humilis (approximately 60)
Chamaerops humilis var. *cerifera*
Chamaerops humilis var. *elatior*
Chamaerops humilis 'Vulcano'
Jubaea chilensis
Livistonia australis
Nannorrhops ritchieana (just about!)
Phoenix canariensis (some 15 plants, several
   forming trunks and have flowered)
Phoenix roebelinii
Phoenix theoprastii
Rhapis excelsa
Rhapidophyllum hysterix
Rhopalostylis sapida
Rhopalostylis sapida var. *chatham*
Sabal bermudana
Sabal minor
Serenoa repens
Syagrus romanzoffianum
Trachycarpus fortunei (100+ to 11m, huge
   variation of growth habits, some wild-
   source collection from Royal Botanic
   Gardens, Kew, most self-seed *in situ*)
Trachycarpus fortunei var. *wagnerianus*
Trachycarpus martinianus
Trachycarpus takil

Trithrinax brasiliensis
Trithrinax campestris
Trithrinax bifabellata
Wallichia densiflora
Washingtonia filifera
Washingtonia robusta

5 Proteaceae

Guy Moore

This chapter is dedicated to the memory of the late Eric Jeffrey, at whose nursery I was first introduced to Proteaceae.

The chapter gives a cultivation guide to members of the family Proteaceae, based on my own practical experience of growing them in Cornwall, and deals specifically with cultivars and species from both sub-families *Proteoidiae* and *Grevilleoidiae*, which will suit many garden situations. It also gives background information on proteas in their natural habitat, to build up a picture of this relatively little-known family.

Left: The King Protea, *Protea cynaroides*. (See page 128.)

History and distribution

Proteaceae is a very ancient family, comprising two sub-families – *Proteoidiae* and *Grevilleoideae* – which are both restricted to the Southern hemisphere. *Proteoideae* occurs principally in southern Africa, with a few species in both Australia and New Zealand. Genera include *Leucadendron*, *Leucospermum*, and *Protea*. *Grevilleoideae* occurs mainly in Australia, with a single species in Africa, some on the south-western Pacific islands, and a few in South America. Genera include *Telopea*, *Hakea*, *Banksia*, *Lomatia*, *Knightia*, and *Embothrium*.

The family existed before Gondwanaland broke up, some 140 million years ago, when dinosaurs roamed the Earth. Today, around 1,400 species, in about 60 genera, make up Proteaceae.

What is a protea?

Proteaceae are, without exception, woody plants – either multi-stemmed shrubs, or single-stemmed trees – never herbaceous, and never annual. The name is derived from the mythological Greek god Proteus, otherwise known as the 'Old Man of the Sea'. He always spoke the truth and could foretell the future, but to extract a prophesy, one had first to catch him, and then keep hold of him while he changed into innumerable shapes and forms, both animate and inanimate, in order to escape. This is perhaps why Carl Linnaeus bestowed the name on the family, the variation in form and habitat being truly remarkable – from the Rewarewa (*Knightia excelsa*) of New Zealand, which at around 30m in height, resembles a Lombardy poplar, with spidery velvet flower buds, to the King Protea (*Protea cynaroides*), the national flower of South Africa, whose blooms can reach the size of a dinner plate!

Often very prominent differences occur within a single species. The King Protea has many recognized forms, from a dwarf at around 1m high, with narrow, rhomboidal leaves, to an upright shrub of about 2m, with broad, orbicular leaves. Only when dealing with such cultivars as *Leucadendron* 'Safari Sunset' and *L*. 'Early Yellow' can colour be used as a truly distinguishing feature. The range within species varies greatly, due to factors such as light and humidity levels; heat, mineral, and nutrient availability.

Proteaceae are one of the finest examples of beauty in the face of adversity. Whether in the Cape floral kingdom or the Australian outback,

Leucadendron 'Safari Sunset'.

the story is basically the same: high exposure, poor soils, low annual rainfall, and seasonal fires. They are so well adapted to these conditions that for cultivation to be successful, close attention must be paid to light levels, soil pH and drainage, air movement, and winter minimum temperatures.

Adaptations to a harsh environment, and implications for cultivation

Proteaceae have sclerophyllous leaves, hence they are stiff and leathery, and will snap rather than bend if folded. Sclerophyllous leaves are very long-lived, and have heavily lignified tissue to stop them collapsing when water is scarce. They keep transpiration to a minimum, so photosynthesis is very slow, but continue functioning long after ordinary leaves have wilted beyond repair. Sclerophyllous leaves are a direct result of nutrient-poor soils, particularly the lack of nitrogen (N) and phosphorus (P), which means protein synthesis is very low. Instead, woody fibres and tannins are formed, making sclerophyllous leaves very unpalatable to both insect larvae and mammals.

Many Proteaceae, such as *Leucadendron argentium*, have tiny hairs or denticles covering their leaves, which give the plant a soft appearance. These hairs are principally for deflecting strong sunlight. They also limit air movement close to the leaf surface, and are very valuable for trapping moisture from mists or low cloud.

When plants of a downy nature are in cultivation in this country, special attention must be given to air circulation and light levels, particularly when growing indoors. Good air movement, but not a cold draught, is essential to keep the ever-present airborne fungal spores (for example, botrytis or grey mould) from settling in the perfect conditions of a downy leaf.

Although many Proteaceae live where fires do not occur, many others are subject to bush fires, and the aspect of their adaptation to this phenomenon most relevant to cultivation is the formation of the lignotuber – a swollen, woody structure situated just below ground level – which contains many dormant buds that are activated if the above-ground parts are destroyed. Plants with lignotubers are recognized by their multi-stemmed habit, a mechanism that enables them to regenerate from the base if the top is frosted, and lets the gardener cut them back hard to stimulate bushier growth.

Leucadendron argentium.

Other points worth noting about fire survival are that some Proteaceae – and bottle brushes (*Callistemon*) – store seed in fire-retardant capsules. Other nut-forming plants (most commonly *Leucospermum* species) have a remarkable association with ants, known as myrmecochory. When nuts ripen, a coat, or elaisiome, is formed, which birds find unpalatable, but ants favour. When the time is right the ants collect the nuts, removing them to their nests underground, out of reach of nut-eating mammals and safe from fire. Many nuts are now 'ready planted', and can germinate when the rains come.

Another adaptation extremely important to cultivation is the formation of proteaceous roots, which assist in the uptake of vital moisture and nutrients, and are twice as effective as ordinary roots. (They can be quite extensive around a plant, so in the garden, care must be taken if hoeing.) Proteaceae do not form associations with soil-borne fungi as do our familiar trees, such as the oak and beech; instead, they form proteaceous roots just below the surface of the soil, which in the wild appear shortly after rain has fallen, as moisture triggers the decay of organic matter.

Summary of cultivation
Soil
In the wild, Proteaceae grow in a variety of stony and sandy soils, from peaty mountain ledges to heavier river silts. These sites are all free-draining, and are generally quite acidic. Proteaceae prefer a soil with a pH of 3.5 to 6.5. To achieve a free-draining, acidic soil, a mix of pine needles, sharp horticultural grit or Perlite, and sharp sand (river-derived, rather than builder's or sea sand) can be back-filled when planting out. If soils are heavy, the addition of peat, or soil mixed with grit (preferably granite) and pine needles, with a layer of crocks in the hole would be advantageous.

Similarly, if the pH is a little high, pine needles or peat should be dug into the soil at least a season before planting. For those hoping to cultivate Proteaceae in a limestone area (pH 7+), pot cultivation may be a solution, using a peat- and soil-based mix, and watering using collected rainwater. It may also be worth considering raised beds, and replacing the existing soil type with a suitable mix.

Planting positions
All the Proteaceae listed in this chapter prefer an open site, exposed to day-long sunshine – with two exceptions: *Telopea oreades* and *Lomatia tinctoria*, both of which tolerate semi-shade.

Raised beds and slopes are most suitable, avoiding spots where moisture and frost accumulate. If plants do not receive adequate light, weak, spindly growth occurs, with increased susceptibility to fungal attack.

Indeed, excessive moisture around the roots will cause root rot, and attack by a soil-borne fungus called *phytophythora*. If a site has poorly drained soil, but is steep enough for little moisture to penetrate, it may still be suitable for many types of Proteaceae.

Proteaceae are generally tolerant of exposure to wind. The larger-leaved species, such as *Banksia robur* and *Telopea oreades*, require a more sheltered position than, say, *Protea subvestita*. All Proteaceae, like the majority of Southern hemisphere plants, benefit from shelter from the cold north and east winds that are most common in January and February. Tolerance of wind and coastal exposure are noted in the list of plants that follows (pages 117–29).

Water
Pot-grown plants require regular watering during dry spells, as roots are unnaturally restricted. Regular watering also keeps peat-based compost from becoming hard and impervious, which would then require prolonged soaking to restore friability. Although the Proteaceae listed favour drier conditions, additional watering during prolonged dry spells would be beneficial, even for well-established plants.

Planting out
Proteaceae can be planted out at any time, even in deepest winter, provided they are fully hardened off; but the optimum time is spring, when the danger of frost is past. Planting at this time will give the plants a full season of growth and acclimatization before the onset of winter. In the absence of frequent rain, plants need regular watering for the first summer.

If soil is stony and difficult to dig, a post-borer is not recommended, as this can pan the sides, restricting root movement and drainage. The hole should be about twice the size of the root ball, and back-filled with a suitable mix to create the best possible soil conditions.

Proteaceous roots are extremely efficient, so when planted out Proteaceae need no additional feed, whether slow-release fertilizer or organic mulch. If a mulch is required for additional frost protection, then straw, horticultural fleece, or pine needles can be used. (In the stock beds at Trevena Cross Nurseries, King Proteas thrive beneath pine trees in a soil pH of 3.5.) Pine needles take several years to decay, so a good layer forms quickly, is long-lived, and gives protection from light frosts. Other advantages with this pairing are low nutrient and moisture levels in the soil, from which agaves and aloes also benefit. This is perhaps an example of perfect companion planting, where both cultivation and aesthetics are enhanced.

Not all gardens can accommodate pines the size of *Pinus radiata* (Monterey pine) or *P. sylvestris* (Scots pine), so two 'dwarfs' are recommended: *P. mugo pumilio*, the Mountain pine natural to central and south-east Europe, which is of bushy habit and grows to about 3m; and *P. sylvestris* 'Beauvronensis', a cultivar of the native Scots pine, which grows to about 1m by 1.5m. Both are suitable for an exposed site, and are tolerant of drought when established.

Protea cynaroides under snow.

Pot-grown Proteaceae, however, appear to benefit from specialist low-phosphorus, slow-release fertilizer, but only after the exhaustion of the 'slow release' within the original compost of the purchased pot. It is necessary to check with the nursery to know how long the plant has been in the pot, and whether they sell specialist protaceous feed. The issue of feed cannot be stressed enough: I have witnessed the death of a *Banksia* after watering from a can retaining residues of tomato feed. Death was sudden and unstoppable.

Weed control

Proteaceae do not accept the cramped, unhealthy, humid conditions that result from being surrounded by weeds. To deal with this, woven PVC film, or weed matting is very effective, while maintaining both water and air circulation. To enhance the overall look, and to keep the film from blowing away, a layer of course bark chips or large, sharp grit can be applied. Natural mulches such as grass cuttings or shredded bark often harbour destructive fungal diseases, and the process of their decay often draws nitrogen from the soil, so should be avoided. However, pine needles have been found to have no detrimental effects on the plants.

If you have already mature Proteaceae, and access to a shredder, old material such as finished flower-heads and dead branches can be spread as mulch. This will form a natural topsoil layer from which Proteaceae can readily feed.

Proteaceae such as *Embothrium coccineum*, or *Banksia marginata*, lend themselves to specimen cultivation in lawns, where grass is allowed to grow close to the trunks. This has the benefit of keeping the soil undisturbed and limiting the area where weeds can infest, but here care should be taken to keep lawn fertilizer – especially high phosphate types – well away from the plants.

Sprays that leave residues in the soil should also be avoided. Pre-emergent and post-emergent sprays have been used by commercial growers for years, with few adverse effects being recorded. Always follow instructions exactly, as careless application of sprays will harm or kill plants and wildlife.

Frost

It is difficult to generalize about the frost-tolerance of Proteaceae, so a hardiness assessment specific to each plant is given in the list of plants that follows.

Frost can damage or kill tender plants in a number of ways. As water freezes in plant tissue, it expands, causing the cell walls to split, and resulting in the collapse of leaves or whole tips, or more drastically the whole plant. Frost also causes drought conditions as moisture becomes inaccessible to roots. Frosty leaves in a position of strong morning sun can be damaged by intense light magnified through frost before thawing. Hosing away the frost before the sun reaches the leaves can help.

Horticultural fleece will offer a few degrees of protection. The best way to apply this is by building a frame that can be handled easily, and minimizing contact of the fleece with the leaves, as this is another cause of fungal infection. Around the base of the plants a temporary mulch of straw; a permanent mulch of pine needles on the soil; or bark or grit on weed matting will also offer some protection against light frosts.

If Proteaceae are in a rich soil and moisture is plentiful, lush long stems will be produced, which are most susceptible to frost as they will not be fully hardened when the frosts come. In milder regions this is a particular problem, as plants will grow sporadically throughout the winter when days are warm enough, leaving new leaves vulnerable to cold snaps. Plants grown in poor, free-draining soils will grow more slowly, and as a result be hardier.

Propagation
Seed
Natural pollination of Proteaceae flowers occurs rarely in this country; however with *Banksia* and *Hakea*, pollination is not unusual.

Proteaceae seeds need a day–night temperature fluctuation of around 12°C. I have found that September or March/April obtain the best results. Night temperatures of around 8°C, and day temperatures of around 20°C are ideal. Proteaceae will not germinate without this difference.

Pre-sowing treatment of some Proteaceae will increase germination chances considerably, and reduce losses by fungal infection.

For *Protea*, *Banksia*, *Leucadendron*, and *Dryandra*, soak seeds for 30 minutes at 50°C with an ethylene smoke disc. Allow them to dry, then dust lightly with a fungicide.

For *Leucospermums* and nut-forming *Leucadendrons*, in addition to the above treatment an additional soak in a 2:1 solution of water and hydrogen peroxide (available under the name Hydrogen Peroxide 10 vols, from chemists) will be beneficial. Immediately after this treatment, sow the seeds in trays or beds, in a mixture of two parts peat or decomposed pine needles; two parts coarse river sand, and one part Perlite or polystyrene pellets. A pH of 5.5 would be best, and sterilization would help limit fungal infection. Place the seeds about 2cm apart; cover thinly with river sand or Perlite, and place in semi-shade. Birds and mice will eat these seeds, so protection will be needed. Do not use supplementary heating, and do not allow the trays to dry out at any time.

When the first true leaves appear, plant on into 1-litre pots, in the same mix used at sowing, and avoiding the use of fertilizer or manure. Specialist slow-release pellets – fish or seaweed emulsions – are available. A cool day or late afternoon is ideal to minimize heat stress.

It is worth noting that *Banksia* fruits are very ornamental – particularly large-flowering species such as *B. menziesii* and *B. grandis*. In their native Australia, the fruits are put to a variety of uses in art and craft – from drinks coasters to children's toys. And 'banksia men', with their open capsules that resemble laughing mouths, have featured in many folk stories.

Cuttings
Semi-hardwood material is favoured for cuttings, as this yields the greatest level of success. Late spring or late summer/early autumn are the best times to take this material. Plants of a downy nature are most susceptible to fungal attack, so avoid nodal cuttings. Some *Leucadendrons*, such as *L.* 'Early Yellow', flower so profusely that it will be hard to find suitable tips; however, these plants seem to strike as well with flowers as without. Cutting compost and after-care is the same as for seed. Rooting can take up to a couple of months, and some plants, including *Protea cynaroides*, may sit completely inanimate for many months before either rooting or dying, so patience is needed.

The importance of hygiene cannot be overstressed, so remove dead cuttings and leaves.

Pests and diseases
Proteaceae in their natural habitat – particularly those in South Africa – are prone to many different pests and diseases. In this country, however,

few pests seem to favour them. Indeed, I have noticed a lack of interest even from rabbits!

Plants growing in rich soils produce lengthy, soft growth that is susceptible to aphid infestation. Aphids may be considered unsightly, but more importantly they can induce infection and reduce vigour. However, they are good food for a number of small garden birds, including blue tits and goldcrests, and predatory insects such as ladybirds. By planting a garden thoughtfully, these natural predators can be encouraged, thus reducing the need for artificial pesticides. A source of water; nesting situations, and the use of plants that encourage insect pollinators are a few ways to attract beneficial predators. In my experience, ladybirds gravitate towards proteas: in the summer, our stock-bed plants all have a healthy population. Perhaps this is because of the shelter offered by their leaves. Any standard pesticide mixed correctly can be used. Woodlice and earwigs can cause problems, in that protea flowers can take up to six months to form, and these insects burrow into the bud, and eat the contents as they do with figs. Plants growing in the right conditions will be strong, and will cope best with pests. Remember always to observe the situation first, resorting to chemical means only as a last resort.

By far the biggest problem facing Proteaceae in this country is fungal infection. *Phytophthora cinnamomi*, known as 'water mould', is a soil-borne fungus that favours poorly drained soil, as it spreads with the movement of water. The first sign is often wilted tips, though the soil is still moist, followed quickly by the browning of leaves and stem. This is unstoppable. As soon as the fungus is diagnosed, it is necessary to remove the whole plant and burn it. A more favourable situation for replanting may bring success.

Phytophthora can form in stagnant water supplies, and be introduced via irrigation. Botrytis, or grey mould, is a common problem in Britain: cool, dark, wet winter conditions are all it needs. Plants of a downy nature are particularly susceptible. Leaves show dark spots and complete loss of vigour, followed by an entire covering of the brown fuzzy spore-mass. Plants indoors need to be closely monitored over the winter, and hygiene needs to be strict. Good air circulation is necessary, without cold draughts.

Avoid pruning and vegetative propagation in winter, and if a tip is infected, cut it back to the next healthy node and improve conditions. Commercially, systemic fungicides are used to keep airborne attack at bay.

The King Protea, *Protea cynaroides*, is susceptible to leaf-spot, particularly potted specimens. The cause is unknown, but healthy plants can usually grow out of it in the spring. Again, a change of situation is what is needed. Plants growing slowly in favourable conditions will be more resistant.

Some Proteaceae worthy of cultivation

Grevilleoideae

Banksia

B. *canei* (Mountain Banksia), named after William Cane, a Victorian nurseryman who first drew attention to this species, is evergreen, and has yellow flowers, 5–15cm long, 4–6cm wide, from late winter to early spring. The leaves, from 2 to 5cm long, and from 0.5 to 2cm wide, are dark green on the upper surface, and white on the underside. The young growth is a pale greenish-brown. The mature bark is smooth, and of a reddish-brown

Banksia canei.

colour, which later turns to brownish-grey, with many lenticels. This rather slow-growing plant will reach a height and spread of about 3m. It requires protection from salt-laden wind; is drought-tolerant when established, and frost-tolerant from an early age. Pruning is largely unnecessary: it will form a full, rounded bush if provided with enough direct sun. Propagation is by seed.

B. ericifolia (Heath-leaved Banksia), was first collected at Botany Bay, New South Wales, in 1770 by Joseph Banks, who gave his name to the genus. It is evergreen, with impressive, fiery orange-yellow upright flower spikes 20–23cm tall, in mid- to late winter. As the name suggests, the leaves resemble those of the ericas: they are numerous, with dark green uppersides and pale, greenish-white undersides, linear and truncate, from 9 to 20cm long. The bark is smooth, becoming corky with age. This large shrub grows well only in an open position. In favourable conditions, it can attain 6m. It is suitable for heavier soil, and will tolerate around -5°C, drought, and coastal exposure once established. Considering that this plant is killed by bush fires in the wild, pruning into old wood is not advisable. Propagation is by seed sown in autumn,

Banksia ericifolia.

or by semi-hardwood cuttings. This is one of the easiest Banksias to grow.

B. grandis (Bull Banksia), a splendid evergreen, was first collected by Archibald Menzies at King George Sound, Western Australia, in late 1791. The flower spike, produced in late spring to early

Banksia grandis.

summer, is a magnificent tower of yellow, up to 45cm high. The species name refers to the size of the leaves, which are over 45cm long, the margins appearing like large teeth. New growth is pink-brown, maturing to bright green. The bark becomes thick with many ridges, of a grey colour, with age. This is a versatile plant, living in coastal sands, open woodland, and heath in its native habitat. It is slow-growing, and will reach around 6m in sheltered, favourable conditions. It needs an open site, but coastal exposure will limit growth. When established, it will tolerate about -5°C, and drought. Propagation is by seed. This Banksia has a lignotuber, so hard pruning to stimulate more bushy growth is possible.

B. integrifolia (Coastal Banksia), is a highly adaptable, evergreen tree, collected by Joseph Banks in

Banksia marginata.

1770 at Botany Bay. The flowers are pale yellow, and form a cylindrical tower, up to 15cm high, from autumn to spring. The species name refers to the entire margins of the adult leaves, which are narrowly elliptic, but vary in shape, and are arranged in whorls of three to five. They are from 4 to 10cm long, with bright green uppersides and white undersides; new growth is pale brown and velvety. The mature bark is brown with many rough lenticels. Living in coastal dunes, an adult tree will attain 25m, but conditions would have to be exceptionally favourable for this in cultivation. It is suitable for heavier soils; is frost tolerant to about -6°C, and tolerant of coastal exposure and drought when established. Propagation is by seed and semi-hardwood cuttings in autumn. This Banksia has a lignotuber, so pruning is possible.

B. marginata (Silver Banksia) is another highly adaptable evergreen, first collected by Luis Née in 1793, from between Port Jackson and Parramatta, New South Wales. The flowers are produced from mid-winter to spring, and are pale yellow, arranged as a short, upright cylinder, 5–10cm high and 4–6cm wide. The leaves are narrow, lin-

ear, and scattered, 1cm wide and 10cm long, with bright green uppersides and white undersides. The young growth is pale or pinkish-brown; the bark is smooth grey, developing many fine lenticels with age. Living on rocky soil – quartzite, sandstone, limestone, and granite – this Banksia is easy to grow, and makes a shrub or tree ranging from 1m to 12m, with or without a lignotuber. Some forms will sucker if the roots are disturbed. It is frost-tolerant to around -10°C, and tolerant of coastal exposure and drought when established. Propagation is by seed.

B. menziesii (Fire wood Banksia), is named after Archibald Menzies, the naturalist and surgeon aboard the *Discovery* expedition of 1791–5. It is evergreen. The flowers are white and red, opening to a fiery red and yellow, arranged as a cylinder or ovoid, 4–12cm high, and 7–8cm wide. The leaves are long, with toothed margins, scattered, of a grey-green colour with lighter undersides, up to 25cm long and 4cm wide. New growth is pale brown and velvety. The bark is thick, greyish-pink or pale brown. *B. menziesii* is found in deep sand in low woodland and tall shrubland near the coast of Western Australia, where the rainfall is between 35 and 90cm per annum. Slow-growing, it can produce a stunning tree of 10m, or a shrub of 3m, with a lignotuber. It is tolerant of frost to around -4°C, and of some coastal exposure and drought when established. It needs particularly well-drained, acidic soil, and plenty of shelter from very cold winds. It is not the easiest Banksia to grow, but is very rewarding. Propagation is by seed.

B. praemorsa (Cut-leaf Banksia) is a striking evergreen, first collected by Archibald Menzies from King George Sound, Western Australia, in 1791. The species name means 'bitten off', referring to the appearance of the leaf apex. The cylindrical flower head is 30cm high and 10cm wide, opening to reveal a fiery red and yellow coloration. The leaves are scattered, with serrated margins, up to 6cm long and 2cm wide, with deep green uppersides and pale green undersides. New growth is pale greenish-brown; the mature bark is rough and flaking. This shrub is found naturally on sand, or sandy loam over granite or limestone, and prefers a neutral soil (pH 6). It has no lignotuber, and reaches a height of about 4m. It is tolerant

Banksia praemorsa.

B. robur (Broad-leaved Banksia), an evergreen first collected by Luis Née between Port Jackson and Botany Bay, New South Wales, in 1793, has an almost peacock-blue bud, the flowers opening pale yellow to light orange, in spikes up to 20cm high, between autumn and spring. The foliage is particularly attractive: the leaves are serrated, up to 30cm long and 20cm wide, with dark green uppersides and pale, rusty coloured undersides. New growth is reddish-brown and velvety. The bark is smooth. This species will produce a sprawling shrub to 3m. It is tolerant to around -5°C, and of heavier soils and higher humidity than most Banksias. However, it is not drought tolerant; it needs shelter from wind, and is not suitable for coastal situations. Propagation is by seed.

B. serrata (Saw Banksia) was named from its sawtooth edged leaves. This evergreen was first collected by Joseph Banks at Botany Bay in 1770. It is pale grey-blue in bud, the flowers opening to pale yellow, arranged in spikes 7–15cm tall and 9–12cm wide, between midsummer and midwinter. The leaves are 7–22cm long and 2–4cm wide, with serrated edges. They are glossy green on the upperside, and pale grey underneath, sometimes downy on both surfaces. New growth is pale red-brown; the mature bark is grey-brown. *B. serrata* occurs

of frost to around -4°C, and of coastal exposure and drought when established. Good drainage is essential. Propagation is by seed, and less successfully by semi-hardwood cuttings.

Banksia robur.

Banksia serrata.

naturally on coastal plains, and consolidated sand-dunes, varying from a shrub of 3m to a tree of 16m. It is slow-growing and long-lived; frost-tolerant to about -4°C, and tolerant of coastal exposure and drought when established. Propagation is by seed. It can be pruned hard into old wood.

B. speciosa (Showy Banksia) was first collected at Esperance Bay by Jean Labillardière in 1792. Its beautiful flowers give it its Latin name. The buds are silvery, opening to lemon-yellow, appearing in late summer to autumn. The flower heads are ovoid, from 4 to 12cm tall, and from 9 to 10cm wide. It is evergreen, its leaves being divided into many triangular lobes, from 20 to 45cm long, and from 2 to 4cm wide; the uppersides are deep green, and the undersides white. New growth is pale brown, with rusty branchlets. The bark becomes smooth and grey with age. *B. speciosa* is found naturally on consolidated sand-dunes, with an annual rainfall of 40–50cm. This species can produce a shrub of around 8m, without lignotuber. It is tolerant of drought and coastal exposure, and requires a particularly well-drained soil. It is tolerant of frost to around -5°C. Propagation is by seed.

Banksia spinulosa.

B. spinulosa var. *spinulosa* (Hairpin Banksia), was first collected by John White *c.*1792 near Sydney, New South Wales. The species name refers to the sharp teeth on the leaf margins, the common name to the distinctive hooked styles of the flowers. The golden-yellow to red-orange flower heads, cylindrical in shape, are about 20cm tall and 4–6cm wide, appearing in winter. The leaves are from 3 to 12cm long, and very narrow, with dark green uppersides and white undersides. The new growth is pale rusty- or brownish-green. The bark matures to a reddish-brown with many lenticels. This slow-growing, evergreen shrub can attain 3m, and is found naturally on sandy loams or clay loams on coastal plains. When established it will tolerate frost to around -8°C, coastal exposure, and drought. It will accept light shade and a fairly heavy soil. Hard pruning will stimulate a bushier growth. Propagation is by seed and semi-hardwood cuttings in autumn.

B. spinulosa var. *collina* was first described as a species by Robert Brown in the early 1800s, the name *collina* referring to the hilly locality where it was found. This variety differs from *B. spinulosa* var. *spinulosa* only in its broader leaves.

Dryandra

D. praemorsa (Urchin Dryandra), whose species name – as with *Banksia praemorsa* – refers to the 'bitten off' appearance of the leaves, flowers in spring and early summer. The flower heads go through several attractive stages, from solid ovoid buds opening to bright yellow shaving brushes, up to 6cm wide. An evergreen, *D. praemorsa* is holly-like in appearance, with leaves medium-green above to whitish on the undersides, 14cm long and 4cm wide. *D. praemorsa* is a shrub of up to 2m, needing a very well-drained, acidic soil, and full sun. It will tolerate frost to -5°C; drought, and coastal exposure when established, but will require sturdy staking if exposed to strong winds. Light pruning after flowering will encourage a bushier habit. Propagation is by seed.

Embothrium

Embothrium coccineum (Chilean fire tree) is a beautiful, erect and slender evergreen tree from high-rainfall areas in the Andes of South America, which makes it quite easy to grow in this country. The flowers are of a fiery orange-red, and spi-

Embothrium coccineum.

3m by 3m. Because of the speed of growth, if plants are in good soils it is advisable to prune them when young, to allow the roots to equal the size of the top growth, and so improve stability. Young plants can be pruned heavily, but as specimens mature do not cut back old wood. Fast growth is a mixed blessing, because it also produces very brittle wood, which is why this *Grevillea* is not suitable for exposed sites or coastal situations. It prefers well-drained soil, but is tolerant of heavier soil conditions. It is hardy to around -10°C. Propagation is by semi-hardwood cuttings.

G. juniperina, whose name refers to its juniper-like leaves, is a highly desirable, very hardy, and adaptable evergreen shrub, widely used from Australia to California. It has many different forms, even colour variants including red and yellow. It grows to around 2m by 2.5m, with leaves varying in length from 1cm to 3cm. The flowers are carried in dense clusters, mainly in late winter, spring and early summer. *G. juniperina* is tolerant of drought, fairly heavy soils, and frost to around -10°C – probably more. It requires full sun, and prefers well-drained, acidic soils. Propagation is by seed, but progeny may vary a great deal. Named varieties propagate by semi-hardwood cuttings from late spring to early autumn.

G. robusta (Silky oak), whose common name refers to the smooth, oak-like timber, and the species name to its strong growth habit, carries fiery, orange-yellow flowers on brush-like racemes up to 15cm long, during spring and early summer. A mature specimen in full flower is a magnificent sight. The leaves are fern-like in shape, and dark green. New growth varies in colour from whitey-green to a pale orange. In its natural habitat of rain forest in northern New South Wales, it forms a tall, straight tree of 30–40m; however, in cultivation it rarely exceeds 16m. *G. robusta* is tolerant of well-drained or heavier soils, provided that adequate moisture is available. It requires a very shel-

dery in form. It is a prolifically flowering tree, and when seen in full flower is a magnificent and striking sight. The tree can attain 5m in height, and is frost hardy to around -10°C when established. Avoid lime, phosphates, and prolonged summer drought. Propagation is by seed, semi-hardwood cuttings, or removal of rooted suckers.

Grevillea

G. hookeriana, or *G. hookerana* hybrid form, has crimson-red, toothbrush-like flower heads of up to 10cm long and 8cm wide, all year, most abundantly in spring and summer. The leaves are slightly spiky and 'fishbone' in appearance, with dark, glossy green uppersides and pale grey undersides. This is a fast-growing, evergreen shrub, which reaches

tered site in full sun. Young plants tolerate light frost, and well-established specimens will take up to -7°C. This plant assumes a deciduous habit in British gardens.

G. rosmarinifolia is evergreen. Its name refers to its rosemary-like leaves, which are like needles, from dark green to glaucous grey, and 3.5cm long. Although there are many variants, cultivated forms generally make dense shrubs of up to 2m. The flower clusters are typically 'spidery' in appearance, up to 5cm across, and produced in flushes in spring and autumn, with colours ranging from deep red and white to variants of green/yellow or cream. This is an easy plant to grow, being tolerant of drought, coastal exposure, and frost to around -7°C when established. It requires a well-drained, acidic soil in full sun, and accepts hard pruning.

Hakea

H. epiglottis, a very tough evergreen, forms a shrub of 2–4m in height, with creamy-yellow flowers of 'spidery' appearance in summer. The dark green, needle-like foliage is very ornamental, particularly on the young, deep crimson stems. It is tolerant of drought, some coastal exposure, and frost to around -7°C when established. It needs a well-drained, acidic soil, in full sun. Propagation is by seed or semi-hardwood cuttings.

H. laurina (Pincushion Hakea) is a slender, evergreen shrub or small tree, of 2.5–5m in height. Flowers emerge from buds covered in scaly brown bracts, to form golf-ball-sized red and yellow 'pincushions', in autumn and early winter. The foliage is laurel-like; indeed, the leaves are elliptic, deep green, and up to 15cm long. Young growth is a soft, gold-bronze, and mature foliage turns an orange-brown before falling. It is tolerant of heavier soils, drought, and frost to -4°C once established. This is a shallow-rooting plant that is suitable only for a sheltered position in full sun. Propagation is by seed, or semi-hardwood cuttings.

H. lissocarpha (Honey bush) is a beautiful, slow-growing evergreen bush, which grows up to 1m high, and bears

creamy-yellow flowers in flushes throughout the year. The leaves are spiny and finely divided, ranging in colour from pale yellow to dark orange. It is tolerant of dappled shade, drought, some coastal exposure, and frost to -7°C when established. It needs a well-drained soil and full sun, and may be hard-pruned. Propagation is by seed or semi-hardwood cuttings.

H. nodosa (Yellow Hakea) is a dense, bushy, evergreen shrub with heavily scented, golden, spidery flowers produced in abundance mostly in autumn, making this a very desirable garden plant. The foliage is soft, dark green and needle-like in appearance, between 1 and 5cm in length. It is tolerant of drought and frost to around -7°C when established, and needs well-drained, acidic soil in full sun. Propagation is by seed or semi-hardwood cuttings.

H. sericea (Silky Hakea) is a dense, erect shrub, producing sweetly scented, white or pink flowers of slender, curly appearance, in summer. It grows to around 5m in height, with silky-haired branches carrying clusters of narrow, stiff, needle-like leaves between 5 and 8cm long. It is tolerant of drought, and frost to -7°C when established, and needs well-drained, acidic soil, in full sun. Propagation is by seed or semi-hardwood cuttings. It is evergreen, and an excellent screening plant.

Hakea sericea.

H. suaveolens, syn. *H. drupacea*, a large evergreen shrub or small tree, between 3 and 5m in height, bears sweetly scented, spidery, white flowers, mainly in summer. The leaves are finely divided, stiff needles, with soft, light green, hairy new growth. It is tolerant of coastal exposure; a slightly higher pH level than is usual for hakeas, and around -6°C when established. Propagation is by seed or semi-hardwood cuttings.

Knightia

K. excelsa 'Rewarewa' (New Zealand honeysuckle), the only Proteaceae in our collection native to New Zealand, is an upright evergreen tree of about 7m in height, with a spread of 2m. It bears crimson-brown, spidery flowers in spring and summer that are very attractive to bees and butterflies. The seedpods are also ornamental. Leaves are linear, coarsely toothed, and pale green. Young foliage is soft, and a creamy-brown. It is tolerant of light shade, close planting, and frost to around -5°C, becoming hardier with age. Drought and high exposure are to be avoided. It prefers a moist, but free-draining, acidic soil. Propagation is by seed. Pruning is unnecessary.

Knightia excelsa 'Rewarewa'.

Lomatia

L. ferruginea, an upright, evergreen tree from Chile and Argentina, has brownish-orange flowers in summer, and stiff, very dark green, fern-like leaves. It grows in rain forest in the wild, and will tolerate damper, more shady conditions than most of the Proteaceae. It grows to around 20m, but usually much less in this country. It requires a hot, sheltered spot, but is frost-tolerant to around -7°C. Propagation is by seed.

Lomatia ferruginea.

L. tinctoria is a low, spreading, and suckering evergreen shrub, growing to around 1.2m in height and spread. Its leaves are of a lighter green than *L. ferruginea*, and more slender, but they retain the fern-like arrangement. Native to Tasmania, and growing in dry, open places at up to 1,000m, it is tolerant of drought, and frost to about -7°C, possibly more with age. Propagation is by seed or semi-hardwood cuttings.

Stenocarpus

S. sinuatus (Queensland fire wheel tree) is an upright, non-spreading tree, rarely exceeding 3m in this country. The flowers are unusual, deep red in colour, and perhaps resembling the spokes of a wheel. The leaves are a glossy dark green, and very variable, from entire, to broad and oak-like. *S. sinuatus* is tolerant of heavier soils and slightly damper conditions than many Proteaceae, but it does need a hot, sheltered situation, in sun or semi-shade. Protection from cold winds is required, especially when young, as the foliage is easily damaged. It is frost-tolerant to -4°C, becoming hardier with age. Propagation is by seed, and by cuttings, which, if taken from mature branches, produce flowering plants at a younger age. This is a rewarding plant to grow.

Telopea

T. burgundy is a natural hybrid between *T. oreades* and *T. speciosissima* (see below), which forms a small evergreen tree of about 4m in height. Its flowers are dense, shallow domes of deep red tinged with purple, up to 10cm across, and borne at any time between winter and late spring. The leaves are a deep green colour, and large – up to 20cm long and 4cm wide. This is an easy plant to grow; tolerant of varying soils; drought- and frost-tolerant to around -10°C. Propagation is by seed and semi-hardwood cuttings.

T. oreades (Gippsland, or Victoria Warratah) is a beautiful evergreen Australian tree, which after many years reaches a height of about 12m, producing deep red flowers in spring, arranged in shallow domes of 7–10cm across. The leaves are a glaucous green, often tinged with red or dark purple, and from 8 to 25cm long and 2 to 5cm wide. This is a relatively easy plant to cultivate. It accepts varying soil types; prefers a sheltered position, in either dappled shade or full sun, and is tolerant of frost to around -15°C once established. Propagation is by seed and cuttings.

T. speciosissima is an evergreen of variable size, from 1 to 4m in height. The flowers, borne mainly in spring, are large, red globes, surrounded by red bracts, from 8 to 15cm in diameter. The leaves are dark green, irregularly toothed, with prominent veination, 10–14cm long, and 2–4cm wide.

This is not the easiest plant to grow. *T. speciosissima* requires an open, airy site in full sun, and prefers acidic, very free-draining soil. Hard pruning is required after flowering to maintain a tight bush habit, as it tends naturally towards an open, straggly form. Although tolerant of some coastal exposure, it is better suited to a more sheltered position, due to its shallow root system. It is hardy to drought, and to frost to around -10°C. Propagation is by semi-hardwood cuttings in early summer, or fresh seed.

Proteoidiae

Leucadendron

L. argenteum (Cape silver tree) is an upright, evergreen tree, which can reach up to 10m high in very favourable conditions. It is a dense plant while young, but becomes more open with age. Flowers appear in the form of golden cones on branch tips in summer, followed by larger, more conspicuous scaly seed-heads in autumn. The magnificent foliage is green, but has a distinct silver appearance due to a thick covering of silky hairs, making it particularly attractive when rippling in the breeze. A beautiful plant, *L. argenteum* is not the easiest to grow: it is prone to fungal infection, and is very fussy about drainage. It is best grown in a hot, dry, airy, but sheltered position, in full sun. It is tolerant of some coastal exposure, and frost to around -5°C, getting hardier with age. The first few years are the most vulnerable. Propagation is by seed or cuttings, with seed producing by far the best results. *L. argenteum* is dioecious.

Telopea speciosissima.

Leucadendron argenteum.

L. galpinii, an evergreen shrub with neatly curving branches, reaches some 2m in height in favourable conditions. Its flowers are conspicuous, silvery cones borne on branch tips in summer. The leaves are pale green and hairless, with a pink edge, linear, truncated, and twisted. This is a relatively easy plant to grow, being tolerant of drought, frost to around -5°C, and some coastal exposure when established. It is dioecious, and propagation is by seed or cuttings.

Leucadendron galpinii.

L. laureolum, syn. *decorum*, is a densely bushy, evergreen shrub that can reach up to 2m high and as wide. The flowers are golden cones set among very showy golden bracts, borne on the branch ends in summer. The leaves are broad and softly hairy, of a mid-green colour with a distinctive dark tip. This is an easy plant to grow, being tolerant of drought and frost to around -8°C when established. Propagation is by seed or semi-hardwood cuttings.

L. 'Maui Sunset' is a desirable evergreen hybrid that grows to about 1m by 1m. The flowers, which appear in autumn and throughout the winter, are tiny cones borne in the centre of attractive, stiff, creamy-white bracts edged in red, which fade to pale yellow in spring. The leaves are a light, glaucous grey-green with a red edge and a light covering of hairs. This is an easy plant to grow, being especially suitable for pot cultivation. It is tolerant of drought and frost to around -6°C, as far as

nursery experience shows. Propagation is by seed, or semi-hardwood cuttings.

L. 'Safari Sunset', a very vigorous evergreen hybrid, can attain over 2m in height. Its flowers are tiny, and appear at the centre of very showy, cream and red bracts. The leaves range from dark green to a very dark red. This plant is densely bushy by nature, but pruning after flowering is advisable to maintain a sturdy structure. It is an easy plant to grow, being tolerant of fairly heavy, rich soils, a higher pH than most, and coastal exposure. It is frost-tolerant to -12°C when established. Propagation is by cuttings.

Leucadendron 'Safari Sunset'.

L. salignum, the most widely distributed leucadendron in its native South Africa, is one of the easiest to cultivate as it accepts a variety of soil types, quite strong wind exposure, and frost to about -9°C. It is evergreen, with tiny flowers set among beautiful bracts that vary from shades of yellow through to shades of red, in late summer and throughout the winter. As its name suggests, the foliage resembles some species of willow in appearance, with a deep green colour frequently tinged with red-orange. *L. salignum* can reach 1–2m in height and spread. Propagate by seed, but semi-hardwood cuttings will perpetuate a particular variant.

L. salignum 'Early Yellow' is a neat shrub of some 1.5m in height and spread. The tiny flowers are set among yellow bracts, and are borne from late summer through the winter. The leaves are slender and glaucous. The plant is tolerant of drought, frost to around -8°C, and varying soil types.

L. salignum 'Fire Glow' is another evergreen variety suitable for pot cultivation, as it has a neat habit and grows to between 1m and 1.5m in height and spread. Its flowers are tiny, and set among fiery red bracts in late summer and throughout the winter. The leaves are slender and glaucous, edged with red. The plant is tolerant of drought and frost to about -8°C. Propagation is by cuttings.

L. strobilinum is a sturdy evergreen shrub of around 2m in height and spread. The flowers are silvery cones set among creamy-white and gold bracts, borne in spring. The leaves are deep green and broad, with a fringe of tiny hairs at the margins. The plant is tolerant of frost to -6°C and wind exposure, when established. Propagation is by seed or cuttings.

L. tinctum is a low, evergreen, bushy shrub of about 1–1.5m in height and spread. The flowers are borne in winter among stiff bracts of red or orange and green. The leaves are sturdy and broad, varying in colour from pale green tinged with orange to deep green tinged with red. *L. tinctum* is an easy plant to cultivate, being tolerant of wind exposure, varying soil types, and frost to around -7°C when established. It is one of the more suitable species for pot cultivation. Propagation is by seed or cuttings.

L. uliginosum is an elegant, evergreen shrub that grows to around 2m in height and spread, although it is frequently smaller in Britain. The flowers appear in early summer among lime-yellow bracts. The leaves, often tinged with pink, are covered in a mass of tiny hairs, giving the plant a silver appearance. It is tolerant of wind exposure, drought, and frost to around -6°C. Propagation is by seed or cuttings.

Leucospermum

L. cordifolium, a variable, evergreen shrub that reaches about 2m in height and spread, has impressive flowers that range between 10 and 20cm in diameter, being either yellow or orange, or red tipped with yellow, and borne in spring to midsummer. The glaucous leaves are stemless, and resemble curved hearts. Although this is regarded as one of the easiest leucospermums to grow, it tends to be vulnerable to fungal infections in damp conditions, particularly when young. However, it is tolerant of drought, and frost to -4°C, perhaps more with age. Propagation is by seed and cuttings.

L. muirii is an erect, bushy, evergreen shrub that grows to 1.5m in height, with a spread of 1m. Its flowers, borne from spring to midsummer, are bright orange to red, and between 2 and 3cm in diameter. The leaves are glaucous and broad, and end in varying numbers of small, blunt teeth. The plant is vulnerable to damp when young, but tolerant of drought and frost to around -4°C, perhaps more with age. Propagation is by seed or cuttings.

Protea

P. caffra is a variable, evergreen species ranging from an erect shrub or small tree of 3–8m in height, to a multi-stemmed shrub of 1–3m, with lignotuber. The flowers comprise pink or carmine bracts, loosely arranged around orange perianth segments, borne in summer. The leaves are glaucous, broad, and hairless. In the nursery, young specimens of *P. caffra* have survived a snow covering over three days, and temperatures as low as -5°C. Propagation is by seed and semi-hardwood cuttings.

P. coronata, an erect, evergreen, bushy shrub attaining perhaps 2m in height, matures into a gnarled plant. The flowers are small, and surrounded by large, stiff, green bracts that overlap, giving the overall appearance of a green pepper. Each bract is edged with fine white hairs. The leaves are variable – either silvery-green and very hairy, or bright green and hairless. *P. coronata* is tolerant of a wide range of soil types, drought, and frost to around -2°C, becoming hardier with age. A relatively easy protea to grow, it is, however, vulnerable to damp, particularly when young. Propagation is by seed, or semi-hardwood cuttings.

P. cynaroides (King Protea) is the best-known of all the proteas, being prized for its magnificent flowers, which range from 10cm to often 30cm across, and resemble large, robust water-lilies. These blooms comprise large, crimson, cream, or dark pink overlapping bracts, and light pink to white perianth segments. The leaves vary in size and shape from broadly orbicular to narrowly rhomboidal, and are usually a rich green colour, with a distinctive red margin. This is an evergreen, often straggly shrub, of 1–2m in height, that responds well to hard pruning. Flowers tend to appear on three- to four-year-old stems, at different times of the year, according to the origins of the parent of the seed. King Protea are distributed right across the Cape floral kingdom. They are tolerant of coastal exposure, drought, and frost to around -7°C when established. Propagation is by seed, or semi-hardwood cuttings. (Photo page 110.)

P. eximia varies from a prostrate shrub to an erect tree of some 2–3m in height. It is evergreen, and the flowers are borne throughout the year, emerging from beautiful egg-shaped buds of tightly arranged, black-tipped bracts. When open, the flowers comprise loose bracts – red at the top, fading to a cream colour at the base. The perianths form an egg-shape in the centre, with a deep crimson point. The leaves are broad and oval, ranging in colour from glaucous to deep purple, almost always with a distinctive red margin. A relatively easy protea to grow, *P. eximia* is tolerant of a relatively high soil pH, drought, wind exposure, and frost to around -5°C when established. Propagation is by seed, or semi-hardwood cuttings.

P. grandiceps is a slow-growing, long-lived (20+ years) protea, forming either a prostrate shrub with a spread of around 2m, or an upright, bushy shrub of 2m in height. It is evergreen, and flowers mainly in summer, the flowers comprising bracts of a dark reddish colour, tipped with white hairs

Protea eximia.

arranged tightly around a white centre. *Grandiceps* translates from the Latin as 'large or noble head', and indeed the blooms range from 10 to 15cm in diameter. The leaves are generally oval; glaucous green with a red margin; up to 14cm long, and 9cm wide. Originating from altitudes of between 1,000 and 1,700m, in the wilds of South Africa, *P. grandiceps* is quite easy to cultivate, being tolerant of frost to around -7°C, drought, and wind exposure when established. Propagation is by seed, or semi-hardwood cuttings.

Protea grandiceps.

P. laurifolia, the 'laurel'-leaved protea, forms a dense, evergreen shrub that reaches around 3m in height, after many years. The flowers are borne mainly in winter, ranging in colour from a pale yellow-green to a pale pink. The bracts are tightly arranged, and tipped with distinctive black to very dark purple hairs. The leaves are elliptic, glaucous with a red margin, and can be up to 17cm long. This is an easy protea to grow, being tolerant of drought, wind exposure, and frost to -6°C. Propagation is by seed, or semi-hardwood cuttings.

P. 'Pink Ice', an evergreen hybrid, is one of the easiest proteas to cultivate. It grows to around 1.5m in height, usually less, with an equal spread, and is tolerant of slightly heavy soils, drought, and frost to around -7°C when established. The flowers are a rich pinkish-red, and are borne throughout the year. The leaves are linear, and of a dull glaucous colour with a white midrib. This is one of the more suitable proteas for pot cultivation. Propagation is by semi-hardwood cuttings.

P. repens, formerly *P. mellifera* (honey-bearing), as it produces nectar prolifically, is an evergreen, eventually erect, many-branched shrub that grows to around 4m. It bears flowers in summer comprising tightly overlapping, hairless bracts coated with a sticky substance, and varying from cream to green to a reddish colour. The leaves are principally linear, glaucous, yellow, and hairless. This is one of the most widespread of all the proteas across the Cape floral kingdom, and is therefore relatively easy to grow; tolerant of drought, coastal exposure, and frost to around -6°C when established. Propagation is by seed and cuttings.

P. scolymocephala, a charming, gnarly little evergreen shrub, grows to around 1.5m in height, often less, with an equal spread. It is almost *Leucadendron*-like in appearance, with slender branches covered in thin leaves up to 5cm long and 6mm wide. The Latin *scolymocephala* refers to its thistle-like flower heads, borne profusely from late winter to early summer. The flowers comprise openly arranged bracts of a reddish-cream or green colour around similarly coloured perianths. This is a relatively easy protea to cultivate, being tolerant of coastal exposure, drought, and frost to around -6°C when established. Propagation is by seed, or semi-hardwood cuttings.

P. subvestita is an upright, evergreen shrub that grows to around 2.5m in height, without ligno-tuber. The flowers, borne in summer, are attractive, and comprise open, cream to pinkish bracts tipped with thick white hairs, surrounding upright perianths. *P. subvestita* lives at altitudes of between 1,200 and 2,300m, making it an easy protea to grow. It is tolerant of drought, wind exposure, and frost to around -10°C when established. Propagation is by seed, or semi-hardwood cuttings.

Protea subvestita.

P. venusta – the species name *venusta* translates as beautiful, or lovely – is hardy, evergreen, and adaptable, making this is a very desirable protea. Originating from altitudes of between 1,700 and 2,000m, *P. venusta* forms a dense, spreading shrub of around 3m, attaining a height of only 70cm. The flowers, which consist of creamy green, red-tipped bracts surrounding fluffy white perianths, are borne mainly in late summer. The leaves are blue-green with a red margin. The plant is tolerant of varying soil types, wind exposure, drought, and frost to around -7°C, possibly more, when established. Propagation is by seed, and semi-hardwood cuttings.

6 Bamboos and Restios

Michael Bell and Les Cathery

The true grass family is one of the largest groups of flowering plants, and a very important one within the ornamental garden. Most are small species, although some grow to over two metres tall, and some of these large species are also ever-green. Two sub-families within Gramineae/Poaceae comprise species that are mainly monumental in size and form, and their delicate profile and evergreen properties impart a unique quality to our gardens. Restios (Restionacaea) are mainly shrub-like in size, with elegant, feathery culms, and interesting flowers and seeds. Bamboos (*Bambusoideae*) range in size from arborescent species down to ground-cover plants. Both groups contain many recent introductions that include plants of great potential to the adventurous gardener.

Left: *Chusquea culeou.* (See page 143.)

Bamboos add an exotic touch to a garden, creating a tropical atmosphere.

Bamboos

Michael Bell

It comes as a surprise to most people that Britain is one of the best climatic regions in the world for growing temperate bamboos, and that the western seaboard zones are the most favourable within the British Isles. This huge and diverse family of plants is little used, and its potential within adventurous gardening rarely exploited. There are species and forms to suit all gardens, and their unique qualities can fill many needs, but they are widely misunderstood. This is mainly due to the legacy of unwise selections introduced to many gardens towards the end of the nineteenth century.

Background to the cultivation of bamboos

Temperate bamboos evolved from tropical species, and during this process some developed a running rootstock that gave them a considerable advantage over competing species. These running species are to be avoided at all costs in a garden setting, except for one or two that are slow-growing.

They are uncontrollable even in very large estates, for they mostly have the qualities of a huge, indestructible couch-grass. However, at least half of the temperate species retained the tight, clumping root system of their tropical ancestors, and these are the species to use in most garden settings.

Geographical and climatic relationships of bamboos

Bamboos cultivated in temperate areas originate in two main climatic regions. Those from lowland China, Japan, Taiwan, and adjacent countries are from regions with very cold winters and very hot summers, compared with England. Most are robust plants with running roots. Those from the colder regions are completely hardy, but our lack of summer heat often severely curtails their size, and with some species their invasive qualities, which is no disadvantage within a garden. As these zones near the tropics, the temperate plants gradually change to clumping, tropical species. This chapter will recommend some of the less invasive temperate plants, but they do have the potential to get out of control if the site is warm or fertile, and this should be considered before planting. Some of the tropical species can withstand a few degrees of frost, but again our lack of summer heat is usually the reason for them failing to prosper in this country.

The other climatic regions that have evolved temperate species of bamboos are the high mountains of the Himalayas and the Andes. These vast areas have experienced great evolutionary pressures, and have given rise to a huge number of species. Each isolated valley often contains its own distinct forms in addition. Species range from those growing in subtropical valleys to high elevations, in every conceivable combination of conditions. The majority are clumping species, and they include some of the most cold-hardy plants we cultivate, as well as those requiring the choicest locations, and all the skills of the gardener. It is among the latter species that the adventurous gardener will find the most interesting and challenging plants. Many hundreds of species and forms remain to be discovered and recorded by botanists, and often new introductions have only the introduction number and brief collection details to guide the grower. Many mountain species will not tolerate high summer temperatures, and Britain's mild, damp climate enables us to grow most of these to perfection, in addition to the lowland species. This combination of conditions that enables us to grow both lowland and mountain species makes your garden one of the best places in the world for growing bamboos!

All bamboos add to the tropical effect – not just the large-leaved species. The well-behaved, elegant, small-leaved plants possess the form of the clumping tropical species, and add an exotic touch. There are very few evergreen plants other than bamboos that have a tropical air, and even fewer that are reliably hardy. Almost all that can be brought to mind have thick, leathery leaves with a waxy cuticle for winter protection. A few bamboos have strong leaves, but these do not compare with the thick, rigid leaves of the *Fatsia*, for example, and most bamboos have thin, delicate leaves. The leaves have a flexible stalk, which allows them to move with every breath of wind and rustle like few other plants. Sound is a quality as essential in a garden as scent, but with very few opportunities. Apart from grasses, only a few deciduous trees, and water, possess this potential.

Bamboos come in many different natural profiles, and can be pruned into others. But the big

Planting to suit your site: bamboos in a small garden.

The horticultural value of bamboos

Above all other attributes, the ability of bamboos to evoke a tropical atmosphere is probably the most obvious. The large, evergreen leaves of some species are equalled by few other hardy plants. Some of the *Sasa* and allied species have leaves over 60cm long, but these are mainly rampant species to be avoided at all costs. With a careful selection of species, and a knowledge of their potential problems, disasters can be overcome.

advantage in most situations, particularly in small gardens, is that their size is completely predictable. They reach full height within a few years, and then do not grow taller. Only the base diameter increases with age – unlike most small trees, which are slow to reach the desired size, but then keep on growing. The height of bamboos varies only with the fertility of the site, which can be controlled. If you desire a specimen plant with the form of a weeping willow or a shuttlecock, a hedge, ground

Planting to suit your site: the yellow-stemmed bamboo *Phyllostachys vivax* 'Aureocaulis' forms an open screen in this garden.

cover, a grove, or individual, wide-spaced culms (canes), then with wise selection there is a plant to suit your site and need. In addition, bamboos do not rob large areas of soil of nutrients, and they do not undermine foundations or seek out drains.

In Cornish valleys, the Victorian gardener's aim was usually to produce an idealized Himalayan valley, even though *Trachycarpus* and *Dicksonias* abounded. Bamboos are as inherent to the Himalayas as rhododendrons, and were originally planted in quantity. Due mainly to neglect, most of the choice plants died out during the twentieth century, leaving only the rampant and less desirable species. Today, there is great potential in all our gardens, and we are beginning to understand that form should not always be sacrificed to colour. There is much more to a good garden than a brilliant, but brief, display of colour in the spring.

Characteristics of bamboos

The great majority of temperate bamboos have no problems with our growing conditions. Pro-

vided that they are protected from drying winds and, in a few cases, extremes of temperature, they are very adaptable plants. They are not fussy about soil or location, within reasonable limits, and can grow without aftercare when established. They are natural survivors, and south-west England and Ireland's benign climate suits them admirably.

To get the plants off to a good start; to pander to those of borderline hardiness, or to accommodate any unknown needs of new introductions, we need to understand a little about their requirements. Bamboos are a family of plants with a distinct mode of growth, and unique botanic features, and certain requirements are fundamental to all genera and species. However, we grow plants from a vast range of conditions, and they therefore have their individual needs, many of which are not fully understood. Without knowledge of the microclimate of their location, these particular needs can only be deduced by experience, and this is the case with most new introductions that we encounter. Here lies the challenge to the keen gardener, and the unique opportunity for mild gardens – just as over a century ago, when these exotics of unknown hardiness and potential were first introduced into this region. But the difficulties should not be over-emphasized. Most bamboos are very easy garden plants, and in time the majority of the new introductions will undoubtedly be found to be completely hardy over most of Britain and Ireland.

Bamboos are part of the extensive grass family, and have inherited their botanic features; but these have been modified to suit the unique growth pattern of bamboos. The culms grow in the spring or early summer to full height – often over 6m in a few weeks. Thereafter, they do not increase in height or diameter, and each culm lives for ten years or more. They are the fastest-growing terrestrial plant, and this massive surge in growth draws heavily on the food reserves of the rest of the bamboo. To accommodate this, the continuous growth pattern of other plants has been modified to a two-phase system, with culm growth usually in the first part of the year, and rhizome growth in the latter part of the growing season. In some species this is reversed, while in others – where our weather does not match that of their native lands, or sometimes during propagation – the biology becomes confused and random. But it is always two-phase (culms–rhizomes), and this is one of the distinguishing features of a bamboo. It is often this unseasonal late growth, or the soft growth of small plants that have not produced woody culms, that is vulnerable to our winter conditions, and so some new plantings may need temporary winter protection for a year or two.

If a bamboo is starved of nutrients or water before or during culm growth, its overall height will be reduced; while if a drought happens later in the year, the rhizome growth will be inhibited, and consequently the number and spacing of new shoots the following spring. Temporary drought or starvation does not result in a period of dormancy followed by a resumption of normal growth, as is the case with many other plants. If adverse conditions happen in a regular pattern every year, growth will be permanently influenced.

A new shoot of *Fargesia robusta*. The number and spacing of new bamboo shoots is affected by the availability of nutrients and water.

In the wild, the natural bamboo zones are limited as much by fluctuations of rain as fluctuations in temperature and, even more importantly, the inter-relationship between these patterns. Many bamboos come from areas of heavy summer rain and dry winters, so in this country it is wise to ensure

adequate water and feed in the summer, and perfect drainage – particularly with new plantings and recent introductions of unknown provenance.

In most areas of the UK, we have a moisture deficit in the summer, but bamboos can usually accommodate this when established, although it will influence their growth if severe, as with any other plant. Probably only the high rainfall zones of the UK have annual rainfalls equalling that experienced by most wild bamboos, but even in these regions the rain falls mainly in the winter. As would be expected with such requirements, soils should ideally be high in humus, moisture-retentive, but also free-draining. Bamboos can be heavy feeders if healthy, and can grow to full size in a few years if well fed and irrigated.

Although it is not advisable to subject obviously delicate species to high winds, our winter storms usually cause bamboos few problems. Unlike most other temperate evergreens, bamboos do not possess protective mechanisms to reduce transpiration through the leaves during high winds, and therefore dehydration is always a danger, particularly in specimens with frozen roots, or if recently planted on the west coasts. Our winter winds are usually very humid or even wet, and do not normally give problems. Less strong, but continuous summer winds can be more damaging, and sometimes leaf curl can be seen even on well-established plants. Most species can be transplanted within a garden very easily, and so when growing plants new to cultivation, or of borderline hardiness, it is best to grow them to a good size in a nursery plot before moving them to a more exposed situation. Salt spray and salt in the soil is very damaging, and even seaweed as a manure should be avoided.

We read of or see bamboos growing in the wild as understorey in open woodland, or on the edge of woodland, but we should not assume that a shaded location is necessary. Some species do require some shade, and show their resentment to strong light by curling their leaves on the side facing the sun, but the majority are probably starved of light in our northern gardens. Not only do bamboos grow considerably nearer the Equator than here, but those woodland species are usually growing at high altitude (some over 4,000m), where we would have to use eye and skin protection. Even in their open woodland, light levels would normally be higher than found in our open conditions. Many species are severely retarded by our woodland conditions, but some mountain species can accommodate some shade. New introductions are best acclimatized to our full sun as soon as they are growing well, unless this causes obvious stress, such as leaf curl.

Growing bamboos

All new acquisitions should be planted out as soon as possible if growing well. Their great need for water can lead to all sorts of watering problems with pot plants, particularly in the confines of a greenhouse if you are at work all day and do not have an automatic watering system. Plant them into their permanent location if they are large and have few arduous requirements. If they are small, of borderline hardiness, or an unknown introduction, they are best planted in a nursery bed where temporary protection can be given if necessary. Top-dress with well-rotted manure, and water regularly, and in 12 months they will be ready to move. Bamboos are mostly shallow-rooted, so incorporating fertilizer into the soil is not necessary.

Plants in pots are very vulnerable to winter cold, because of their evergreen leaves and lack of any means to reduce transpiration. All pot plants – even the toughest – should be protected from temperatures below freezing. Species of unknown cultural requirements should be kept slightly on the dry side until the spring, as they could originate from zones with a dry winter, or where moisture is locked up as snow.

Bamboo species

Until recently, the Royal Botanic Gardens at Kew were at the forefront of naming Himalayan species of bamboo, and considerable progress has been made in categorizing the genera and species from this region. But many new introductions are best referred to by their introduction number until a positive name is established. The other region of interest to the adventurous gardener is the Andes. There is experience of this region in North America, but there are

a vast number of South American bamboos, so information is scant on this side of the Atlantic, and naming is unreliable in this important region too. The largest problem for the horticulturist is knowing the climatic conditions required by a new introduction, rather than the correct name.

Himalayan and Chinese species

Of the large number of species introduced into cultivation during the late nineteenth century, only a few could be considered as requiring the special conditions of our most sheltered areas, and none requires any horticultural expertise. These few species are vulnerable to neglect, and so are now rare in old gardens, while the more robust species have become almost naturalized, and in some cases invasive. The more vulnerable species have some very special qualities, and should be seen much more often. They are listed below.

Himalayacalamus falconeri (formerly *Arundinaria falconeri*) is one of these special plants, for although it grows to perfection in Cornwall and other parts of the south-west, provided it is sheltered from the wind, it flowers and dies about every 60 years, and in over-grown gardens its seedlings do not prosper. It is a very large, impressive, clumping species, with small leaves, and culms up to 7m high. It survived at Penjerrick, where it flowered *c*.1990. Seedlings were planted in several gardens, and now it can also be seen at Glendurgan, and as a small plant in both Fox Rosehill Gardens, and Carwinion Bamboo Garden.

Himalayacalamus falconeri – a large, clumping species.

Himalayacalamus falconeri has a slightly smaller form, with striking variegated culms in panels of cream, pink, and green. This has proved of more interest to gardeners, and can be seen at Fox Rosehill Gardens, Trebah, Carwinion Bamboo Garden, and a few other locations. It also spread from survivors at Penjerrick, where several plants can still be seen. The species was incorrectly named *Arundinaria hookeriana* by early gardeners, but this is a different species with blue culms that is described below. The correct name of the variegated plant is *H. falconeri* 'Damarapa', but it is probably still seen more often under its incorrect title.

Himalayacalamus asper.

Himalayacalamus falconeri 'Damarapa'.

The true *Himalayacalamus hookerianus* is also in cultivation. This is similar in appearance to *H. falconeri* 'Damarapa', but is slightly less hardy, and has striking blue, waxy new culms that age to yellow in shade, or purple in the sun. As with all but the toughest bamboos, the young plants with soft growth are vulnerable to winter damage. This species – and any other slightly tender bamboo – should be planted out as large plants with woody culms, and perhaps given winter protection from the wind during its first year.

Several other *Himalayacalamus* species of unknown hardiness have been recently introduced to cultivation, and these should be treated as above until experience is gained. All have the delicate appearance of the genus. *Himalayacalamus asper* is almost identical to *H. falconeri*, but has smaller leaves. *Himalayacalamus porcatus* grows to about 6m, and is identified by prominent, ridged culms. *Himalayacalamus cupreus* comes from high altitudes, and so is potentially the most hardy; it is identified by long internodes, and prominent, copper-coloured hairs on the culm sheaths.

Another plant that was confused with *H. falconeri* is *Drepanostachyum falcatum* (formerly *Arundinaria falcatum*, or *A. falcata*), but visually this is totally different. Confusion probably arose because of the similarity of their names. *Drepanostachyum falcatum* is slightly more vulnerable as it needs a well-protected spot, and flowers and dies about every 15 years. Well grown, it is a spectacular plant, its large culms arching from a compact

Drepanostachyum falcatum.

base under the weight of a myriad of tiny leaves, to almost sweep the ground. In Cornwall, it survived only at Bosloe, but flowered and died recently, as did a more recent planting at Trengwainton. Small plants are often seen in garden centres as imports from New Zealand, under the incorrect name *Bambusa gracilis* (or sometimes *B. gracillima*).

Two other members of the genus *Drepanostachyum* that can be cultivated in sheltered gardens of the south-west, and probably elsewhere, are *D. khasianum* and *D. microphyllum*. They are very similar in appearance, with tall (approximately 4m), compact, upright growth, and very small, delicate leaves. *Yushana boliana* (formerly *D. intermedium*) is similar, but more open at the root.

Phyllostachys edulis.

Drepanostachyum khasianum.

The only old introduction that is a real challenge to growers is the giant bamboo, or Moso of the Orient (*Phyllostachys edulis*). All of this genus originate in lowland China, and are perfectly hardy with us, but the main attraction with this species is to try to get it to produce an open forest of its giant culms in our cooler summers. A few Cornish gardens grow culms to about 8cm diameter, but it is usually seen much smaller, although in its native regions it can grow up to 18cm in diameter by 20m high. Good-sized plants can be seen at Fox Rosehill Gardens, Bosloe, Trebah, Penjerrick, and a few other south-western sites.

Phyllostachys edulis has spread all over the Far East in suitable locations, but it originates from climatic zones 8 and 9 in subtropical monsoon regions (hot, wet summers, and cold, dry winters). It needs winter cold to induce dormancy, and its size is then dictated by the summer condition. The best plants in China are from areas that record mean summer temperatures of 26–29°C, and annual rainfall of between 800mm and 1,800mm, with the majority falling in the growing season. *Phyllostachys edulis* has acclimatized well in the warmer parts of Japan, but where summer temperatures are too low it requires very heavy feeding to compensate. In addition to these challenges, growers should be aware that this bamboo has a reputation for being a difficult plant that is very slow to get established, and is not happy in pots. You should buy a large, healthy plant showing good rhizome activity, and perhaps keep it during the summer in a large pot in full sun, where the heat to the root should get it off to a good start. It will need an open, south-facing slope to give it good summer heat, and very heavy irrigation and feeding with composted horse manure. This species has a running rootstock, but in this instance the challenge is to induce it to grow vigorously, not to prevent its spread.

Numerous new introductions are being cultivated in a few gardens, mainly from the little-explored regions of the Himalayas. These are usually unnamed species, of unknown garden merit, and some probably new to science. They have all been selected from the wild because of certain potential, so although some of the following descriptions are of little use, those species should not be rejected if you come across specimens. They mostly belong to the genus *Fargesia*, which has been subdivided recently (by some authorities) by adding *Borinda*.

A number of plants were introduced recently into The Netherlands under the reference Yunnan 1 to 6. Yunnan 1 to 3 all proved to be different forms of *Borinda albocerea*. Its specific name refers to the white/blue bloom of the new culms, a prominent feature of many new *Borinda* introductions. They age to yellow, and the published Chinese literature on this species gives an ultimate height of about 4m. None of these forms has given any cultural problems in Cornwall, and they are very ornamental.

At Carwinion Bamboo Garden, a very fine specimen of Yunnan 4 is growing in the valley. This was imported with the incorrect name of *Borinda edulis*, and was subsequently identified by Kew as *B. lushuiensis*, from very immature material, so this latter name requires confirmation. This young plant is already about 6m tall, of upright stature, with blue/green culms and subtropical bearing. It is reputed to have limited hardiness,

Borinda albocerea.

Yunnan 4.

Yunnan 5.

Borinda perlonga.

but at Carwinion and other sites in Cornwall it has no cultural problems. This is a fine, fast-growing plant of great potential here, and is highly recommended.

Yunnan 5 is a strange, half-climbing species with squat leaves. Even its genera is uncertain. My first plant died quickly in a shaded location, so it probably needs some cosseting, but a replacement seems happy, so far, in a more open, exposed site.

The name of Yunnan 6 has been confirmed as *Borinda perlonga*, a hardy species with short branches, and an ultimate height of probably about 4.5m. Culms develop a purple colour in the cold. *Borinda fungosa* is a very similar species, but its culms turn a bright red during cold conditions. It was introduced by seed, and young plants were of disappointing hardiness, although larger, tougher plants are now established in some gardens. It needs dry winter conditions until it is established, and is generally less hardy than *B. perlonga*.

Borinda angustissima is a tall (7m) species, grown occasionally. It is slightly tender, but very elegant, with tiny, narrow leaves, and a compact form. A similar, more readily available plant is usually sold, incorrectly, as *Fargesia yulongshanensis*. This also has small, narrow leaves, but noticeably uniform dark green leaves and culms. This species has been identified as a small-leafed clone of *F. albocerea*.

Although not commercially available at the time of writing, *Borinda papyrifera* has great garden potential, and therefore will no doubt be available in time. It is very large (up to 8m), with well-spaced culms of a striking grey-blue, with obvious longitudinal striations. Culms age to a contrasting ochre, and leaves and branches are large. Its hardiness has yet to be assessed, but gardeners in the south-west of England, and probably most of the rest of the UK, should have no problems.

A number of collections have been made under the tentative name of *Borinda grossa*. This is also a

Borinda papyrifera.

Borinda frigidorum.

species with great potential, but not yet commercially available. The true species has outstanding blue culms up to 12m high. Many introductions are probably not hardy, and none seems to originate from plants of this stature, but no doubt some will succeed in Cornwall and southern Ireland, and will make impressive plants.

Borindas have the same tight, clumping growth as *Fargesias*, but they come from a different region of the Himalayas, which has had a lot of attention recently. They have different inflorescences, and more delicate leaves. *Fargesias* are mainly hardy in this country and are evergreen. *Borindas* can be evergreen, or may partially shed their leaves in the cold. The evergreen group that includes most of the above species is mainly less hardy than the *Fargesias*, while the following deciduous species are mainly very hardy, but some have cultural problems – particularly with small plants – if they originate from areas that have a dry winter.

In the deciduous group is collection SICH 987, which has the unpublished name *Borinda muliensis*. This is one of the highest-altitude bamboos, but it needs a dry winter when a small plant. It came from imported seed, so its potential is as yet unknown. *Borinda frigidorum* is also a high-altitude species, with very variable height in the wild, but this may be due to local over-grazing. It can reach 3m in the wild. Another high-altitude species in cultivation is the true *B. yulongshanensis*, which has been seen growing at over 4,200m, and is also unlikely to have problems with our winters. It grows to 7m tall, with a delicate appearance that belies its hardiness.

Not all recent Himalayan introductions are *Borindas*: there are one or two *Fargesias*. *F. rufa* seems to be a tough, dark green, small bamboo, although if correctly named it reaches 5m high in the wild. Its potential size in this country has not yet been found, but its dark, glossy leaves, small

Fargesia rufa.

Fargesia scabrida.

size (if maintained), and clumping roots should be of great value in the garden, as most small bamboos are invasive. A plant that is sold as *F. scabrida* also has great potential, for it has instantly recognizable reddish branch bases that contrast beautifully with the dark green of the rest of the plant. The imported material was reported as being taken from a large plant, but all cultivated material is still very small, and published material from China gives a medium height for this species.

Members of the genus *Chimonobambusa* originate from medium mountain elevations of China, with cool temperatures and year-round high humidity. They are understorey plants, and even with our low light levels seem to benefit from some shade. In their native lands, the high rainfall coincides with the growing season, and in this country summer conditions probably determine the vigour and size of the plant. Some species do not grow well without some coastal influence and wind protection. One of these is *C. quadrangularis*, which

already grows in profusion in some south-western gardens. Its recently introduced forms 'Suow' and 'Nagamineus' – both with yellow, rectangular cross-section culms interspersed with dark green panels – will probably be of more interest to the adventurous gardener.

Chimonobambusa tumidissinoda is another special member of this genus, with its bizarre, hugely inflated nodes and very elegant form. Its eventual size in this country is not known, but young plants can be seen at Carwinion Bamboo Garden, Trebah, and Trevarno Estate Gardens. All plants of this genus are rampant spreaders in mild areas, and need strict control even in large gardens. *Chimonobambusa utilis* probably has great potential in a large garden, with a height up to 10m, but is not presently in cultivation.

The genus *Thamnocalamus* comprises mainly elegant, clumping plants with small leaves, which are very attractive in the garden. Most have no problems with the weather in southern England, but

Chimonobambusa quadrangularis.

Chimonobambusa tumidissinoda.

Thamnocalamus crassinodus 'Kew Beauty'.

Thamnocalamus crassinodus 'Gosainkund' is more sensitive, and new growth is very liable to winter damage. It is a natural form requiring some early care, and is best grown in a sheltered spot, where it will develop into a leafy fountain with striking blue-grey new culms.

South American species

The South American genus *Chusquea* contains many temperate species that require similar conditions to those of the *Chimonobambusa*. They detest high summer temperatures and dry air, and for this reason as much as our mild winters they grow best in south-western gardens. There are very few species in cultivation, but they are all very imposing. Although completely hardy, *Chusquea culeou* is usually a large, regal, upright species, with masses of short branches and small leaves, giving a 'fox brush' effect. There are many clones of this species in cultivation, each of distinct appearance. It resents any root disturbance, and therefore it

Chusquea culeou.

Chusquea montana.

Chusquea gigantea.

Chusquea nigracans.

is best to select a good-looking and well-grown specimen in a pot, and plant it in its final position.

Very similar, but larger and with wide-spaced, but none-running culms, suitable for creating a grove effect, is *Chusquea gigantea*. This is often erroneously labeled as *C. breviglumis*, a name also erroneously used for a dwarf species that is not commercially available. There is a scandent bamboo with near-horizontal culms that is almost certainly a form of *C. culeou*, but which is sold as *C. quila*. There are also various small *Chusqueas* sold

Chusquea cumingii.

Chusquea valdiviensis.

Chusquea deliculata.

as *C. montana*, *C. nigracans*, and *C. alpina*, but some authorities think these are also often misnamed regional forms of *C. culeou*.

Chusquea cumingii is a special species growing to about 1.5m or more, with short, stiff branches and leaves. It likes full sun, and even in the southwest needs some winter protection until it is well established. Another species requiring our mild winters is the very vigorous *C. valdiviensis*. This is

a climbing species that has a fascinating mode of growth, but no great beauty. It can be cut to the ground even here by a really bad winter, but has so much energy that it quickly rises again when well established. It will rapidly swamp shrubs and small trees, and is best trained up larger, non-ornamental species or solid hedges. The true *C. quila* has a very similar mode of growth, and similar hardiness. It is a smaller and supposedly less vigorous species, and although there have been reports of several introductions, it is not known now in cultivation.

Chusquea deliculata is a very delicate-looking climbing species that is grown only in the temperate house at Kew, and seems to be destined to remain there, although it probably has great potential for growing in our most favoured gardens. There is a very similar, unnamed species already in cultivation in Cornwall.

There are vast numbers of *Chusquea* species awaiting introduction, and many would probably be suitable for cultivation in the mild gardens of the south and west. Some of the most desirable are *C. uliginosa*, as it grows in marsh conditions; the beautiful *C. leonardiorum*, *C. lehmannii*, and *C. loxensis*. In addition, there are some very unusual species awaiting introduction in that other heat-intolerant South American genus, *Neurolepis*. This genus contains some particularly strange plants that like similar conditions to the *Chusqueas*, and can be found growing at elevations up to 4,300m, so there is great potential for adventurous gardening with *Neurolepis*.

Another mountain genus rarely cultivated is *Ampelocalamus*. It comprises only a few species, which have rough culms and projections on the nodes to enable them to scramble up other plants, or to hang down cliff-faces. Culms are generally long, and small in diameter. *Ampelocalamus scandens* was introduced by seed, and found to be of disappointing hardiness; however, I found a dry, neglected, pot-bound specimen growing outside in central England, which gave a clue to its requirements. This was subsequently planted in a well ventilated, abandoned greenhouse with very dry soil, where it has thrived without any attention. The location was not a favoured area of Cornwall, and it has shown no damage from sub-zero temperatures or drought. It probably originates from cliff-faces, and therefore perfect drainage is perhaps an essential requirement. However, I have experience of only this one specimen.

Hot, lowland species

All the above, with the exception of *Phyllostachys edulis*, are high-elevation species, but there are some other genera from the hotter lowland areas that need our mild winters. *Pseudosasa amabilis* is the species used in China for the commercial production of canes for export. It is a very tall, stately species, growing up to 13m in its native lands, but it fails to thrive in most of the UK. I have found no problems with it in a cold Cornish garden, but it probably needs a location that traps all the summer sun, and good growing conditions, in order to achieve a large size.

The Japanese are very selective when choosing their garden plants, and they cultivate very few species of bamboo. In the warmer regions, *Sinobambusa tootsik* is grown in nearly every garden, because of its large, upright stature, and because its branches can be pruned to form a compact ball of foliage at every node. Its requirements are exactly as those of *Pseudosasa amabilis,* and it can

grow up to 7m tall, but it will lose its leaves in cold winds. It has a very brightly variegated form called 'Albostriata' (or 'Variegata'), which will be more attractive to some gardeners. *Sinobambusa intermedia* is a slightly smaller species that can also be grown. Even smaller, at 2–3m, is *S. rubroligula*, which develops brown-purple to almost black culms if given a sunny spot.

Sinobambusa intermedia.

Other lowland species spread into tropical zones, and many of these possess the ability to withstand a few degrees of frost. As mentioned above, our cool summers are usually the reason why these fail to prosper, but there is much potential here for the adventurous gardener. In Britain, little is known about these species and their ability to adapt to our very cool, uniform climate, and therefore there is much to be discovered. *Bambusa multiplex* (syn *B. glaucescens*) and its various forms are known to be among the most suitable, and are fairly easily obtained as unwise imports from warmer countries. For most gardeners they should remain as indoor plants, or in pots for moving into a greenhouse during the cool months. *Bambusa multiplex* 'Riviereorum' is a dwarf form that is accepted as being the hardiest. It can be seen growing outside at Kew, but is practically static there. The USA includes large areas suitable for growing tropical species, and growers in that country list over 70 species that are in cultivation, and that will stand a few degrees of frost. There is a vigorous, unnamed *Bambusa* species growing in Tresco Abbey Garden, so we are very close to providing the correct conditions for some tropical species.

Sources of further information

Many of these new introductions are fairly easy to obtain from the specialist bamboo nurseries and suppliers listed in *The RHS Plant Finder*; in magazines, and in the list of Nurseries, Specialist Suppliers, and Societies at the end of this book. Some growers aim to stock the unusual, while others restrict their range to more common commercial species, but a few enquiries should soon locate some interesting plants. You may have to put your name on a waiting list if you insist on a certain species, and many of the plants listed above are not available commercially at the time of writing. Almost certainly these will be available very shortly if they are found to be desirable species.

Restios

Les Cathery

Restios are perennial herbs – a little-known group of plants belonging to the sub-family Restionaceae, with great potential for horticultural use.

Origins and habitat

Restios are plants of the Southern continents. They are a distinct sub-family, and an example of parallel evolution, their nearest relatives being the rushes, Juncaceae. There are around 30 genera of Restionaceae, with some 330 species. Approximately 170 of these grow in temperate Australasia, but by far the largest number and variety of forms are to be found in South Africa, where some species – *Chondropetalum tectorum*; *Thamnochortus insignis*; *T. erectus*, and *Cannomois taylori* – have been used for thatching, while shorter species are sometimes used for making brooms.

Thamnochortus insignis: male flowers.

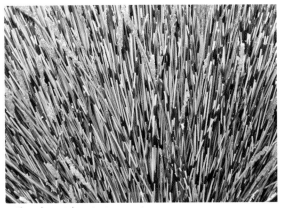
Chondropetalum tectorum: stems.

In their native habitats, restios tend to grow mainly along leats and streams, enjoying light but frequent moisture, and free-draining, slightly hungry soils. Their primary requirement is air movement, and for most a light situation.

Habit

Restios are mostly clumping or tussock-forming, making them ideal subjects for landscape gardening – particularly those of architectural stature. Some restios are rhizomatous, and of these a few can be invasive – for example, *Hypodiscus*, *Willdenowia*, *Chondropetalum microcarpum*, *Ischyrolepis eleocharis*, *I. leptoclados*, and *Dovea macrocarpa*. However, don't panic: *Elegia capensis* may resemble the invasive Horsetail rush *Equisetum*, but the similarity is purely superficial. In fact, even some of the alleged invasive restios are worthy of investigation for ground-cover potential. With this in mind I have tried *Willdenowia incurvata*, and frankly, I wish it would invade a little faster!

The plants are dioecious – that is, having male and female flowers on separate plants. The males

Ischyrolepis subverticillata – male.

Ischyrolepis subverticillata – female.

Ischyrolepis subverticillata – female flowers.

Hedgehog-like dome of *Chondropetalum tectorum*.

of some species bear many sterile branches, which give them an attractive, feathery appearance, while the females generally bear few, if any. It seems reasonable to suppose that the sterile branches have evolved to aid pollen distribution, and that the females lack them because they need to remain more upright in order to collect pollen, and to support and distribute the seed, which is sometimes heavy. The flowers have three petals and three sepals. They are wind-pollinated, so the males produce profuse yellow anthers, while the females have white, pink, or occasionally green or crimson styles, which are very pretty and worthy of close scrutiny.

Restios have a dual rooting system. The fine matt of surface roots is adapted to absorb heavy dew rapidly, to tide the plant over the heat of day. The deeper roots have evolved the ability to die back when under stress, and regenerate when conditions improve. Long-lived and low-maintenance,

the versatility of these plants in the garden is limited only by your imagination. There is something for every situation – from 20cm ground-cover to 3m architectural statements; from upright clumps through hedgehog-like domes, to plumed, weeping giants. Restios make excellent foils for large-leafed exotics, and are particularly effective around a water feature.

Growing restios in the UK

My own garden is a short distance from Land's End, Cornwall, and as such may not be considered typical. However, the restios have been unmoved by gusts of 185kph (115mph), and even salt spray leaves them unmarked. The foliage on some may be a little singed by persistent cold, dry, north or east winds, but it soon recovers in the spring. Despite the usually mild winters here, they have survived -7°C with very few losses, and those only in young potted plants. Like most plants, they are happier

Ischyrolepis subverticillata – left: female, and right: male – in a garden near Land's End, Cornwall.

in the ground, and the secret for getting them and other Southern hemisphere plants through the cold spells is to mulch and keep them moist at the roots, bearing in mind that for many the winters are usually cold and wet in their natural environment. (The whole subject of maintaining moisture at the roots during cold spells is worthy of further research.)

Restios do not appear to suffer from any of the usual pests and diseases, apart from the occasional little nibble by inquisitive rabbits or mice which, finding little sustenance in them, soon move on to more tasty treasures.

On very lean soils, dead foliage should not be removed until it collapses, as the plant will draw nourishment from it. However, in practice it may not be possible to leave dead, faded foliage on most species, because it is extremely attractive in its own right, and highly desirable to flower-arrangers. I have known a cut stem of *Ischyrolepis subverticillata* to keep its form and flower heads for over three years: what more could you ask for?

Propagation

Seed propagation

All restio seeds have inhibited dormancy: most respond to smoke and/or heat, but some have other inhibiting factors yet to be discovered. They are all diurnal: that is, they need temperature fluctuations in order to trigger germination – typically, 8–10°C at night, and 20–28°C by day. Exposing seed to fresh smoke is not easy for the amateur, but impregnated paper discs are available from Kirstenbosch Botanic Garden, Cape Town. However, while looking into alternatives, I found that Australian research into germination of *Banksia* seeds had isolated the active ingredients from the smoke. They are ethyl and ammonia. In 2001, I decided to experiment with seed collected from my own *Ischyrolepis subverticillata*, which is usually a difficult subject. The control yielded 3 per cent; the trial, 92 per cent. The following is my most successful method to date:

- Sow in pots; water-in with proprietary Cheshunt Compound (ammonia); keep

Cannomois virgata: restios are ideal subjects for landscape gardening.

moist for approximately two months, maintaining temperature fluctuations.

- Allow to dry out for one month; then re-water with Cheshunt Compound, and stand in a propagating frame with two or three ripe bananas (ethylene). Maintain temperature fluctuations and watering regime.
- As soon as sufficient germination occurs, remove from the propagating frame, and move to semi-shade outside to increase air movement.
- Prick out and pot on as soon as roots show at the base of the pot. Always over-pot, and do not let the seedlings dry out completely until they are planted out and established in their final position.

Allowing the seeds to dry out before rewatering has the effect of condensing seasons, and can be repeated with difficult subjects. Bananas have long been used to force-ripen fruit – an effect brought about by the ethylene gas that they produce. They seem to ripen the seed and break dormancy, and the Cheshunt Compound gives a quick Nitrogen 'fix' to encourage rapid growth. I have since tried the same treatment on both African and Australian Proteaceae, with marked improvements in germination.

Vegetative propagation

Restios do not like root disturbance, but divisions can be successful provided common sense is used. Do not remove old culms, as the plant will draw energy from them. Cut the plant into two or four equal parts, and over-pot. They will take approximately one year to recover, and must be kept moist until established.

Cannomois virgata.

Restio quadratus.

Recommended shortlist

The following are all from South Africa. They, and a number of new introductions, are currently growing in my garden:

- *Askidiosperma chartacea* – 1m, erect tussock, many flowers on female spikelets; fairly hardy.
- *Askidosperma esterhuysenae* – 1m, forming colourful dome; flowers cream turning to chocolate.
- *Calopsis paniculata* – 2m, beautiful weeping habit; seems hardy.
- *Cannomois virgata* – 3m+, upright, graceful clumper, impressive new shoots.
- *Chondropetalum hookerianum* – 30–80cm, domed tussock, damp areas, spectacular accent plant; hardy.
- *Chondropetalum mucronatum* – 2m, thick, upright stems; slightly tender.
- *Chondropetalum tectorum* – 1m+, handsome, domed tussock.
- *Elegia capensis* – 2–3m, looks like a clumping *Equisetum*; likes damp areas, and shelter from cold, dry winds.
- *Ischyrolepis subverticillata* – 2m, arching plumes, one of the few shade-tolerant restios; hardy.
- *Restio quadratus* – 2m, erect, square scapes, beautiful, branched specimen plant; hardy.
- *Rhodocoma capensis* – 2m, arching stems with fine foliage; elegant and hardy.
- *Rhodocoma foliosa* – 1.5m, beautiful, plumed feature plant; hardy.
- *Rhodocoma gigantea* – 2–3m, stunning, variable plant; hardy.
- *Staberrhoea aemula* – 50cm, erect tussock, beautiful male flower heads; fairly hardy.
- *Thamnochortus cinereus* – 1m, silver-grey, feathery plumes.
- *Thamnochortus insignis* – 2m, 'thatching reed', very attractive tussocks with decorative flowers; hardy.

Askidiosperma esterhuysenae.

Rhodocoma foliosa.

Cannomois virgata – female.

Rhodocoma gigantea – male.

Elegia capensis.

Thamnochortus cinereus.

So far, I have been able to obtain the seed of only one Australian restio – *Baloskion tetraphyllum*, a 2m+, bright green, very attractive plant, which seems hardy. Other Australian species that may be worthy of trial are:

- *Anarthria scabra* – 80cm thick, upright, prominent leaves and stems.
- *Chaetanthus aristatus* – 80cm, tufted.
- *Desmocladus castaneus* – 30cm, tufted, verticillate clusters of branchlets.
- *Hypolaena pubescens* – 80cm, numerous slender branchlets, covered in long hairs.
- *Lepidobolus chaetocephalus* – 40cm tufted, males have spherical spikelets.
- *Loxocarya gigas* – 2m, graceful nodding culms with fine, sterile branches on lower parts.
- *Meeboldina scariosa* – 1m pale green, nut fruited.

7 Hedychiums and Others

Edward Needham

Few plants are more evocative of the temperate Himalayas than the hedychiums. Their lush foliage tells of unfailing warmth and abundant rain; their intricate flowers, richly scented, speak of dim forests and the attentions of giant moths.

They are plants of the lower mountains, and range from Nepal, through eastern India and Burma, into Yunnan and Indo-China. It is therefore not surprising that when they were first introduced in the mid-nineteenth century, it was assumed that they would require the protection of a heated greenhouse. As a result, only a few of the more showy kinds retained a hold in cultivation outside botanic gardens.

More recently, interest has been rekindled by the introduction of fresh material, and by the realization that a number of species are reasonably happy with conditions in the warmer parts of the British Isles. But they are not always seen at their best, due to a widespread misunderstanding of their needs. Their exotic appearance, and obvious affinities with subtropical plants such as the cannas, have led to the belief that they are best given the warmest and sunniest available position in the garden. Being plants of great vigour and adaptability, they will certainly grow and flower there, after a fashion, but they will only reach their full potential during an exceptionally wet summer.

Left: *Hedychium gardnerianum*: the paler form commonly grown in Cornwall. (See page 162.)

Hedychiums

Most of the species that concern us here come from the temperate forests, between about 1,600 and 2,500 metres. They make their growth and flower during the season of monsoon rains from June to September – a cycle which coincides with the more reliably warm period of our own climate. Those from the higher part of the range find our normal summer temperatures quite acceptable, and are in fact difficult to grow in areas with hot summers, such as the southern USA. And although some from the lower forests would benefit from more consistently warm conditions – as distinct from very high temperatures – than our climate can offer, and do not attain the same luxuriance here as in the wild, many flower successfully nevertheless.

The greatest need of all the hedychiums is for moisture. Despite benefiting from nightly downpours of rain, they are often to be found by the banks of streams and other very wet places, though in part this may be due to the greater accumulation of rich soil there. Humidity also remains very high, and this is particularly important at flower-ing time. For due, presumably, to rapid transpiration in the drier and less buoyant air of the open garden, the blooms of many kinds collapse when exposed to the direct rays of the sun.

The most suitable environment for these plants is therefore the semi-shade and more stable microclimate of a sheltered tree and shrub garden. There they will provide an effective contrast of form and foliage, and flower when there is comparatively little colour from other plants. Nevertheless, care should be taken to avoid competition from tree roots, and for best results they should be watered at the first hint of drought.

The hedychiums from the subtropical lowlands – and these include many of the showier species, and the hybrids derived from them – are of a somewhat different character. They are accustomed to higher temperatures throughout the year, and have a more extended flowering season during the dry sunny days that follow the end of the monsoon rains. As might be expected, with few exceptions they are not a success in the open, either growing too slowly to produce flower buds at all, or failing to open them in the dank chill of

Hedychium densiflorum 'Sorung' in a woodland garden in west Cornwall.

late autumn. Nevertheless, it says much for the resilience of this genus that many will not only survive, but increase in warmer areas. For example, *Hedychium coronarium*, the 'fragrant snowy garland' from which the genus takes its name, and now cultivated throughout the tropics, has long been grown at Trengwainton near Penzance, though it has never flowered there. Nurseries sometimes recommend these flowerless kinds for 'subtropical' bedding, but there is little point in this as many of the hardier kinds are equally effective. Several are deciduous and give a touch of yellow autumn colour in late October, and some offer the bonus of quite showy seed-heads, the tri-valved capsules opening to reveal an orange interior set with red seeds – a gift for flower-arrangers.

The species from the high forests are the first to flower, and the season commences in the early days of August with *Hedychium densiflorum* in its many forms. In Nepal it is quite common at around 2,400m, often in the company of such well-established garden plants as *Rhododendron arboreum*, *Cardiocrinum giganteum*, and *Magnolia campbellii*. It differs from other species in producing, as the name implies, close-packed racemes of many small flowers. In most forms they open almost simultaneously, and are very short-lived. Superficially they resemble the blooms of some of our native orchids such as *Gymnadenia conopsea*, and by an odd coincidence have something of the same scent.

Hedychium densiflorum is one of the hardiest species: a Ludlow and Sherriff collection (LS&H 17393) from the Tibetan side of the Himalayas has succeeded as far north as Castle Howard near York, but it is a rather stubby plant with weak orange flowers. For milder gardens, 'Assam Orange', a Kingdon Ward introduction from the Khasia Hills, is far better – graceful in habit, with thick-petalled flowers of rich colour, and often generous with its spires of red seeds. The common Nepalese form is attractive enough, but the blooms are so ephemeral that few gardeners would wish to give it space. However, a collection from a relatively low altitude on Phulchoke mountain near Kathmandu (S.582) has larger flowers of an attractive pinkish-orange, somewhat longer lived than most. This was introduced by A.D. (Tony) Schilling, who botanized in Nepal in the 1960s, and helped set up the botanic garden at Godewari at the foot of the mountain.

Hedychium densiflorum 'Assam Orange'.

Occasionally *Hedychium densiflorum* appears to mutate into something quite exceptional. The form called 'Stephen' was discovered, again by Tony Schilling, in the Dudh Kosi valley south of the Everest region, where it occurred as scattered plants over quite a small area of the evergreen oak forest. It is in every respect twice the size of the typical plant, and has flowers of a pale apricot yellow with an orange centre. From dusk to dawn, if nights are warm and humid, it gives out a spicy scent, subtle but pervasive, and thereby draws to itself numerous moths, so ensuring a plentiful crop of the colourful seed-heads. It is possible that there is now more of 'Stephen' in cultivation than in the wild, as that stretch of forest has since been burned through and opened up for grazing. Nevertheless, it does not appear to be widely grown: perhaps the description of the flowers in the RHS Dictionary as 'pale yellow or dirty yellow' – a slander I can only attribute to the mistakes in cultivation alluded to above – has been a factor in this. The contribution of the eponymous 'Stephen', incidentally, was to be born in the year of its discovery. It would be surprising if in the

Hedychium densiflorum: left: 'Sorung'; right: 'Stephen'.

Hedychium spicatum.

vastness of the Himalayas other superior forms did not exist, and visitors to Nepal, particularly to the east of the country, should keep a look out for them. Unfortunately, to find them in flower one would have to brave the mud and leeches of the monsoon, but in the autumn they may be detected by their larger seed capsules (*H. spicatum* also has large capsules, but in a much looser raceme). Such was the case with a single plant, growing in a stand of the ordinary form, that caught my eye when travelling through the wild country between the Dudh Kosi and the Arun valley. This proved to have flowers only slightly smaller than those of 'Stephen', but of a deeper shade. Lacking suitable relatives, I have called this plant 'Sorung', the name of the scattered Sherpa village at whose outskirts it grew. Planted together, and in association with *Hydrangea villosa*, the two forms set each other off to great effect. In almost complete shade, and in rich vegetable soil dredged from a nearby pond, they have both attained 2m, with solid racemes 25cm tall or more.

Hedychium spicatum occurs in much the same habitat as *H. densiflorum*, but is even more wide-

spread and adaptable. In very wet areas it may even be seen growing epiphytically on the branches of trees, and encircling their trunks with its rhizomes. The flowers open a few at a time from an open raceme, and are white with an orange centre. They have a large bi-lobed lip, and have been likened to resting moths. Many forms have rather insubstantial blooms and look commonplace unless really well grown, but all are attractive in seed, which is set freely. My best form, which is possibly variety *acuminatum*, came from the same stretch of forest as *H. densiflorum* 'Stephen'; the flora there generally is, or was, particularly rich, and it is possible that these more luxuriant forms evolve as a result of especially favourable conditions of soil and climate. It has very long, ribbed leaves, and much fuller racemes of flowers. A variety that originated as seed from Darjeeling has a reddish rather than orange centre and flowers later, in early October. To the best of my knowledge, reports of *H. spicatum* with yellow flowers are due to the reluctance of some botanists to work in the field, for the flowers do indeed turn yellowish when wilted or dried. In Nepal the dried rhizomes are used to

Hedychium yunnanense.

scent clothes chests, and the flowers are presented as offerings to the Kumari, or living goddess, a young lady residing in one of the Kathmandu temples.

Hedychium spicatum extends into south-west China, where in places – as, for example, on the Western Hills near Kunming – it grows alongside *H. yunnanense*. The latter is even more variable, and in some cases the two are difficult to distinguish. Botanically, the leaves of *H. spicatum* are downy beneath, whereas those of *H. yunnanense* are glabrous. In general, *H. yunnanense* has much broader leaves and a narrower lip to the flowers, which tend to open more at a time. An early introduction by Roy Lancaster (L.633) has a wispy raceme of small flowers opening almost simultaneously, pretty but ephemeral. A form found by a waterfall above the ancient walled city of Dali has a compact head of bloom somewhat like *H. ellipticum*, though less colourful, while another from the hills on the other side of the Erhai lake is larger in all its parts, with quite the showiest seed-head of any *Hedychium* that I know.

Hedychium venustum, another Himalayan, has flowers of better colour and substance than most forms of *H. spicatum*, and long, upright leaves. Under good conditions it can grow very tall, and the blooms then look a little small in relation to the foliage; in the right position it is nevertheless a graceful and imposing plant.

Hedychium forrestii is even larger and more impressive in growth, perhaps the finest of all the hedychiums in foliage, with long, dark green leaves on stems up to two metres high, but it needs shelter as it is easily flattened by wind. The flowers appear several at a time from a stout raceme that has an almost sculpted appearance. It has been compared to *H. coronarium* in bloom, which flatters it somewhat as although the flowers are larger than in the other species that I have described, they are rather spidery in effect, because of the narrow lip and petals. It is said to have a narcissus-like scent when grown in a greenhouse, but in the open this is imperceptible. *Hedychium forrestii* is a native of Yunnan, where it appears to be rare; so far as I can ascertain, most plants in cultivation are derived from a collection by Joseph Rock from an

Hedychium forrestii and *Dicksonia antarctica*.

ing a few plants in any garden whose flowering comes as a special event rather than becoming commonplace through over familiarity. Unfortunately, it does not seed and is slower to increase by division than other species. *H. ellipticum* is something of a puzzle. Claims that it occurs up to 3,000 metres are doubtfully correct, as recent reports all speak of it as a plant of rocks and cliffs in the transition between the subtropical and temperate zones at no more than 1,500 metres. The form I grow was collected by Christopher Grey-Wilson in one of the lower valleys north of Kathmandu, where it grew over boulders by the river (GWPH 247). Other *Hedychiums* from this altitude flower in the autumn and retain their leaves over winter. *H. ellipticum*, however, is the first of the Nepalese species to flower, in mid-July (some weeks later in our cooler summers), and it dies down in autumn – possibly because the meagre soils of its habitat dry out very quickly once the rains have ceased.

The species I have described is that listed in Hooker's *Flora of British India* (1894), and in Polunin and Stainton's *Flowers of the Himalayas* (1984). Recently, a plant has been offered under this name, imported from an Indian nursery, which is described as a subtropical species ranging from the Himalayan foothills to Thailand. Although somewhat similar in flower, in all other respects it is clearly a completely different plant, and has no value in the open garden. I have been unable to discover whether this is simply a case of mistaken identity, or due to changes in taxonomy.

All the plants discussed above die down naturally in late autumn; but at somewhat lower altitudes, where frosts are slight, the hedychiums retain their leaves throughout the year. In cultivation in Britain they will be cut down by the first sharp frost, but this does not affect their subse-

unrecorded location. The yellow-flowered plant from northern Vietnam, tentatively identified as *H. forrestii* var. *latebracteatum* when it was first introduced, is now called *H. maximum*.

Hedychium ellipticum is, by contrast, dwarf, and seldom attains one metre. It is a handsome foliage plant, with broad, strongly ribbed leaves, and the pure white flowers appear in a dense head surrounded by a veritable firework display of long, orange stamens. It is always much admired when in bloom, its only fault being that the show is all too brief; but there is much to be said for hav-

quent performance. They include a complex of forms currently regarded by most botanists as varieties of *H. coccineum* – like many Himalayan plants, they appear to be in a state of continuing evolution, and the same might be said of the science of taxonomy. Several forms have long been in cultivation, and have retained their place in the greenhouse flora by reason of their colourful flowers; but their potential in the open garden remained largely unsuspected and untried until the coming of the plant called 'Tara'.

'Tara' came from Nagarkot, a hilltop resort at the edge of the Kathmandu valley with views of the great Himalayan peaks from Daulagiri to Makalu. It was introduced by Tony Schilling, and named to celebrate the arrival of his daughter; but the name is also the Nepali word for 'star'. At its best, 'Tara' is among the most resplendent of hedychiums, with large racemes of orange flowers with a reddish centre and long filaments. As each of the bracts contains several flower buds, it lasts longer in beauty than many species. It is attractive in foliage too, with glaucous stems and leaves. It was collected as seed, and as the resultant plants showed little variation the name covers a group or 'grex' of several clones. There does, in fact, appear to be some variation, for instance in the degree to which the flowers are scented – though as with other species this may depend largely on environmental conditions. With me it is quite strongly fragrant, with a fruity scent that is very attractive to wasps. These, however, are of the wrong shape to effect pollination: like other species with long stamens, it is likely to set seed only in years when hawkmoths are prevalent. In flower colour too it varies a little, but again this may be due to weather conditions rather than to any

inherent trait, for it is noticeably richer when temperatures remain fairly high. Of greater importance, in that it ensures a longer succession of bloom, is that some clones appear to have a greater number of flower buds in each bract. The form I grow has three, but up to six has been reported. 'Tara' grows best in a rich but open soil, and in at least semi-shade; in my experience it is quite useless in the open, because of the speed with which the flowers wilt and fade when exposed to sun – a factor surely not taken into account when it was given an Award of Garden Merit, as well as an Award of Merit and

Hedychium coccineum 'Tara' and *Strobilanthes wallichii*.

a First Class Certificate by the Royal Horticultural Society.

The botanical status of 'Tara' seems likely to remain controversial, as in a forthcoming revision of the genus it will apparently be included as a form of *Hedychium gardnerianum*. My own observations suggest that it is no more, and no less, than a typical form of a plant fairly widespread in central Nepal at about 2,000 metres, though not at all common except on the ridges surrounding the Kathmandu valley, where grazing is controlled and the forests preserved. It may be seen, for example, on Sheopuri, where Nathaniel Wallich did much of his collecting during his visit to Nepal in 1822. I therefore wonder whether it is not the plant to which the name *H. aurantiacum* was originally applied. It is also possible that it has long been in cultivation as a greenhouse subject, for a plant received from the Edinburgh Botanic Garden is similar both in appearance and in garden performance.

The name 'aurantiacum' was eventually subsumed into *Hedychium coccineum*; of late it has reappeared in some lists, though not necessarily in relation to the same form. Other early introductions were also given the status of varieties, and although it may not be the current taxonomic usage, it is useful to retain these for horticultural purposes. *Hedychium coccineum* var. *coccineum* — in other words, the typical form — has flowers of a particularly pleasing shade of orange-red, but it is less easy to grow and flower than the 'Tara' forms, and probably needs more warmth; nor have I yet flowered var. *carneum*, with 'flesh pink' blooms. But a plant from one of the upper tributaries of the Arun River, and which fits the description of var. *angustifolium* in having long, ribbon-like leaves and cinnabar-red flowers, is easy to grow and flower, albeit in a relatively open position. It seems less troubled by sun than most hedychiums.

Plants of *Hedychium coccineum* imported from Indian nurseries may be crosses between several forms, as the result of being grown from seed. In the interests of botany, material from recorded wild sources should be carefully preserved and propagated only by division.

Hedychium gardnerianum was dubbed by Wallich the 'Queen of the Hedychiums'. Almost certainly he would have found it on Sheopuri, where it may still be seen, but I first made its acquaintance in the wild in a ravine running off the Trisuli Khola, the torrent that drains the sacred Gosainkund lakes. Even out of flower it was indeed an impressive sight, hanging down from the wet cliffs in great swathes of foliage: how much more so must it be when crowned with tall racemes of rich yellow flowers, with their long red filaments filling the air with an exotic scent. In cultivation it is more modest in growth, but the blooms are the same. The true Nepalese plant is finer in colour than the pale form commonly grown in Cornwall, but the latter seems easier to grow and flower. In the wild it grows at a somewhat lower altitude than the 'Tara' forms, and in cultivation blooms later.

Plants from still lower in the temperate forest find it difficult to reach the flowering stage in cultivation before the onset of colder weather. *Hedychium thyrsiforme* may be described as an evergreen version of *H. ellipticum*, with similar but more lustrous leaves, so that it is worth growing simply as a foliage plant. That is usually as far as it gets in the open, for although every year it forms flower buds, none of them open even in an exceptionally warm October. The flowers are similar to those of *H. ellipticum*, but in a larger head, and the stamens area creamy-white. One source describes it as a 'giant' of a plant, but the form I have, which came from the lower slopes of Phulchoke, grows to only about one metre, and so is one of the few species comfortably housed in an average greenhouse.

On the basis that our autumns are becoming later by two days each decade, it seems possible that *Hedychium thyrsiforme* will be a success out of doors by the year 2050, perhaps earlier in very warm gardens by the shore. Although enthusiasts for the genus may be tempted to think that global warming may have its advantages, they should consider that in more temperate climates hedychiums can become rampant weeds: in the Azores, *H. gardnerianum* has become a serious menace, strangling even young pine trees with its rhizomes; and in New Zealand, hedychiums and related plants are banned from cultivation altogether.

The plants described above all have an exposed raceme of flowers that open within quite a short period. The remaining species produce their flowers in succession from a cone-like head of overlapping bracts, often over several weeks. The best-known plant of this type is *Hedychium coronarium*. According to some sources, it occurs up to 1,900m in the eastern Himalayas, but these records may

Hedychium maximum.

relate to the outer hills, which are less under the influence of the great peaks, and it is not a success in the open garden. *Hedychium flavescens* is still considered to be simply a variety of *H. coronarium* by some botanists, but it differs in foliage as well as in its yellow flower colour, and currently seems destined to become a species in its own right. It certainly grows more readily, and has been a success in some gardens apparently, though I have yet to flower it. In the East this plant is often planted around Buddhist shrines, and has even found its way to Emei Shan (Mount Omei) in Sichuan, where it is naturalized along ditches and watercourses around the Baoguo monastery at the foot of the mountain. Although clearly an escape from cultivation, for a time Chinese botanists regarded it as a distinct species, *H. emeiense*.

Another very fine species on the verge of being a success in really warm gardens is *Hedychium maximum*, of which there have been a number of introductions in recent years from the mountains of northern Vietnam. Even in the open it is quite a massive plant, and regularly produces flower heads, but although in my own fairly shady garden it sometimes manages to open a few of its scented, apricot-yellow flowers, they emerge too late to develop fully; mostly they simply rot. In a cold greenhouse, provided one has one large enough, it can be quite magnificent.

Hedychium greenii is similar in form, but otherwise seems to have no close relations within the genus. The stems and undersides of the leaves are maroon-red, and it has the peculiarity of sometimes producing bulbils in the axils of the leaves. It is recorded as growing on low hills in Bhutan and northern India, often in marshy ground. For this reason it is sometimes suggested for waterside planting. Although such a position might suit it – and many other species – in some ways, it is likely to be too cool to induce flowering. Even against a warm, half-shaded wall, many of the flower buds fail to materialize in a cold autumn, but in a really warm October it is a great success: at its best it is one of the prettiest species, the fluted, fan-shaped lip being orangered with a yellow centre, and carried all through the month.

In one of his books on his travels in upper Burma, Frank Kingdon Ward relates how one of

Hedychium greenii.

Unnamed yellow species of *Hedychium* from Gongshan.

Cautleya spicata. Above: in flower. Below: the seeds.

the joys of the autumn landscape was the number and variety of *Hedychium* species. No doubt many of these would be beyond the scope of our gardens; but perhaps as a foretaste of what is still to come is an as yet unnamed species from near Gongshan, just to the east of the Gaoligong ridge separating Yunnan from Burma. This is of medium height, and produces an almost club-like head of many bracts. From these throughout September there emerge a succession of clear yellow flowers, opening several at a time. They have a broad lip and staminodes, giving them a rounded appearance quite different from those of other species. It is certainly one of the finest introductions of recent years, and one of the most dependable.

Cautleya

Cautleya is a small and diminishing genus, for most of the former names have been reduced to synonyms of *C. spicata* and *C. gracilis*. By far the best species for the garden is the form of *C. spicata* formerly known as *C. robusta*. It is quite common in eastern Nepal, in much the same habitats as *Hedy-*

chium densiflorum. It grows to about 70cm, with elegant, lance-shaped leaves, and deep yellow flowers shaped somewhat like the gaping beak of a bird. They appear from among a sheaf of maroon-red bracts that persist after the flowers have fallen and eventually, in warm gardens, produce large, translucent seeds resembling grey pearls, so that this plant remains decorative for longer than most of its tribe. The other species commonly available is *C. gracilis* (*C. lutea* and possibly *C. cathcartii* are synonymous), a variable plant, widespread from the Himalayas to west China. It is similar in form to *C. spicata*, but smaller and less colourful, and with red seeds. Although suffering by comparison with its larger cousin, it is an attractive plant, and increases readily.

Roscoea

Their size, and their need for shade, limit the use of hedychiums in smaller gardens. The roscoeas, however, are almost all quite small, and are rather more tolerant of sun, although it is vital to keep them moist during growth. *Roscoea auriculata* has long been in cultivation from Sir Joseph Hooker's collections in Sikkim, sometimes under the name of the very closely related *R. purpurea*. The distinctions between the two are in fact still in question, particularly as the latter ranges from Himachal Pradesh to the extreme east of Nepal, where it gives place to *R. auriculata*, only to reappear in Bhutan. From a gardener's point of view the relevant difference is that *R. auriculata* blooms earlier, very soon after the leaves appear in June. In good forms the flowers are a deep, rich purple, enhanced by the small white staminodes at their centres. The forms of *R. purpurea* in cultivation have come from more recent collections in Nepal. This species has a wide range of habitat, even colonizing cleared or disturbed ground where there is some protection from grazing animals, and is often to be seen in the walls of cultivated terraces. On some of the ridges surrounding the Kathmandu valley, where grazing is controlled, its grassy leaves grow so thickly as to form a kind of turf. Plants from central Nepal have flowers of some shade of lilac-purple, but forms with white or bi-coloured flowers occur in the east, and one or two are sparingly in cultivation. A variety with blooms of a startling shade of red (variously described as 'coral red', 'geranium red' and 'burgundy red'), and given the name 'Red Gurkha', was collected in the Ganesh region about ten years ago, and is held at Kew; but it seems slow in reaching the outside world. All these flower quite late, from July to September,

Roscoea purpurea.

and vary considerably in stature. The taller forms look very well planted alongside hedychiums such as *Hedychium ellipticum*, and all associate well with the several forms of *Geranium wallichianum*, a frequent companion in the wild. Some plants have purplish stems and are attractive at all stages of growth.

Of the remaining Nepalese species, only *Roscoea alpina* – a dwarf plant with variously coloured flowers – is at all common in gardens; even then *R. scillifolia* – a much smaller Chinese species – is often offered under this name. *Roscoea nepalense*, which is confined to the west of the country, is also suited to the rock-garden rather than the border, but has quite large, pure white flowers. *Roscoea capitata* bears its rather small flowers aloft on a short stem: they open several at a time and may be any shade from white to magenta-purple. It is found only in the area of the Trisula river, north-west of Kathmandu. *Roscoea tumjensis* was described from plants found in the relatively dry Shiar Khola valley, where they were blooming when the leaves had scarcely emerged from the soil; but in wetter parts of its range, and in cultivation, the leaves are well developed at flowering time, and the plants are then similar to the larger forms of *R. purpurea*. When fully grown, it is the tallest and most robust of all the roscoeas, making an upright stand of foliage over a metre high.

In China, Roscoeas have much the same range as the hedychiums in Yunnan and southern Sichuan, but at somewhat higher altitudes. Because they shed their seeds early, they have largely eluded collection by this means, and most introductions have been through limited plant collections, and so take some time to reach general circulation. However, *Roscoea cautleoides*, and a mid-purple form of *R. humeana*, are well established in cultivation. *R. humeana* is, by common consent, the finest of the genus, for the flowers are carried several at a time, and are very large in relation to the size of the plant, the dorsal petal and lip being of equal length. Visitors to Lijiang may see it at its best on the wide, stony plain, a former lake bed, that lies east of the shining peaks of the Jade Dragon Mountain, Yu Long Shan. There, in May, it erupts by the thousand, not only from the ground, but from fissures in the weathered outcrops of magnesium limestone, in every shade from mauve-purple to almost white, with here and there a plant with pale yellow flowers. These colour variants are gradually coming into circulation, and a very dark purple, almost black, form is sometimes available under the name 'Inkling'. *R. humeana* is perhaps somewhat more tolerant of dry conditions than other Roscoeas, and in well-ordered gardens may seed itself about.

Roscoea cautleoides occurs in the same areas, but is a plant of open forests. It too has both yellow and purple forms, often growing together in about equal numbers. In this case it is the yellow form that is more often seen, and is the only yellow-flowered species generally available. As seen near Lijiang, the purple variant is in fact of an unattractive leaden hue, but a variety of colours have been reported, including white and pink. The flowers are carried on a tallish stem, and appear singly, with a large bi-lobed lip and smaller dorsal petal.

The other Chinese species are so variable in size, colour, and time of flowering, that any description based on a particular form may not hold good for the species as a whole. For example, *Roscoea scillifolia* – a widespread and readily grown alpine plant, which often seeds itself – is available

in two forms: one with very small pink flowers; the other taller, and with larger dark purple ones, so that it has been questioned whether they are in fact the same species; but numerous intermediaries occur in the wild. *Roscoea tibetica* is found in upper Burma and Bhutan, as well as in south-east Tibet, and is locally abundant in clearings in sub-alpine forests and alpine meadows in northern Yunnan and south-west Sichuan. In some forms it is close to *R. scillifolia*, but the plants in cultivation have much larger flowers and are charming subjects for the rock-garden. Even so they vary in height, some flowering almost at ground level, while others are relatively tall. *Roscoea debilis* and *R. praecox* are related species from further south in Yunnan and at lower altitudes, and are little-known in cultivation; from photographs, *R. praecox* appears quite desirable, and flowers before the leaves appear.

From further west, in Burma and Assam, comes *Roscoea wardii*. It does not appear to be in general cultivation, if at all; its introduction is greatly to be hoped for, as Kingdon Ward thought highly of it, and described the flowers as being of a 'rich Tyrian purple'. *Roscoea australis*, also purple, has an isolated distribution in western Burma, in the Chin Hills and Mount Victoria. It has long been grown in the Edinburgh Botanic Garden, and is now reaching more general cultivation.

Roscoeas are readily raised from seed, reaching flowering size in from two to four years.

Other genera

Of late, a number of other genera – *Zingiber*, *Curcuma*, *Amomum*, *Kaempferia*, and so on – have been imported from Indian nurseries and offered as possible subjects for the open garden, simply on the grounds that they have been known to survive a few degrees of frost during their dormant period. However, this ignores their need for much warmer conditions throughout their growing season than our climate can provide. The few hardier sorts may be described as plants for the curious, rather than good garden subjects, for the flowers are not very showy, and are carried at ground level amid a forest of leafy stems.

Zingiber mioga, from China and Japan, is of interest as an edible relative of the culinary ginger, *Z. officinale*. In this case, however, it is the young shoots that are eaten, though probably not often as it is said to induce forgetfulness. The pale

Zingiber aff. *mioga* from Lu Shan.

yellow flowers have a largish, shovel-shaped lip, and are produced in clusters at the base of the stems, but are easily overlooked. However, a form or related species from Lu Shan in Jiangxi Province has larger and quite noticeable deep yellow flowers; in the wild, they are succeeded by bright red seed capsules, opening like starfishes on the ground; but these do not always mature in our cooler climate.

Zingiber mioga has at times been classed as an *Amomum*. This genus also contains one or two fairly hardy species. An unidentified plant from Yunnan has been quite successful in a damp spot, and produces purplish-pink flowers, like small pleiones, amid purple stems. Grown on a raised bank, so as to be closer to the eye, it is a pretty and intriguing subject. The Chinese flora contains many other similar plants, some at least on the verge of hardiness.

8 Climbers

Charlie Pridham

The use of climbers can lift a garden from the ordinary, providing height, colour, and often scent. Unlike trees and shrubs, climbers do not always need their own space, but can share with other plants. Climbers that disappear below ground in winter can even be used on shelterbelt planting to provide seasonal interest. Because they take up little space at ground level, it is often possible to grow several climbers in close proximity to one another, extending the interest over a long season. As gardens become smaller, so the need to make the best possible use of vertical space becomes ever more pressing.

There are many good and hardy climbers to choose from, and gardeners could play safe and stick to those. However, the large increase in the number of houses with conservatories has extended the range of less hardy climbers that are readily available, and there are now many exciting plants to be found in nurseries all over the country, especially in Cornwall.

Left: *Bomarea hirtella*. (See page 172.)

Below is an alphabetical list of climbers that range from slightly less than hardy to tender. All will succeed in unheated conservatories, and gardeners in milder areas who cannot resist taking a chance may like to try them outdoors – all are growing outside without cover in at least two counties of the UK. Brief propagation tips are given, just in case!

With regret, some of my favourite climbers have been left out, as they are perfectly hardy. Others have been excluded because I was unable to stretch a point, and have had to admit they are probably too tender. Hopefully, gardeners will know their own plots and be able to decide just how far they can push the boundaries. But it never ceases to amaze me how plants can defy perceived wisdom, and grow in both unlikely latitudes and aspects – gifts to those brave enough to try.

Akebia

A. quinata with five-lobed leaves; *A. trifoliata* with three lobes, and *A.* × *pentaphylla* – a hybrid of these two – are all vigorous evergreen, or semi-evergreen twiners with attractive leaves. As with other members of the Lardizabalaceae, their flowers are strongly scented (sweet chocolate in the case of *Akebia*). Hardiness is not normally a

problem, as they come from winter-cold regions of Japan, China, and Korea. However, in a mild maritime climate they will come into flower early (February on), and the flowers may be damaged by frost. Wall protection (even a northerly aspect) will ensure reliable flowering, but fruit-set is rare. Propagate by semi-ripe stem cuttings on bottom heat. Plants will also layer themselves. Left to its own devices, *Akebia* will reach 12m.

Andredera

A. cordifolia (formerly *Boussingaultia baselloides*) came originally from tropical South America, but will behave as an herbaceous twiner in our maritime climate, dying back each winter to a tuberous rootstock; reshooting the following May, and often reaching 6m in a season. Its common name of 'Sweet mignonette' alludes to the light but pleasant fragrance of the small flowers, which are carried in many-flowered panicles during late summer. It needs warmth to ensure flowering before the year draws to a close, and good drainage to prevent rotting of the tubers. Propagate by dividing the tubers; or by nodal stem cuttings in summer, which are easy.

Andredera cordifolia.

Araujia

A. sericofera, 'Cruel plant', is an evergreen, twining member of the Asclepiadaceae (milkweeds), originally from South America. In milder gardens, it

Akebia quinata.

Araujia sericofera.

does well in the sun and will reach 7m, producing bunches of scented white and pink flowers from midsummer on. (The scent is more noticeable in enclosed areas of a garden.) These are followed by large, egg-shaped seedpods full of silky seeds. A sunny wall suits this plant best. Propagate from seed, or nodal stem cuttings in summer, using hormone rooting powder to stop the cut stems bleeding.

Aristolochia

A. macrophylla is hardy, and has wonderful, large, kidney-shaped leaves, but its flowers are on the small side, and not often freely produced. However, *Aristolochia* contains many climbers and there are several more tender 'Dutchman's Pipes' with larger flowers, many of which, including *A. chrysops* and *A. kaempferi*, also flower as younger plants and would be worth trying. All are potentially large (7m), but can be maintained at smaller sizes: *A. sempervivens* is smaller at 3m. Unfortunately, all of them seem to be targeted by snails and slugs. Plants are easily raised from seed, but home-grown seed may not be produced on more tender species. There are good specimens of several *Aristolochia* species at Pine Lodge Gardens near St Austell, Cornwall.

Asteranthera

A. ovata, a small, evergreen creeper is best grown as a ground-covering creeper. It comes from Chile, where it grows much larger – to 3m – but in the UK it is unlikely to exceed 1m, and does best in moist, sheltered woodland as it dislikes both hard frost and cold winds. The flowers are red, tubular, and showy, appearing in June and July. The plants are easily propagated from stem cuttings during the growing season.

Berberidopsis

B. corallina bears many deep crimson flowers in late summer, which hang down from the handsome, evergreen foliage. It comes from Chile and does best in moist soils, which are acid to neutral, but if happy, it will tolerate alkaline conditions. It looks wonderful growing through and hanging out of conifers, where it can reach 6m high. Propagate by 10cm-stem cuttings on bottom heat and mist in July.

Berberidopsis corallina.

Billardiera

B. longiflora, a small, slender climber to 2m high from Australia, is ideal where something larger would swamp the host. The small, yellowish flowers are pleasant, but the real beauty lies in the large, shiny, blue/purple fruits (white and pink fruiting forms are also known). In coastal areas it can be grown in the open through shrubs, but elsewhere wall protection is required. It is easily propagated from seed.

Bomarea

Climbing relatives of the *Alstroemeria* from South America, *Bomarea* are proving no less hardy, and will succeed in similar situations. *B. caldasii*, with its large heads of orange flowers, is perhaps the most flamboyant, and climbs rapidly to 5m. *B. hirtella* (photo page 168) is smaller, and will succeed in pots. Other species such as *B. edulis*, *B. cardieri*, and *B. salsilla* are possible, but not easily obtained. Seed production is good on established plants, and this is the best method of propagation, as they dislike root disturbance. There are large plants of *B. caldasii* at Tregrehan, near Par, Cornwall.

Bomarea caldasii.

Bougainvillea

Outside, *Bougainvillea* should be regarded as a real challenge, and indeed temperatures below -3°C are likely to cause damage. Nevertheless, I know of several private gardens in Torbay, and at Point in Cornwall, where it flowers outdoors without protection. The three species in horticulture – *B. spectabilis*, *B. glabra*, and *B. peruviana* – and a naturally occurring hybrid, *B. × buttiana* (still sold as 'Mrs Butt'), are all from winter-dry parts of tropical South America, and tend to be deciduous in temperate climates. The stout stems have thorns, and the small flowers are surrounded by brightly coloured bracts. Such is the mixing over the years that the straight species are unlikely to be encountered, but each parent imparts different characteristics, and many cultivars tend towards one more than the other.

Bougainvillea hybrid.

Bougainvillea peruviana is the most delicate, and will not tolerate any frost. *B. spectabilis* tends to flower following cool, dry weather, while *B. glabra* flowers continuously. Although there is not a lot of difference between the latter two for hardiness, in cooler, temperate climates the *B. spectabilis* cultivars do best, as they are happier to go dormant in winter; these tend to be the purples and reds. The dryer they are during dormancy the better. They often shed many of their leaves when growth resumes in spring, and flowering should occur in summer. If grown under an overhang of house roof, on a south-facing wall, watering is more easily controlled. Generally, variegated cultivars are less hardy and flower less well outdoors in cooler, temperate climates.

Propagation by 20cm hardwood cuttings in winter is not often feasible, due to lack of material, although it can be quite successful in a frost-free greenhouse or frame. Layering is a good system; semi-ripe, 10cm nodal cuttings taken in summer, on bottom heat and treated with hormone rooting powder also work well. In warm climates, *Bougainvillea* can be very large, but on the edge of hardiness they are unlikely to exceed 3m.

Campsis

C. radicans from the USA, *C. grandiflora* from China, and their hybrid 'Madam Galen' are the main plants encountered in gardens. All have large, showy red to orange tubular flowers on the shoot tips during late summer. Growth can be rampant – 10m or more (but they can be reduced annually) – and in the case of *C. radicans*, self-clinging; but all three are best tied in. Perversely, the milder winter areas often have cooler summers, and flowering can be late and unreliable. These do best in full sun on a hot wall. *C. grandiflora* is the least hardy, but none are difficult. Propagation of the species is easy from stem cuttings in June, but 'Madam Galen' requires mist and bottom heat (or layers). *Campsis* is often seen poking above the walls of hidden gardens in late summer in Truro, and there is a good specimen at the RHS Garden Rosemoor, in Devon.

Clematis

There are so many good, hardy varieties that it seems hardly worth the risk to grow tender clematis, although some of the more marginal ones do have a good scent. New Zealanders *C. paniculata*,

Clematis paniculata.

C. forsteri, and Asian *C. fasciculiflora* are all evergreen and scented, but flower early in the year. Unfortunately, under glass clematis are magnets for whitefly and red spider mite.

Clematis fasciculiflora, which originates in southwest China and northern Vietnam, flourishes at Roseland House, near Truro, and would reach 10m or more if not cut back hard each year after flowering.

Clematis are best propagated on bottom heat, from stem cuttings taken early in the year, either nodal or inter-nodal (the latter method provides more cuttings per length), or from seed for the species. (*Clematis* from New Zealand have differ-

ent male and female plants, and both are required for the production of viable seed.)

Clematoclethera

There are three species of *Clematoclethera*: *C. integrifolia*, *C. lasiociada*, and *C. strigillosa*. All are large, vigorous plants (10m) related to *Actinidia*. They originate in north-west and west China, and all have small, white, scented flowers. None are seen often in cultivation, but they are sufficiently hardy to cover walls and trees in sun or semi-shade. Propagation is by 15cm nodal cuttings, under mist in June.

Eccremocarpus

Eccremocarpus (Greek 'hanging fruit') belongs to the Bignoniaceae, but only one of the five species is at all common in horticulture – *E. scaber*, which comes from subtropical parts of Chile and Peru, and was introduced to the UK in 1827. Given warm conditions, it will remain evergreen and flower all through the year, but at temperatures below 0°C it will tend to become herbaceous in habit, reappearing from the rootstock each spring, and flowering all summer. With modest rootstock protection it will survive temperatures down to -9°C. The tubular flowers are carried in bunches, and there are forms with flowers that are yellow, orange, red, and red with yellow tips. It is a rapid grower, and soon bounces back if it suffers during the winter. Climbing by tendrils on the leaves, it can be scrambled over other plants. *E. scaber* is easygoing in its requirements, and easy to propagate from surface-sown seed on bottom heat, or stem cuttings in the summer. Both seedlings and cuttings can be expected to reach 4m, and to flower the same year.

Ercilla

E. volubilis is an evergreen, scented climber that flowers in early spring. Introduced from Chile, it will self-cling if given some help, and if grown up trees would reach 10m+. Tough, reliable, and wind-resistant, it is easy to propagate from stem cuttings. Its main drawbacks are that it becomes very dense and heavy, so needs trimming back to prevent it tearing off whatever it is growing on, and the flower clusters (which are pale pink, scented powder-puffs) turn black as they go over, and take their time to drop. However, it remains a useful plant for awkward places.

Ercilla volubilis.

Gelsemium

G. sempervirens is an evergreen twiner with small, shiny leaves and yellow, scented, jasmine-like flowers in spring. It comes from the southern USA, where it reaches 6m, and does best on a warm, sunny wall. Nodal cuttings on bottom heat strike readily during summer.

Hardenbergia

These small, evergreen climbers from Australia look charming growing through other plants, their small violet flowers carried in long clusters in early spring. *H. violacea* is the more successful species outdoors, but *H. comptoniana* could be tried in very mild gardens. There are named forms with varying coloured flowers of pink, pale lilac, or white, but none looks as effective as the strong violet of its natural state, which is easily raised from seed. Seedlings will flower the same year, but will take several years to reach their full size of 3m. Named forms can be raised from nodal stem cuttings taken during summer. This plant needs careful siting, as winter damage will prevent flowering.

Hibbertia

H. scandens ('Guinea flower', 'Golden guinea vine', 'Snake vine') is the only true climber from a large family of tropical plants that will both grow and flower out of doors in the UK. It comes from Australia, where it is found from coastal south-eastern New South Wales to north-east Queensland. A vigorous, glossy-leaved, and evergreen twiner, reaching 4m on a wall in the UK, it has bright yellow flowers of 5–6cm diameter in early summer, and from a distance looks not unlike a climbing *Hypericum*. It is not fussy as to soil type, but as with any plant growing on the edge of its range, wet, cold sites should be avoided. It will suffer some leaf loss or damage below 0°C; stems will remain intact down to -2°C, but below this the plant will often be killed to the ground. However, as long as the rootstock has been protected with loose mulch, regrowth will be rapid. Choose a warm wall, or grow through sheltering evergreen plants. Propagation by seed is sometimes slow and erratic; but cuttings are easy – nodal stem cuttings 6–10cm long, taken any time the plant is in growth. Bottom heat, mist, and hormone treatment will speed things up, but are not essential. *H. scandens* does well around the coast, and there are good flowering specimens at Lamorran House Gardens, St Mawes, Cornwall.

Hibbertia scandens.

Holboellia

It is difficult to know why *Holboellia* have a reputation for being tender: both species grow vigorously in a maritime climate, and can be grown up trees and on structures, as well as against walls, reaching 6m. They have wonderful, glossy, evergreen leaves, and the flowers are highly scented (male and female flowers are carried separately on the same plant, and are either greenish-white or pale purple, depending on sex), appearing in spring. Occasionally, squat, sausage-shaped fruits are borne. The species originates in Central China to the Himalayas, and I suspect lack of summer heat and suitable pollinators in the UK to be the reason for poor fruit-set.

Holboellia latifolia is said to be more tender than *H. coriacea*, but I have not noticed a difference. Both can be propagated from seed if found; otherwise use nodal stem cuttings in mid- to late summer. *Holboellia* are common in Cornish gardens, and there is a huge specimen of *H. coriacea* at Trehane, near Tresillian.

Holboellia coriacea.

Hydrangea

There are several climbing hydrangeas, of which *H. seemannii* from Mexico is a really good evergreen. It is self-clinging, and does well on sheltered, shady walls and tree trunks, where it can reach 10m. Slow to start, then vigorous, it has beautiful white, scented, lace-cap flowers in summer. The leaves are dark green and leathery, and look good all year if kept out of the winter wind. Propagation by stem cuttings from spring to autumn is straightforward, but can be slow – mist and bottom heat help. Established plants can layer themselves.

Hydrangea seemannii.

Jasminum

The following are some less hardy jasmines. All except *J. polyanthum* should be considered difficult.

J. azoricum, from Madeira, is evergreen and grows to 4m or more, with white, star-shaped, scented flowers in flushes throughout summer and autumn. (*J. angulare* is similar, and more free-flowering, but difficult to obtain.)

J. dispermum, from the Himalayas, is a 5m-plus evergreen that looks similar in leaf to the hardy *J. officinale*, but the flowers, which are white, flushed pink, and scented, are carried in large terminal cymes, any time between early autumn and early summer.

J. grandiflorum – normally encountered as the form 'De Grasse'. The true plant is widely grown for its essential oils in India, where it is known as 'Pitchy', and is probably too tender except under glass. It can be kept to around 2–3m by pruning in spring. The highly scented flowers are 5cm in diameter, and appear on and off all year, with bigger flushes in the cooler months.

J. mesnyi, from south-west China, is an evergreen, with scandent stems about 4m long where happy. The yellow, semi-double flowers are large and beautiful, but have little or no scent. They appear in spring.

J. polyanthum, from China, is an evergreen often sold as a house-plant. However, it can be very good outdoors. If protected from strong winds, it will stand a couple of degrees of frost and may reach 5m. The strongly scented white flowers are carried in large trusses over a long period in spring, summer, and autumn.

J. sambac is of stiff, evergreen habit. I have yet to see a large plant doing well outside, which, as it comes from India, is perhaps not surprising, but as it will take a light frost under glass it may be worth experimenting with. It flowers in flushes from spring to autumn, and the waxy flowers have an exceptionally strong fragrance. It is often seen as the forms 'Grand Duke of Tuscany' and 'Maid of Orleans'.

Kennedia rubicuunda.

Jasmines can be propagated by stem cuttings, nodal or inter-nodal, during the growing season, but *Jasminum sambac* and *J. azoricum* can be slow to root. Several tender Jasmine species thrive at Lamorran House Gardens, St Mawes, Cornwall.

Kennedia

K. rubicunda is one of a group of small, evergreen, Australian twiners, related to *Hardenbergia*, but having red, pea-like flowers in spring. It requires a warm wall, but is unlikely to exceed 2.5m. It is easily raised from seed or cuttings.

Lapageria

L. rosea, named after Josephine de la Pagerie (Napoleon Bonaparte's wife), belongs to the Philesiaceae. The genus contains only one species, *L. rosea*, although there are several cultivars. This evergreen, twining climber comes from the forests of southern Chile, where it is known as the *Copihue*. The people of Chile collect and eat the fruits, as well as making garlands of the flowering stems. The flowers of the wild plants are usually rose-pink to cherry-red, and 10cm long. They hang bell-shaped and waxy, often in bunches. It is not unusual for colour and flower size to vary considerably during the flowering season, which in Cornwall is mainly between July and April, although some flowers can appear at any time.

Due to its home in cool, moist forests, *Lapageria rosea* prefers not to be sited in a sunny, hot place, and often does well on shaded or north walls. It requires a moist soil, rich in humus and with a low pH (below 5.5, ericaceous or acid). The stems arise from a rhizome-type root system and, once settled, growth can be vigorous, with the roots spreading rapidly. Adult growth is frost-hardy, and remains undamaged at -9°C, but new growth, which often starts as early as January, will be damaged below -2°C, or by wind. Wall shelter is therefore a good idea. North walls suit it very well, but further north and east in the UK, the aspect of the wall needs to be more southerly, although always providing shade from strong, direct sun. Properly sited, *L. rosea* will succeed in sheltered gardens throughout the UK and, where happy, produce a plant of 3–4m.

There are a number of cultivars, but not all are readily available now:

- 'Alba' has white flowers.
- 'Beatrix Anderson' has red flowers with white spotting on the outside.
- 'Flesh Pink' has flowers of a pale, clear

Lapageria 'Flesh Pink'.

pink. Both this and 'Beatrix Anderson' were given to Rennie Moffitt at Penheale by E.B. Anderson as seedlings, the seed having originated in the wild.

- 'Nash Court' is an old, red variety, with larger flowers than the species.
- 'Penheale' is a red, with straight, unflared flowers and more lanceolate foliage.
- 'Wisley Picotee' has white flowers with pink picotee edges. This and the next variety were given by the RHS to Rennie Moffitt at Penheale to propagate. (Both are weak growers and hard to propagate.)
- 'Wisley Spotted' has white flowers with pink spots.

There are also a large number of American cultivars.

Propagation

Although division is feasible, *Lapageria* do not enjoy root disturbance, and it is not recommended. Layering is the most popular method: done in January into deep pots, the layers will be ready for severing a year later, but generally require a further year growing on to establish a good root system. Cuttings can be taken under mist and bottom heat at most times of the year. The best material is 2–3mm in diameter (about the same as a computer mouse cable!). It needs at least one good leaf and dormant bud (a two-node

cutting gives better results). Cuttings are not difficult to root, but do take a long time, and although one or more buds may make shoot growth within months, roots are likely to take a year or more. Once rooted, handle the cuttings with care, growing on for a further two years. (I prefer to leave them for a couple of weeks in the mist unit after potting, to settle them in.)

Seed, if sown fresh (still in the sticky goo, which needs washing off immediately prior to sowing), germinates well and quickly. Seed set is variable: the natural pollinators – hummingbirds – are not present outside America. Single plants are not very self-fertile, but hand pollination between plants works well. The snag with seedlings is that the five- to seven-year wait for plants to flower may be rewarded with a plant that flowers sparsely, or with poor flower shape or colour – although, of course, you may get a show-stopper!

On young plants, aphids, slugs, and snails can do a lot of damage, but once established *Lapageria* are trouble-free.

There are many different forms of *Lapageria* at Tregrehan, both inside and out.

Lardizabala

L. biternata is a vigorous twiner to 6m, originally from Chile, and slightly less hardy than *Akebia* or *Holboellia,* with attractive, evergreen foliage. The scented, purple-brown flowers are borne during autumn and winter, and wall protection is advised. The large, edible, sausage-shaped fruits are seldom produced in cool climates. Propagate by semi-ripe stem cuttings on bottom heat. Plants will also layer themselves.

The front elevation of Tregothnan used to support a good specimen of *Lardizabala biternata*. It has been moved while building work is carried out, but will be relocated.

Lathyrus

L. pubescens, a perennial, blue-flowered pea from South America, will do well in a sunny spot that is not too wet in winter, and will reach about 2m. The flowers are scented, and appear in bunches from spring on. Seed production is erratic unless hand pollination is carried out, but once seed has been obtained it is no more difficult than any of the other peas to germinate and grow. However, a hard winter will kill it.

Lonicera

In addition to all the wonderful hardy and scented honeysuckles available to the gardener, there are some that are more of a challenge. All are twiners that require their own space, as they would quickly choke other plants.

L. hildebrandiana, a very large and vigorous evergreen, has succeeded in a number of Cornish gardens over the years. The leaves and scented flowers are large, and growth is rampant. However, it comes from Burma and is tender, and only the best of sunny situations in mild gardens will ensure success. Presently, one of the best specimens may be seen at Tregrehan, near Par, where it reaches 6m. However, it is capable of being much larger – up to 30m or more.

L. sempervirens, as the name implies, is an evergreen. The bright red, tubular flowers are carried in bunches on the shoot tips, and are pollinated by humming-birds in its native America. Sadly, this means that the flowers are not scented. Its hybrid *Lonicera × brownii* is more reliably hardy, but more orange in colour, and it too is not scented. Wall shelter is useful for *L. sempervirens*.

L. similis 'Delavayi', from western China, is like a refined version of *L. japonica*. The evergreen foliage is large and healthy, not suffering from the mildew that can so disfigure *L. japonica*. The long, tubular, scented flowers are white to pale yellow, and produced abundantly over a long period from midsummer on. This is not a particularly tender plant, and is well worth the space. It does not need a wall to succeed in milder parts, and makes a large plant of 6m or more if unpruned.

Lonicera can all be propagated by semi-ripe nodal or inter-nodal cuttings. Bottom heat and mist help, but are not critical.

Macfadyena

M. unguis-cati is an evergreen, self-clinging climber, capable of climbing to the top of large trees. According to its provenance (it is found throughout South America and the West Indies), it should die at the first hint of cold, but I have found that it survives well outside, provided the tubers are below the frost-line. However, as yet its large, yellow, trumpet flowers have not been produced, and I have seen it flower in the UK only under glass. It may be worth experimenting with this to see whether different seedlings would behave differently. If a free-flowering form were found, it would be easy to propagate, as it roots wherever it touches the ground. There is a plant flowering in the large greenhouse at Probus Gardens.

Mandevilla

M. suaveolens, from Argentina, does very well on a south or west wall with good drainage, producing lots of large, white, scented flowers during summer. It is deciduous in habit; a vigorous grower, and can cover a large expanse of wall. Under glass it defoliates in response to red spider mite attack, and can look a mess. Summer stem cuttings, or seed, can be used to propagate it. Sadly, other *Mandevilla*, like the beautiful pink-flowered, evergreen 'Alice du Pont' are too tender for outdoors if winter goes below 0°C.

Lonicera similis 'Delavayi'.

Mandevilla 'Alice du Pont'.

Mutisia

There are a number of species of *Mutisia* to try. These South American climbing daisies attach with tendrils, but unfortunately can be difficult to establish, for reasons that are not always clear – it is not normally cold that gets them. They require good, well-drained soil in a sunny position, plus something to scramble through or up, which also serves to shade the roots. When growing well, all have very attractive, large, daisy-like flowers during late summer, and all tend to look tatty in winter – but so do a lot of other climbing plants!

M. clematis is the least hardy, and has the smallest (almost red) flowers, at 4.5cm diameter. However, the buds and seed-heads are large, and it is the easiest to grow. It reaches 3m or more in height.

M. decurrens has bright orange flowers up to 12cm across. It is one of the best known, but most difficult to get hold of! Height 2–3m.

M. ilicifolia has lilac-pink flowers, 6cm across, with holly-like leaves. Height 2–3m.

M. oligodon has pink flowers, 6cm across. It has a marked tendency to sucker, and is low-growing at just 1–2m.

M. subulata has pink flowers, 7cm across, and reaches a height of 2–3m.

Mutisia can all be propagated by seed (which may be of low viability) – which should be surface-sown on bottom heat – or by stem cuttings in summer (avoid moving on the cuttings until well established). Division of the rootstocks may look tempting, but should be avoided because they dislike root disturbance. There is a fine specimen of *M. subulata* at Higher Truscott, near Launceston.

Pandorea

Named after the pre-Greek Earth goddess Pandora, because of the box-like seedpods that release masses of seed, they belong to the Bignoniaceae family. Two species likely to succeed in our gardens are *Pandorea jasminoides* and *Pandorea pandorana*.

P. jasminoides (Bower vine, or Bower of Beauty, syn. *Bignonia jasminoides, Tecoma jasminoides*) comes from rain-forest areas of north-eastern New South Wales and south-eastern Queensland, Australia. It is a large, vigorous, evergreen twiner reaching 6m in the UK, with bunches of large white, pink-throated trumpet-shaped flowers, from midsummer until early winter. These are faintly scented, like marshmallow sweets. The shiny leaves are divided into seven leaflets, and seem untroubled by pests. The 10cm seedpods are freely produced. *P. jasminoides* is tolerant of most soil types, but good drainage is essential. It is drought-tolerant once established. Avoid overfeeding, as this can lead to a lack of flowers. Indeed, pot-bound specimens often flower the best. Put it on a warm wall, or grow it through evergreens for protection (it also makes a wonderful conservatory climber); it is happy in full sun to semi-shade. It will generally be undamaged down to 0°C, but below that it will lose leaves, and below -4°C the stems are likely to be killed; but the plant will grow again from the base if this is protected by mulch. The more damage the plant suffers, the later the flowering will start. The main criteria for flowering this plant out of doors is the preservation of as much foliage as possible. A position out of cold winds is therefore essential. Propagation from surface-sown seed on bottom heat is quick and easy. Cuttings (which are required for named cultivars) can be nodal or inter-nodal, and root quickly with or without mist; bottom heat and hormone treatment are advantageous, but not essential. Cuttings may be taken any time during the summer.

There are a couple of named cultivars:

- *P. jasminoides* 'Rosea Superba' – as for the species above, but the flowers are pink with a deeper pink eye.

Pandorea jasminoides 'Rosea Superba'.

- *P. jasminoides* 'Lady Di' has all-white flowers (syn *P. jasminoides* 'Alba').

Pandorea pandorana (Wonga-wonga vine, syn. *Bignonia pandorana, Pandorea australis, Pandorea doratoxylon, Tecoma australis*). This is another vigorously twining evergreen, bearing masses of foxglove-like flowers in spring. It is also from New South Wales, Australia, and will easily reach 6m in the UK. The flowers are typically cream/white with purple or pink staining, and spotting on the insides. The leaves are divided into five leaflets. Young seedlings can have much more finely divided leaves, giving rise to the number of different names this species goes under. It is largely pest- and trouble-free. The 8cm-long seedpods are freely produced. Tolerant of most soil types, and showing good salt resistance, it is hardier than *P. jasminoides*, tolerating temperatures of -1°C without damage, but due to its earlier flowering it is less likely to recover from a harsh winter in time to flower. It does well on a sunny wall, and can look stunning with *Wisteria*.

Propagation from surface-sown seed is easy and rapid, but plants are variable both in appearance and cold-tolerance. Cuttings are not quite as quick as *P. jasminoides*, and nodal cuttings on bottom heat during summer give the best results. Mist and hormone treatment are an advantage.

Available cultivars include: 'Alba' with all white flowers; 'Golden Rain', which has rich gold flowers with deeper coloured tips, and 'Ruby Heart', which has much pinker flowers.

There are good plants of *Pandorea jasminoides* at Roseland House near Truro, and in May the specimen of *Pandorea pandorana* is in full flower at Polgwynne, Feock – both in Cornwall.

Passiflora

There are many species and hybrids of these evergreen tendril climbers. The best-known and most often cultivated is *Passiflora caerulea*, the blue passion flower, but there are several others worth trying if attention can be paid to protecting the rootstock from both cold (nothing below -1°C) and wet – a combination of the two is likely to prove fatal. The top-growth's survival is of little consequence, as *Passiflora* flower on their new growths. The base of a warm wall is a good site; another trick is to plant inside a greenhouse, and train the stems through a hole to the outside (the opposite of the treatment of grape vines). The status and origins of most of the *Passiflora* below are the subject of much discussion: most originate from South America but are now found in many parts of the world.

P. actinea is early-flowering, and scented. The blue and white flowers hang down like sea anemones. It is evergreen where happy, and will reach 4m.

P. 'Amethyst' is a beautiful, free-flowering, small passion flower, with large amethyst-coloured flowers all year if suitably protected. It is good for growing up other plants. This evergreen grows to about 3m, and will often lose leaves in winter before recovering in spring.

Pandorea pandorana 'Golden Rain'.

Passiflora 'Amethyst'.

P. × *caerulea-racemosa*, about the nearest to a hardy red passion flower, also has beautiful flowers, freely borne. Size and growth-habit is similar to *P.* 'Amethyst'.

Passiflora × *caerulea-racemosa*.

P. × *exoniensis* is a lovely deep pink to red hybrid, one of whose parents is *P. antioquiensis*, itself a beautiful species with very long flower stems (up to 1m). It is not often seen in its true form, and is in any case better under glass (most plants turn out to be *P.* × *exoniensis*). By crossing this with *P. mollissima*, a vigorous evergreen is produced, which flowers from midsummer on. The large, 12cm-diameter flowers hang down on stems 10–15cm below the shoots. It flowers best in cool, moist conditions, is vigorous, and will reach 6m.

P. mollissima, the 'banana' passion flower, has clear, light pink, hanging flowers, slightly smaller than those of *P.* × *exoniensis*. The foliage is smaller, and less deeply lobed. Fruit production is more reliable, especially if flowering starts by midsummer, but this plant also prefers cool, moist conditions.

P. 'Purple Haze' is one of a number of *P. caerulea* × 'Amethyst' hybrids. Combining the hardiness of *P. caerulea* with the colour of 'Amethyst', it is free-flowering and vigorous. I have not noticed any fruit being produced.

Species passion flowers can be raised easily from seed, most flowering in their first season. Nodal stem cuttings in summer are also very easy – some root in just three days!

Podranea

P. ricasoliana from South Africa has beautiful large, pink, trumpet-shaped flowers, and the plant appears to survive outdoors suffering only minor damage down to -4°C, and coming through -8°C of winter frost. However, the late flowering period – even in subtropical areas – means that it often fails to flower in cooler maritime climates. Nevertheless, if you do well with *Campsis*, you may wish to try this in similar hot, sunny situations, as it grows vigorously, and is easy to propagate from stem cuttings during summer.

Rhodochiton

R. atrosanguineum, from Mexico, is a 3m evergreen that wraps its leaf stems around its support to climb. Many would regard it as an annual, or at best a short-lived perennial, but this is not important as it is so easy to replace, and so quick to get to flowering size. Wine-red bracts top the deep purple flowers, and remain long after the flowers, greatly enhancing the display. Without frost, flowering is continuous. This is an extremely useful climber for growing into other plants in sunny situations. It is easy to raise by surface-sown seed or summer cuttings.

Rhodochiton atrosanguineum.

Rosa

Many beautiful climbing and rambling roses, both species and hybrids, are perfectly and reliably hardy. However, there are a few special roses that are worth taking additional trouble to grow. Generally, roses need to ripen their wood for it to be winter-hardy, so in the cooler, milder west some of these less hardy sorts do best on a warm wall.

R. banksia is available in both yellow and white, double and single forms, and all but the double yellow 'Lutea' have a good scent. From China originally, it has the potential to be very large (7m plus). Growth is vigorous, and flowering (which requires older wood, so go light on the pruning) takes place early in the year, during spring. Individual flowers are small, and carried in many-flowered bunches. Spring frost is a danger for this rose, as the buds are vulnerable.

Rosa bracteata.

R. bracteata, from China, has evergreen foliage, which is attractive and disease-resistant, and makes a good foil for the large, strongly lemon-scented, single white flowers from midsummer on. It needs a warm wall to do well, where it can reach 5m. Its hybrid 'Mermaid' is less tender, and has large, pale yellow, scented flowers.

R. laevigata, originally from China, is now the state flower of Georgia, USA. In a cool climate it merely survives, seldom producing the masses of large, single white flowers for which it is famous. If it is happy it will ramble to 6m, and try to flower early (typically May), when it has often not

fully recovered from the winter. Slightly more reliable is its reputed hybrid 'Silver Moon', although this is more liable to get black spot.

Since roses are so promiscuous, sowing seed even for the species is a waste of time (unless you want something new), but nodal stem cuttings 15cm long in late summer and autumn root readily in a cold frame.

Bosvigo, near Truro, Cornwall, has a very well-trained *Rosa bracteata* against a wall, which is stunning in flower.

Schisandra

There are a number of extremely attractive, deciduous species that can be grown in cooler maritime climates, although the evergreen sorts are less successful. The flowers resemble small magnolia blooms. Part of the beauty of these plants lies in the strings of often brightly coloured fruits; however, these will not be produced from just one plant as the different-sexed flowers of *Schisandra* are on separate plants. As with hollies, it is necessary to have two plants of different sexes. All look good on walls, and hanging from large shrubs and trees, and will reach 5–6m.

Schisandra rubriflora.

S. chinensis, from Japan and China, is a large plant with small white or pale pink, scented flowers in late spring, which are followed by scarlet berries on long strings.

S. grandiflora, from the temperate Himalayas, has pale pink flowers in May and June, which are also followed by strings of scarlet berries.

S. rubriflora, from western China, has deep crimson flowers in late spring, followed by the trademark strings of bright scarlet berries.

Schisandra are easy to grow from seed, if this can be obtained, but less so from cuttings – the right stage of semi-ripeness is required for reliable rooting, and the resulting plants need to have made growth before they go dormant for the winter.

Semele
S. androgyna, from Madeira, is rampant and evergreen, and related to 'Butcher's Broom'. It is unusual in that its small, green-white flowers appear around the leaf margins, followed by large, bright red berries. It will not tolerate much frost, but as it will grow in shade it can be grown under trees, where frost danger in milder gardens is reduced. The outline of the large, shiny, pinnate leaves, each with many small individual leaflets, makes this a very attractive plant. The berries are a bonus. It will grow to 4m in the UK. Propagation is from seed or division of rootstock.

There is a large specimen scrambling under the palms at Lamorran House Gardens, St Mawes.

Senecio
S. scandens, with wide distribution across Asia, is a vigorous grower, up to 6m, with masses of yellow daisy flowers in late summer. Unfortunately, it is likely to become a pest anywhere it does not die of cold during the winter. Propagation is by seed sown in spring, but viability is sometimes low.

Solanum
S. laxum 'Album' (syn. *S. jasminoides* 'Album'), from Brazil, is a vigorous evergreen to 9m. The form 'Album' is a better garden plant, and will be covered in large bunches of white flowers, each with a yellow beak in the centre, from early summer until after midwinter. To keep it looking good, the mass of growth can be tidied up in the spring. This is one of the best climbing plants for a rampant and free-flowering effect. Propagate from nodal cuttings during summer; the resulting plants are quick to grow on. Seed-set is rare in cooler climates, which is fortunate because the seeds are poisonous.

Solanum laxum 'Album'.

Sollya
S. heterophylla, a small, evergreen twiner from Australia, seldom exceeds 2m. It is extremely pretty, with bunches of small, sky-blue, bell-shaped flowers being produced all year where it is sheltered and happy. Small, sausage-shaped fruits follow – removal of some of these will help to keep

Sollya heterophylla.

flowering going. It needs a sunny, sheltered site in mild gardens to over-winter happily. Propagation from seed is straightforward, as are stem cuttings in summer.

Stauntonia

S. hexaphylla is related to, and closely resembles, a *Holboellia*, and is just as scented. It comes from Japan and Korea.

Tecomaria

T. capensis, Cape honeysuckle, comes from South Africa. It is an evergreen, with bright orange-scarlet flowers in late summer and autumn, and is both self-clinging and twining to 4m. It needs a hot, sunny wall, not just to get it through the cold of winter, but because without a hot summer, flowering will not have started before winter sets in. It does well under cold glass, however. Nodal stem cuttings during summer are a good way of propagating it.

Trachelospermum

Trachelospermum are evergreen and self-clinging climbers, with scented flowers in summer. It would be difficult to ask for more: give them a sunny wall and there is no catch!

T. asiaticum, from Japan and Korea, is a vigorous, close-clinging plant with neat evergreen leaves, which are a yellowy-green, and often colour up in winter with fiery reds. The scented flowers are a dull yellow colour, and are produced in great quantities during summer. This is the hardiest of the two main species, and numerous forms are in cultivation, and will reach 6m or more.

T. jasminoides, from China, is a vigorous self-clinger, with larger and greener leaves than *T. asiaticum*. Its scented flowers in summer are also larger, and nearer pure white in colour, but not produced in such profuse quantities in some forms, and especially not on young plants. This will do best on a sunny wall, and will reach 7m. There are several named forms : 'Majus', 'Wilsonii', 'Japonicum', 'Tricolor', and 'Variegata'. The variegated forms tend to flower less well, but make stunning foliage plants.

Propagate by nodal stem cuttings after flowering, using hormone powder to stop the flow of milky

Trachelospermum asiaticum.

sap on cut stems. Bottom heat certainly speeds things up, but is not essential. All are slow in the early stages of growth.

There are several different *Trachelospermum* growing on the walls at Roseland House near Truro, Cornwall.

Tropaeolum

Tropaeolum are herbaceous climbers from South America that die back to their underground storage root systems in winter. They will reach 5m during the growing season if happy.

T. speciosum, whose bright red flowers are freely produced during late summer, looks stunning growing through evergreens, but is not for everyone. It does better in the cooler, wetter north and west, often thriving on the north sides of yew hedges. Its roots behave not unlike bindweed in the way they travel around below ground. Propagation is from seed, or by division of the roots.

T. tuberosum 'Ken Aslet' grows from tubers that are not unlike knobbly potatoes. It is important to grow named forms, as the straight species will not flower before the autumn equinox. These earlier flowering forms produce their burnt-orange flowers from midsummer on, and should be propagated by division of the tubers or cuttings, not seed.

Tropaeolum are common in Cornwall, and I was intrigued to see *T. speciosum* growing through hedychiums at Lamorran House Gardens, St Mawes.

Wattakaka

W. sinensis is another of the milkweeds (*Asclepiadaceae*). With evergreen foliage, and bunches of scented flowers in summer, it looks not unlike a *Hoya*. Find this a spot to its liking – a warm and sheltered wall – and it is a rampant grower, nowhere near as tender as once thought. Occasionally, a good crop of viable seed is produced, and this is a good method of propagation. It is doing well in private gardens in St Erme, near Truro, and in the Mendip hills!

9 Ferns, Clubmosses, and Horsetails

Chris Page

Ferns, clubmosses, and horsetails are primitive plants of mostly mild, moist climates; of shady, damp places, and are of inherent grace of form. Once established, they are undemanding of attention, providing a recurring source of inspiration through their soft textures and the changing seasonal patterns of their fronds. In cultivated landscapes, all add a sense of the primeval; of sheer verdancy, luxuriance and tropicality; and, best of all, their graceful beauty and exquisite delicacy of architectural form bring a sense of tranquillity, and even magic and romance to a garden's quiet corner.

Left: *Onoclea sensibilis* from North America: detail of frond in cultivation, Gillywood, Cornwall. (See page 194.)

The tradition of cultivation of 'exotic' ferns in Britain is well illustrated by these, which have long been in successful cultivation under glass in Glasgow.

Background to the cultivation of ferns

Ferns and their close relatives, the horsetails and clubmosses, are descended from some of the oldest plants in the world: they have been found as fossils dating back nearly 400m. years. They have early associations with humans, especially in medicinal use, and in many societies their curious forms have endowed them with overtones of magic and mystery. In recent times, they have been sought and nurtured by enthusiastic collectors and dedicated growers, as tender, heated glasshouse subjects; half-hardy cool glasshouse plants, and fully hardy species that thrive outdoors, especially in the high rainfall and humidity of our Western climate.

Their most widespread use as horticultural furnishings reached a peak in Victorian times, having close links with the history of glasshouses and conservatories. Subsequently, ferns declined in general appeal through the first three-quarters of the twentieth century. Since then, they have enjoyed a gradual reawakening of interest, especially among gardeners in the mild, moist climate of Cornwall, where some of the best diversity of cultivated ferns can be displayed most reliably and naturally, not just in greenhouses, but in outdoor gardens, where they have a horticultural appeal of their own.

Geographical and climatic relationships of ferns

World-wide, in the wild, ferns are an immense group, with more than 12,000 known species. There are also well over 500 allied plants – mainly clubmosses and horsetails – which are grouped with ferns under the botanical term Pteridophyta. Collectively these plants represent considerable diversity of form, lifestyle, habitat, and ancientness of geological origins.

Today, in this world-wide perspective, species of Pteridophyta increase greatly in abundance and diversity along a gradient from cooler latitudes of both hemispheres to the humid tropics. In the latter – especially in habitats of cloudy climates on tropical mountain flanks, where there is frequent cloud cover, warm, moist winds, and soft, light rain – ferns are the most abundant form of natural vegetation. In such habitats there are characteristically numerous tree-ferns, climbing ferns, and often filmy ferns, as well as dense ground-cover growths of a great diversity of species over steep, rocky terrain, and around small, tumbling rills and streams. There are species that grow in water; others in deep shade, and many are epiphytes.

On a European scale, luxuriance of growth of native ferns generally increases towards the milder, moister climates of the western periph-

Polypodium interjectum – a native species which thrives especially in south-west England – showing croziers in a lane-bank habitat in early summer.

ery. In Britain and Ireland, ferns thrive best in the south-western parts of these islands. In general, islands with mountains and cloudy climates are usually exceptionally rich in ferns. However, in the native British and Irish fern and fern-ally flora, there are only just over 100 different taxa (including all known hybrids), and many of these are rare. This species-poverty in our native ferns is largely the result of our glacial history, in which a much richer pre-glacial flora was decimated by the Ice Ages. In comparison, the islands of Japan, which were not glaciated, have well over 600 species. These are the sort of fern numbers that we *would* have had if we not been glaciated. So by adding some of the species and genera that are not native, but are hardy, into cultivated habitats, we are returning some of that diversity to levels more appropriate to our latitude, and within an oceanic-fringe insular setting.

The horticultural value of ferns

The luxuriance of numbers of native ferns seen so abundantly in the banks and hedgerows of Cornish lanes emphasizes the elegance and diversity that the cultivated species can also achieve,

and even surpass, in appropriate garden settings. Ferns and other pteridophytes add elements of perennial value to cultivated landscapes in several important ways:

- In terms of garden design, ferns can provide a green background to more gaudy flowering-plant brilliance, or a soft clothing to a hard-sculptured landscape. They have undoubted architectural qualities; the serial, lace-like delicacy of fronds combining with many crown shapes, from upright combs or arching shuttlecocks, to descending cascades. Young spring growth is diverse, surprising, and often spectacular; and when expanded, the form of the fronds contrasts, especially in tree-ferns, with bold and solid upright trunks. Almost all groups have many evergreen species, which add year-round interest. Larger ferns provide a further protective canopy for tender woodland ground cover and mosses, and are good subjects with which to fill a dark but sheltered corner.

A particularly fern-rich valley garden setting at Penjerrick, west Cornwall, in which tree-ferns – *Dicksonia antarctica* – mix with an undergrowth of mainly native species. The similarity of this scene to a wild temperate rain forest is impressive.

- Set within shielding vegetation in dappled shade, beside a clear-flowing stream, a grove of ferns creates a special verdure, embodying a sense of the exotic, relaxation, and romance. Historically, such images were well known, and ferns were linked to the renewal of life. Today, the combination of crowns of delicately arching fronds, and shafts of morning light etching a delicate tracery of dewy fronds, continues to add a measure of beauty and implied purity, mystery and mystique to a garden scene, in a thousand shades of green. (This is an image beloved of commercial advertisers, who use fern fronds on many cosmetic products to imply purity, mystique, and perhaps secret hidden powers of delicate rejuvenation!)
- Ferns are primeval plants, giving a vivid, living reflection of ancient forests. Their presence in a garden, together with clubmosses and horsetails, can provide unusual botanical elements, with a degree of primitiveness and timelessness. In appropriately sited gardens, with mild, moist climates, such as those of the sheltered ravines and valleys of south-western England, the larger species of ferns evoke the luxuriance of the tropics.

Dryopteris affinis – a native species which thrives especially in south-west England, showing characteristic gold-coloured fronds in a lane-bank habitat in early summer.

We still have much to learn about the ecology of ferns in the wild. Direct observations made in their native habitats provide fundamental information. But much additional knowledge can be gained from the careful observation of the same plants in cultivation, especially when reared through their life cycles from spores.

There is a wide array of species and forms of ferns from which to sample. Our knowledge of the totality of the species appropriate to cultivation in almost any climate is incomplete, but there is every reason to believe that a considerable array of little-tried species will thrive in the mild, moist climate of south-west England, and in Cornwall in particular. There are real opportunities for exploration in experimenting with new introductions, their hardiness, and appropriate habitats in cultivation.

Here I have presented possible choices of ferns by habitat and type, starting with those most suited to the beginner, and working towards those that are more for the specialist:

- ferns for average garden soils
- marsh and waterside ferns
- tree-ferns
- epiphytic ferns
- filmy ferns
- terrestrial colony-forming ferns
- ferns of rocks, walls, and other dry habitats
- clubmosses
- horsetails
- ferns of the future.

I hope that this chapter reveals something of their diversity and form, and echoes something of their general beauty.

Thus, the disciplines of science and horticulture come together in the study of ferns, and the value of recording and exchanging information with other fern-growers and garden-owners can make fern culture exciting, and the exchange of that information inspiring. Ferns offer several features of distinction and interest in their own right. Together, these are aspects that make the growing of ferns dynamic, and spiritually, horticulturally, and scientifically rewarding.

Ferns for average garden soils

A useful range of basic ferns, particularly for beginners, comprises those that grow readily, with a litttle shade, shelter, and moisture, in ordinary garden soils. For the most part they are denizens of the temperate forest zones, especially the North Temperate. Such ferns are popular in cultivation because of their general garden usefulness, characterized by the proven hardiness and cultural requirements of the species most widely available; their adaptability to many garden settings; the diversity of form they collectively represent, and their convenient size: most vary from plants the size of a primula to that of a small shrub.

Almost all are long-lived, reliable in cultivation, and need little attention once established. Most are also relatively simple to propagate from spores, and with a little experience can be propagated this way by the hundred.

The species most widely available belong to a range of genera, most of which have several (some many) species, although usually only a few that are easily available commercially. A selection of more commonly available genera for ordinary garden soils, which are worthy of cultivation, includes *Athyrium, Phyllitis, Gymnocarpium, Thelypteris, Pteris, Dryopteris, Lastreopsis, Polystichum,* and *Cyrtomium.* Of some of the species of these – for example, *Athyrium, Phyllitis, Dryopteris,* and *Polystichum* – there are also numerous cultivated 'varieties', or cultivars, with variously crisped, forked, and otherwise anomalous fronds. Most of of these selections are Victorian in origin. These clearly have a place, especially in association with gardens that reflect such a historic period in horticulture.

Top: *Phyllitis scolopendrium,* and below: *Polystichum setiferum,* showing croziers in spring. Both are native species which thrive especially in south-west England.

Adiantum pedatum – from western North America: detail of frond in cultivation, Halgarrick, Cornwall.

Polysticum polyblepharum – from southern Japan – thriving in a Cornish garden: detail of fronds in spring.

Dryopteris crispiifolia – from the Azores – thriving in a Cornish garden: detail of croziers in spring.

Among the hardiest, the overall group includes several large native species of attractive visual appeal, such as the Male fern (*Dryopteris filix-mas*); the Lady fern (*Athyrium filix-femina*); the Soft shield fern (*Polystichum setiferum*), and the Hard fern (*Blechnum spicant*). Also likely to be hardy in the southwest, but needing much experimentation with cultivation from spores, are the very numerous species of the same genera from the Far East, the Americas and, where appropriate, the Southern hemisphere. Additionally, the genera *Pteris*, *Adiantum*, *Lastreopsis*, and *Cyrtomium* all have many species, varying from half-hardy at present to already just hardy in many Cornish gardens. Other genera, as yet more seldom cultivated, but which are potentially valuable in the garden, and thus worthy of future experiment, include *Phegopteris*, *Ampelopteris*, *Christella*, *Onychium*, *Diplazium*, *Arachnioides*, *Aspidotis*, *Pellaea*, *Ctenitis*, and *Doodia*. Both as genera and species, there are many more ferns, especially in the warmer margins of the temperate zones, which have been little tried, but for which there is much potential.

Of these genera, species of known hardiness in the Cornish climate (though less so elsewhere) include: *Polystichum polyblepharum*, with glossy fronds and spectacularly curled, scale-clad croziers in spring; *P. rigens*, with glossy, serrated pinnae; *P. munitum*, with near-upright, narrow, simply pinnate, ladder-like fronds; *P. braunii*, with soft foliage; *Dryopteris erythrosora*, with copper-pink-tinged young fronds; *D. sieboldii*, with coarsely lobed fronds; *D. crispiifolia*, with crinkled fronds (from the Azores); *Cyrtomium fortunei*; *C. falcatum*, and *C. caryotidium*, all with large pinnae with dentate margins resembling holly leaves, and between which there are differing views as to the hardiest species; *Athyrium nipponicum* 'pictum', with finely cut, pale purple fronds, which are delicately variegated; *Adiantum venustum*, with finely cut maidenhair foliage; *Pteris cretica*; *P. multifida*, and several allied species, with spreading, narrow, finger-like bright green or dark green pinnae; *Lastreopsis* species, such as *L. hispida*, with very finely divided, stiff, sharply triangular blades; and *Blechnum penna-marina*, forming multiple low, compact, dark green rosettes.

A semi-natural pondside planting in a valley garden at Penjerrick, west Cornwall, where many natural and exotic ferns blend to add well to the luxuriance of the planting.

Even though I have described these as species for ordinary garden soils, which are hence ferns particularly suited to the beginner, this does not mean that there is not considerable room for experimentation. For example, the genus *Polystichum* is particularly attractive and diverse in form, and there are over 180 species world-wide – the majority temperate. Many more could be tried.

Marsh and waterside ferns

Marsh and waterside ferns are undoubtedly the second most widely cultivated group of ferns. They include plants with a considerable range of form, and species of occasional spectacular size and longevity. All those mentioned here are in some way associated with wet habitats, although like all ferns, they need good natural oxygenation of the roots, and hence require the water to be moving, and never still or stagnant. The sides of streams, and gently sloping bog gardens with some water movement constantly by the roots are ideal locations.

Croziers of *Osmunda regalis* in cultivation in a Cornish garden, showing their characteristic covering of spring down.

A selection of genera worthy of cultivation includes: *Osmunda; Todea; Adiantum; Onoclea; Matteuccia; Cystopteris; Blechnum; Woodwardia; Thelypteris; Pneumatopteris; Marsilea; Azolla* (free-floating on water surfaces), and *Isoetes* (submerged aquatics). As with the ferns of ordinary garden soils, these genera have between them a number of species in the wild, with differing degrees of hardiness, several of which have been little tried.

Osmunda is usually represented in cultivation by *O. regalis* (Royal fern), some individuals of which are of considerable size and age (perhaps a century or more). Plants thrive in moist, peaty soil beside streams, especially where spring-fed water passes by their roots. *Osmunda regalis* is noted for its large oval pinnules, which repel water droplets like the proverbial duck's back. There are several cultivated selections with reddish or purple foliage, the best of these colours being especially apparent during frond expansion stages in spring.

Closely related, though more rarely grown, is the Japanese *Osmunda japonica*, while *O. cinnamomea* and *O. claytoniana*, from the swamps of eastern North America, add substantial variations in frond form. *Todea* is the Southern hemisphere equivalent genus. It has bipinnate, leathery, bright shiny green, more finely divided pinnules, with serrate margins, and globular sori massed on to the lower or middle pinnae of the frond. In the wild (Australia), it is an equally large plant of similar streamside habitats, of which there must be provenances of suitable hardiness for cultivation in south-west England. Both *Osmunda* and *Todea* have fronds which, in older specimens, reach 1–2m or more in length. The plants eventually form clumps, with massive, fibrous trunks, and such aged individuals can be particularly spectacular.

Onoclea (Sensitive fern, photo page 186), *Matteuccia* (Ostrich fern), and *Thelypteris* (Marsh fern) are genera that contain species from moist streambanks. Their deciduous-fronded species can gradually build up large colonies. Plants of *Onoclea* have separate, fertile fronds, which remain standing through winter. Fronds of *Thelypteris* species are delicate and deciduous, with mostly simply pinnate, upright fronds arising from slender, surface-creeping rhizomes, which characteristically twine among other marsh-loving vegetation. Plants of

Todea barbara, from Australia: detail of fronds in cultivation, summer.

Matteuccia struthiopteris, from North America: detail of fronds in cultivation, spring.

Blechnum capense thrives in many Cornish gardens, often forming patches with shoulder-high fronds.

Blechnum magellanicum: tree-fern habit in temperate rain forest, southern Chile.

Matteuccia have many separate groups of fronds that emerge as beautiful, shuttlecock-like groups of bright green unfurling foliage in spring.

Blechnum (Hard ferns and Deer ferns) and *Woodwardia* (Chain ferns) are mostly evergreen-fronded ferns, and are typical of moist, acidic river-banks. Many *Blechnum* have spectacular, stiff, herringbone-like fronds arising in dense rosettes. The majority of species are half-hardy, although in some Cornish valley gardens there are several long-lived large colonies of spectacular growth, among which *Blechnum capense* forms locally extensive patches by streams. Nevertheless, many species await experimental introduction – especially those from the islands and peninsulas of the Southern hemisphere. Among species of *Blechnum* that are just hardy in the south-west, *B. discolor* is a particular favourite of mine. *Woodwardia* has much larger, arching fronds, which in some species root at the tip. The Canary Island *Woodwardia radicans* can be spectacular when well grown, with fronds reaching 2m or more in length. Although early-season fronds (produced from late February on) may become blackened by frosts, in Cornwall this species produces further fronds in a steadily timed succession, so that there are always some later ones that expand successfully to full size, and from the bud-tips of which new plants can be readily propagated. *Woodwardia unigemmata*, from the Far East, is considered by some to be hardier than *W. radicans*, *W. fimbriata*, *W. virginica*, and *W. areolata*, from eastern North America, especially Florida, are mostly smaller plants, and their overall habits are more creeping and climbing.

Adiantum includes a wide array of forms, of differing degrees of hardiness and size. Native *A. capillus-veneris* naturalizes on old greenhouse mortar-courses, where sufficiently damp, and crevices of waterside rocks, especially limestone. Beside flowing water, *A. venustum* builds clumps with masses of billowing foliage, while *A. pedatum* (with several subspecies of distinctive size and habit) thrives in the high humidity when planted overhanging running streams. Very many other overseas species exist in both hemispheres, especially in the Americas, and although many of these are truly tropical, others that have potential in our climate must also exist.

Woodwardia orientalis, from southern Japan: detail of foliage on expanding frond, spring, on Yakushima Island.

Adiantum capillus-veneris – a rare, native, maidenhair fern – often establishes on old, damp brickwork in milder parts of the south-west.

Adiantum hispidulum, from Australia: detail of fronds in cultivation, Halgarrick, Cornwall.

Polystichum, *Diplazium*, *Cystopteris*, *Asplenium*, and *Bolbitis* include several variously bulbiferous (gemmiferous) members, especially suited to high-humidity, moist rock-surface sites beside flowing, splashing stream-water. Many of the overseas species could well be candidates for future cultivation interest and diversity. Other possible candidate genera of ferns in this category include *Tectaria*, *Stenogramma*, *Cornopteris*, *Pellaea*, *Ctenitis*, *Depuria*, *Camptosorus*, *Lunathyrium*, and several species of *Lycopodium*; while numerous other species, especially of *Adiantum*, *Asplenium*, *Athyrium*, *Diplazium*, *Dryopteris*, *Blechnum*, *Polystichum*, *Thelypteris*, *Cyclosorus*, *Pneumatopteris*, *Cystopteris*, and *Pteris*, are worthy of careful and sensitive experimentation.

Marsilea is a genus of ferns of mainly wet, but well-lit marshy places, which has many tropical species and some temperate ones. A few of these

Azolla filiculoides – the red carpet floating on the water surface – in the wild: Murray River, eastern Australia.

might well be hardy enough in appropriate sites. *Azolla* is an unusual, minute, free-floating, fresh-water aquatic, which behaves rather like duckweed (*Lemna*). *Isoetes* form quill-like rosettes, and are submerged aquatics of clear, fresh-water pools. I am aware of only the *Azolla* being cultivated. These are minute, green plants, which have a moss-like texture, and often turn red-brown in autumn. If unchecked by removal (they make a good fertilizer), they can grow rapidly to cover a whole pond surface within a single season. A landowner in north Cornwall had a large, square pond covered in solid *Azolla* that gave it such a fine, level texture, through which no water could be seen, that a visiting landowner commented (without appreciating that there was still deep water beneath), 'I see you have turned your pond into a bowling-green'!

Tree-ferns

Tree-ferns are probably the most significant, robustly architectural, and widely appreciated group of cultivated ferns, of considerable popular appeal for the milder garden. In Cornwall, there is wide interest in ensuring the success of tree-ferns as cultivated plants, now and for the future. Genera worthy of cultivation are mainly *Dicksonia* and *Cyathea* (the latter of which has segregate genera, which are sometimes recognized – for example, *Alsophila* for the Australian *A. australis*, and New Zealand *A. colensoi*). Other large-fronded relatives that may have some hardy members include *Culcita*, and possibly some *Cibotium*.

There are two main families of tree-ferns: the Dicksoniaceae, to which *Dicksonia* belongs, and the Cyatheaceae, to which *Cyathea* and *Alsophila* belong. Dicksoniaceae are distinguished by having beard-like hairs around the frond bases, while Cyatheaceae have chaffy scales to the frond bases. Most species of Dicksoniaceae are also characterized by their stout, stocky trunks, while Cyatheaceae have more slender trunks, and (at least in the wild) are often taller.

All tree-ferns are slow-growing, but potentially long-lived, with a life-span of well over a century being likely for the large *Dicksonia* species, so they need careful and well-considered initial placement. All, of course, are demanding of moisture and adequate shelter, and always fare best when set within (indeed they demand) other, wind-shielding vegetation, ideally in a habitat of dappled shade. They can be challenging to grow if the environment is not initially correct, for if humidity levels are insufficient, and they are not adequately sheltered, fronds soon become shabby in appearance. But in the right environment, tree-ferns are the epitome of plant charm, delight, and grace, looking especially appropriate when set beside clear, flowing stream-water. So-set, tree-ferns make a strong statement in the landscape, where each must always be treated as an individual specimen, and multiple plantings should have each member set at least 3m apart, so that their frond-tips do not touch when mature.

Because tree-ferns are usually species of the tropics (and especially of tropical mountain flanks), most are still tender, or at best half-hardy, even by present Cornish standards. The numbers of species that are either truly hardy here, or even on the margins of hardiness are, in fact, very few,

Dicksonia antarctica in cultivation: detail of the spectacular croziers in spring, Gillywood, Cornwall.

although it would take only a modest rise in temperature to embrace a considerably greater species array.

The only proven truly hardy species is *Dicksonia antarctica* (Soft tree-fern). This species is Australian, and ranges from the mountains of southeast Queensland to Tasmania. Most of the early introductions to Cornish gardens were imported on ships arriving at Falmouth during the mid-nineteenth century, or earlier, and came as trunks said to have been used as ballast, which probably sprouted on the journey. The Fox family, who, among their gardens at the time, owned the valley gardens of Penjerrick, Glendurgan, and Trebah, and were closely associated with shipping and the import trade, were instrumental in these early introductions. Soon, plantings were made at other gardens too. Such information on origins as exists suggests that the sources for these trunks were the forests of the Blue Mountains, behind Sydney, within the central part of the extensive north–south eastern Australian range of this species. These introductions have performed well, achieving trunk diameters of up to 60cm, and

Dicksonia antarctica: self-sown young plants thriving
in a Cornish garden attest well to the climatic suitability
for this species.

Dicksonia antarctica: introductions originally from the
Blue Mountains, New South Wales, planted in the early
to mid-1800s, thrive in many Cornish gardens. These at
Penjerrick are some of the tallest I know.

trunk heights frequently of 6–9m. Indeed, there
are specimens in one Cornish ravine garden,
which I have climbed (to remove ivy) and measured trunk heights of nearly 14m, and which I
estimate to be some 200 years old. All of these
early-introduced tree-ferns now regularly self-
spore-set in and around many Cornish gardens,
especially where there are disturbed soils beside
paths and streams. In many cases, the sporelings
have been either left to grow or moved to better sites. They grow rapidly and successfully, and
have given rise to further Cornish home-grown
generations from these original New South Wales
specimens.

In addition to these early introductions and
their progeny, during the last decade of the twentieth century, a round of new arrivals as trunks
of *Dicksonia antarctica* was imported from the
mountains of Tasmania, hence from the southern end of the range of the species in the wild.
Coming from mountainous areas with relatively
low winter temperatures, the expectation is that
these introductions may prove hardier elsewhere

than those of the earlier sources. They have been
widely marketed as such. Only time will tell, but it
is perhaps significant that already, within a decade
of these introductions being planted, many are
showing considerable individual variation as well
as producing spore-bearing fronds. These newer
introductions will represent a wider genetic array
than the earlier ones, and this is already being
explored by a research programme in Cornwall.

Besides *Dicksonia antartica,* other tree-ferns
from both Australia and New Zealand have been
more occasionally introduced to England on a
more *ad hoc* basis. These include *D. squarrosa* and
D. fibrosa, both from New Zealand. At present,
all these seem to be on the very margins of current hardiness in west Cornwall gardens, but they
can succeed under cool glass. *Dicksonia fibrosa* has
a trunk up to 30cm thick, and thus approaches
D. antarctica in appearance. *Dicksonia squarrosa*
has a thin, but stiff, rather black, woody trunk,
at most up to 10cm diameter and 3.5–5.5m high,

with a light crown of bright green fronds whose rachis has long, dark hairs standing out rigidly and perpendicularly, like the proverbial cartoon of a frightened cat!

There are also some six or seven species of *Cyathea* and *Alsophila* from Australia and New Zealand, which come into the category of marginal hardiness in present Cornish gardens. All of these should be winter-protected, for instance by straw on the crowns, and, ideally, wrapping the trunks with straw. These include the species *rebeccae*, *australis*, *cunninghamii*, *leichardtiana*, *cooperi*, *dealbata*, and *medullaris*. Based on their wild ecology and locations, the first is probably the least hardy, while the remainder should be varyingly more so, each depending on source. Most have more slender trunks than *Dicksonia*, but make more rapid upward growth under ideal conditions. All differ in details of frond form, scaliness, and colour of trunk and frond. Perhaps the most unusually coloured are *C. medullaris* and *C. dealbata*: the former has black trunks and green fronds; the latter

has a buff trunk with fronds that are bright green above, but distinctly white to bright silver-grey beneath. There are also very many more species (especially of *Cyathea* and its close allies) on many tropical mountains, in both Asia and the Americas. Many of these have yet to be successfully introduced to England, and their provenances experimented with for the purposes of cultivation. As with the New Zealand *Dicksonia*, all can also be considered, initially at least, as candidates for growing under cool glass in a large tub.

In all tree-ferns with rough trunk surfaces – especially *Dicksonia* – old dead fronds that accumulate below the crown *must be left on the plant*, as these are an important frost protection as well as a natural defence against invasion of the crown by climbers (for example, ivy) and large epiphytes. Additionally, in periods of dry weather, trunks should be hosed regularly with fresh water, as the trunks themselves contain many tiny roots. Therefore, all moss growth should be left on, but ivy should be removed.

Typical crowns of the tree-fern genus *Cyathea* are characteristic of cool, mist-shrouded mountainsides of the tropics, sometimes at considerable elevations. These are in the mountains of New Caledonia.

Epiphytic ferns

Epiphytic ferns form a botanically diverse group, with very many species. Almost all are natives of warm temperate to tropical latitudes, including many tropical mountains, hence the majority of their species are most likely to be reliable only in cultivation in cool, or even warm, glasshouse conditions. Much careful and patient experimentation is needed to establish which species can be established in favourable outdoor sites.

A selection of cultivation-worthy genera of epiphytic ferns that includes at least some hardy or marginally hardy members comprises *Polypodium*, *Phymatodes*, *Phymatosorus*, *Rumohra*, *Microsorium*, *Pyrrosia*, *Davallia*, and *Humata*. Of these, *Polypodium* is undoubtedly the most widespread temperate genus, of which only a few species are seen normally in cultivation. It also has three native British species. All species have thickly scale-clad, creeping rhizomes, from which coarsely pinnately lobed evergreen fronds arise. As with the native species, plants are sometimes true epiphytes, and sometimes grow on rocks and (often) on hedge-

Davallia canariensis, from the Canary Islands, as an epiphyte in the wild.

bank-tops. Both lime-loving and lime-avoiding species are involved. Knowledge of the conditions to which the particular species are suited in the wild can thus be particularly useful in adapting sites in cultivation to appropriate suitability. *Phymatodes* and *Microsorium* have simple to coarsely pinnate fronds, and are somewhat similar in form to *Polypodium*, though often larger. By contrast, most *Pyrrosia* have slender, creeping rhizomes, and boat-shaped, simple or lobed, sometimes fleshy fronds. Of these, *Phymatosorus diversifolia* is a particular favourite of mine.

Davallia and *Humata* are widespread, especially in Asia and the Australasia–Pacific regions, where there are many species. Because most of these are in milder climates than are most *Polypodium*, fewer are likely to be hardy, although again experimentation is needed. However, they are beautiful plants, with similar scale-clad, creeping rhizomes to *Polypodium*, but with triangular fronds often finely divided into numerous small segments, giving an overall more lace-like appearance. Most are true epiphytes, spreading along the tops of branches of rough-barked trees in the wild, especially in mossy layers where branches overhang streams. Remarkably few of the overseas species of each of these genera seem to have been much tried in cultivation.

Other epiphytic genera with numerous species in the wild, spanning temperate to tropical (and especially tropical montane) regions, which could thus provide suitable species for introducing to cultivation, include at least *Grammitis*, *Lepisorus*, *Lemmaphyllum*, *Drymoglossum*, *Xiphopteris*, *Arthropteris*, *Rumohra*, some *Asplenium*, *Vittaria*, and *Elaphoglossum*. This list is by no means exhaustive, and other epiphytic ferns await successful introduction and cultivation experimentation. Additionally, of more unusual epiphytic pteridophytes, *Tmesipteris* and *Psilotum* could prove hardy in sheltered locations in Cornwall, the former especially as an epiphyte of trunks of *Dicksonia* tree-ferns, on which it usually grows in the wild, together with filmy ferns, and all of which I have seen arrive on recently imported trunks.

Also to be considered here is the small group of ferns most correctly bracketed as climbing ferns, the fronds of which twine among other vegetation, but which remain ground-rooted at their bases. The most widespread genus of this category is *Lygodium*. It has species in both the

Old and New Worlds, most of which are tropical–subtropical, but some of which occur in relatively high latitudes of both hemispheres. There are also climbing species of *Blechnum* – for example, *B. filiforme* – and the genus *Stenochlaena*. I am not aware of any attempt to introduce any of these outside glasshouses at botanic gardens, but there is certainly potential for experimentation in south-west England.

Filmy ferns

The term 'filmy ferns' refers to the unique feature of these ferns, which is their very thin, membrane-like blade surfaces to the fronds. These are only a single cell in thickness, and thus translucent. The fronds themselves are typically small and delicate, seldom more than a few centimetres long. Clearly such fronds can dry out very easily, and in the wild these ferns are usually confined to either epiphytic or rock-surface sites, either close to streams (especially on rocks or on the boles of trees among mosses), in the spray-zones of waterfalls, or on the branches of trees in cloud forest on tropical mountains.

Hymenophyllum wilsonii: a wild specimen showing the characteristically pellucid fronds of the filmy ferns.

The two main filmy fern genera are *Hymenophyllum* and *Trichomanes*. There are very numerous species of these and related genera throughout the world's wet temperate and tropical rain forests, and some of these, especially from high latitudes and tropical mountains may well prove hardy in cultivation under conditions of careful and sensitive site management. In cultivation virtually all would need similar conditions to those of the wild, in which shade and moisture are constant, and where climates are especially mild. In at least one Cornish garden, I have seen a New Zealand species successfully established around a shallow cave-mouth over which flows a waterfall. Such are clearly ideal sites, and these are unusual and attractive ferns with which much more experimentation is needed, in gardens fortunately endowed with such streamside habitats.

Terrestrial colony-forming ferns

The terrestrial colony-forming ferns have been little used in cultivation. As the heading implies, all are species usually with underground, creeping rhizomes, giving them a tendency to spread, although for most species this is neither excessive nor too rapid. Any tendency to spread may be perceived as a disadvantage in a small garden, but there are many places, especially in larger estate-planting and in more semi-natural garden schemes, where drifts of fronds from a single fern species can offer a worthwhile cultivated purpose.

In the wild, most of these species are forest-margin plants, or species of open, drier forests, thriving in semi-shade, and usually in deep, sandy, well-drained soils. Even in the wild, the majority form relatively small patches, and for most, problems with excessive growth seem unlikely. Similar conditions in cultivation can be anticipated to most likely suit the majority of species.

A selection of genera potentially worthy of cultivation includes: *Culcita*, *Dennstaedtia*, *Microlepia*, *Hypolepis*, *Paesia*, *Histiopteris*, *Lastreopsis*, *Lonchitis*, *Arachnioides*, *Gleichenia*, *Gymnocarpium*, *Phegopteris*, and some *Blechnum*. Although many of the species are relatively tender in present British conditions, there remains enormous scope for cautious experimentation in cultivation. Of these, *Paesia scaberula* is a particular favourite of mine.

Gymnocarpium dryopteris forms attractive ground cover beneath rhododendrons in cultivation.

The temperate rain forest epiphytic habitat of *Selaginella oregana*, with many lichens and mosses, in the Olympic Peninsula, Washington State, USA.

Ferns of rocks, walls, and other dry habitats

It is perhaps little appreciated that world-wide (especially in Mediterranean climates) there are considerable numbers of ferns that grow in dry, rocky habitats, which are technically called rupestral or saxicolous species. Most grow in dry, sunny sites that have one or more dry periods annually. In structure, many have fronds partly clad in scales or hairs. Many have curious frond forms, and some are farinose (with powdery coverings). In terms of temperature tolerance, many experience cold nights in the wild, and so at least some of these might well be suitable for cultivation. The problem in cultivation, especially in Cornwall, is likely to be keeping them dry enough (especially in winter), since under mild, wet conditions, the scales and hairs readily trap water, and such plants are consequently prone to rot.

A selection of potentially cultivation-worthy genera of true dry-zone ferns includes: *Actiniop-teris*, *Cheilanthes*, *Notholaena*, *Pityrogramma*, *Paraceterach*, *Gymnopteris*, and *Ceterach*. Many of these genera contain a range of species. All are particularly suitable for growing in lightly summer-shaded, cool glasshouse conditions, where the glass allows their moisture to be controlled, and especially to keep these plants winter-dry – more akin to conditions for cultivation of alpines. Under such conditions, these dry-zone ferns can be very attractive and rewarding to grow. At least one dedicated pteridologist in Cornwall grows a successful range of species from these habitats, giving them daily attention on domestic window-sills.

In various parts of the world, many other ferns grow in habitats that fall between those of dry-zone ferns and those of either epiphytic or ordinary garden-soil ferns. Some are species of mature rock screes. These include genera such as *Anogramma*, *Anemia*, *Lindsaya*, *Sphenomeris*; some *Elaphoglossum*; *Crypsinus*; *Cryptogramma*; *Doryopteris*; some *Adiantum*; some *Pellaea*; *Pteris*, *Drynaria*; *Pyr-*

rosia; *Pleopeltis*; *Rumohra*; many *Asplenium*; *Camptosorus*; *Doodia*, and some *Selaginella*. Many of these may fare better in our climate than the true dry-zone ferns. There is clearly very considerable scope for experimentation with members of these genera under conditions of cultivation in outdoor sites, perhaps protected from the excesses of winter rain.

Clubmosses

Of the very many clubmosses, cultivation-worthy species are mainly confined to the genera *Selaginella* and *Lycopodium*, in the broad sense (sometimes *Lycopodium* is split into many segregate genera).

Of *Selaginella*, for example, there are some 700+ species in the wild, many of which are often of low, rather moss-like growth. In the wild, most are forest-floor species that spread freely to become semi-epiphytic on fallen trunks and damp boulders, or spread freely over rocks, especially in ravines and by waterfalls. *Selaginella kraussiana* is the most widely cultivated, often establishing freely under greenhouse staging, and sometimes escaping outside in sheltered spots. *Selaginella denticulate* – of rather similar appearance – may join it in similar habitats. Additionally, I have grown the epiphytic *S. oregana* for many years in shady conditions behind a north wall. All require shelter, moderate shade, and especially high humidity to thrive.

Many *Selaginella* species are sold today as (usually unnamed) bottle-garden subjects. These might well be adapted to more external, high-humidity cultivation, especially among rocks by streams in gullies and woodlands. They can be rapidly propagated vegetatively for careful experimentation in gardens with such suitable habitat niches.

A few *Lycopodium* are epiphytic in the tropics, though more temperate members are mostly terrestrial. Most also require high humidity. There seems very little experience of cultivation of most *Lycopodium* and related genera outside botanic gardens, and much horticultural research is yet to be undertaken.

Horsetails

The horsetails, with upright, articulated shoots, are surprisingly little used in cultivation in Britain, beyond specialist collections, although several species could have useful roles to play. Cultivation-worthy species are confined to *Equisetum*, the sole genus, which has two subgenera: subgenus *Equisetum* – the deciduous-shooted species – and subgenus *Hippochaete* – the mainly evergreen-shooted species. Species of both subgenera can be cultivated with equal facility, and the majority are hardy. All have subterranean – sometimes very deep – creeping, slender rhizomes, and avid escapism is a particular feature of almost all species – especially those of the subgenus *Equisetum*.

However, all contribute much to an appropriate garden sitc, when allowed to make bold planting features, for which they are both botanically and architecturally most especially suited. In such situations, the upright form of horsetails, with regular, verticillate, slender branches in perfect whorls, adds strong architectural characteristics. Most horsetails are thus potentially useful in the right place by water, and can be valuable in semi-natural settings, where their tendency to spread is less likely to cause a problem. Alternatively, they adapt well to cultivation in containers, which enables individual species to have appropriate water regimes, and hence to thrive well in the places in which they are most specifically required. Most thrive best in heavy soils.

In recent years, several species have begun to be offered as waterside plants from aquatic plant centres. Those most usually available through this route are *Equisetum fluviatile* (Water horsetail); *E. hyemale* (Dutch rush); *E. variegatum* (Variegated horsetail), and *E. scirpoides* (Arctic horsetail). Others are available mainly from specialist growers.

The spectacular architecture of horsetails is a feature used to great effect in many Japanese gardens, where *E. hyemale* (Dutch rush) in particular is often grown. For sheer beauty, my all-time favourite pteridophyte is a horsetail – *E. telmateia* (Great horsetail), with ivory-white, fleshy main-stem internodes, and immaculately verticillate whorls of bright green, slender, regimentedly ascending branches. *Equisetum sylvaticum*, with gracefully drooping, branches provides a further contrast of form, its shoots looking like miniature pine trees. I (and other specialists) have successfully cultivated these, and many other species, for very many years. Many hybrids are now known, especially among the deciduous-shooted species. All are of intermediate form, between parent species, and make additional subjects of specialist interest.

Equisetum sylvaticum thrives beside running water.

Equisetum telmateia: cones produced in April in the wild can also arise in cultivation in well-established colonies.

Ferns and the future

The above account shows something of the great diversity of form and habitat that are represented by ferns and their relatives, even of those already in cultivation, and which may inspire these and other species to be introduced.

The future of ferns and allied plants as outdoor subjects

Of the 12,000 or more species of ferns world-wide, there must still be hundreds of ferns that have yet to be tried in our climate. For many of those that have been tried, very little selection has been made to deliberately gain the hardiest, or even the most appropriate provenances. Already, the south-west of England has the opportunity, because of wetness and mildness, to grow a substantial number of species that would be less reliable or not possible elsewhere. Under conditions of likely future climatic amelioration, and particularly with milder, wetter winters, the south-west of England is likely to be at the forefront of any such change.

Among other parts of the world having a diversity of species of ferns and allied plants that might well prove hardy in our climate now or in future, are such potential sources as the vast Sino-Himalayan region; Japan and Taiwan; many tropical montane areas of both New and Old Worlds, including the Andes and high-altitude New Guinea, Australia, Tasmania and New Zealand, and the more southerly latitudes of the South American continent; and habitats of distant oceanic islands. There are clearly considerable opportunities for diligent and sensitive experimentation with ferns for future horticultural appropriateness in Cornwall, and in other similar regions.

The future of ferns and allied plants as cool glasshouse and conservatory subjects

It seems fitting to end this account by commending genera for glasshouse cultivation, for these can add very considerably to the diversity and interest of species and form that can be cultivated.

Ferns are highly appropriate to growing in shaded and humid glasshouse and conservatory conditions. Indeed, it was the interest in cultivating exotic plants in Victorian times – especially ferns – that spawned experiments with glass constructions, which led directly to the great Crystal Palace of 1851, and to the glasshouses and conservatories of today. With interest in domestic-scale conservatories developing again in the twenty-first century, more exotic ferns are beginning to be offered for 'indoor' cultivation by many garden centres – as are conservatories of all shapes and styles (and methods of shading) suitable for housing them. What could better complement these structures than a selection of highly architectural ferns, as horticultural furnishings both inside and out, with which the Victorians themselves would have adorned them?

In the south-west of England, and 'on the edge', we are fortunate because suitable glasshouses can mean either cool glass shade, with little additional heating, or glass which is kept a little warmer (say with a minimum of 7–10°C in winter). We can thus provide a buffer against occasional winter cold, enabling an especially wide array of species to thrive.

Terrestrially-rooting, cultivation-worthy glasshouse and conservatory genera include: *Marattia; Angiopteris; Leptopteris; Lygodium; Anemia; Pellaea; Doryopteris; Hemionitis; Gymnopteris;* more tropical species of *Adiantum*; *Pteris*; *Thyrsopteris*; *Cibotium*; *Macrothelypteris*; *Matteucia*; *Tectaria*; *Quercifilix*; *Didymochlaena*; *Bolbitis*; *Leucostegia*; *Doodia*; *Sadleria*, and *Stenochlaena*. Additionally, as warm-water aquatics are: *Ceratopteris*; *Marsilea*; *Regnellidium*; some *Microsorium*, and *Salvinia*. *Acrostichum* is an unusual saltwater-tolerant genus. Mainly epiphytic genera are: *Vittaria*; *Pyrrosia*; *Drynaria*; *Merinthosorus*; *Aglaomorpha*; *Platycerium*; other species of *Pyrrosia*; *Drymoglossum*; *Microsorium*; *Selliguea*; *Pleopeltis*; *Microgramma*; *Lemmaphyllum*; *Belvisia*; *Dictymia*; *Phymatodes*; *Phlebodium*; more tropical species of *Polypodium*; *Goniophlebium*; some *Asplenium* (for example, *A. nidus* group; *A. antiquum*); *Elaphoglossum*; *Humata*; *Scyphularia*; *Davallia*; *Rumohra*; *Oleandra*, and *Nephrolepis*. Of these, collectively, there are hundreds of species.

Clearly, with such an array of genera, there are gaps in our knowledge of which species are already adequately hardy. However, it is evident that, in the event of even modest climatic warming, species of today's cool glasshouse may well become tomorrow's outdoor subjects, growing 'on the edge'.

Sources of further information and materials

There is a vast array of fern species with potential for cultivation. This chapter has concentrated on a synopsis mainly at generic level, because I feel that the diversity of ferns, even at this level, is seldom fully appreciated. Further details and descriptions of many of the genera and their species may be found in some of the books listed in Further Reading, and in the many countries' floras.

While encouraging experimentation with fern cultivation, it is *vital* to stress adherence to sensible restrictions. No wild ferns should be dug up, either at home or abroad: indeed it is illegal to do so in many counties. The movement and importation of plants with attached soil is also illegal, as it can introduce unwanted parasites, insect eggs, and soil-borne diseases.

However (and fortunately), it is easy to collect ferns in the wild as dry spores, and to put them into envelopes, labelled with source, habitat, and species. The collection and movement of spores internationally is not restricted, and (with a few exceptions), most travel well and remain viable for a long time. Spores are easy and light to trans-

One of my favourite ferns: the New Zealand *Blechnum discolor* 'Fishbone Water-fern' in cultivation in west Cornwall.

port; do not harbour disease, and can be posted or carried safely and legally. They can be collected non-destructively from the wild population, and can be rapidly propagated at home to give new young plants in large numbers – which is especially desirable if sensible experimentation with a range of horticultural conditions is to be tried.

Interest in ferns, from both horticultural and scientific points of view – including their rearing and cultivation; identification; nomenclature, and taxonomy – is promoted by the British Pteridological Society, which holds regular meetings about ferns; issues an annual spore-exchange list to members, and can supply various works that include details of spore-growing and fern culture.

In Britain, and in Cornwall in particular, we are extremely fortunate to have a climate especially appropriate to experimentation with cultivation of a great many possible fern species from many parts of the world. In doing so, we are continuing a tradition begun by the Victorians, and are thus both reviving and taking forward some of the best aspects of experimentation and building on our heritage of Victorian culture.

10 Some Uncommon, Untried, or Tender Plants

Rob Senior

To the 'experimental, venturesome gardeners' whom W. Arnold-Forster addressed in *Shrubs for the Milder Counties* (1948), the last chapter in his book – 'Uncommon, Untried, or Tender Shrubs' – is the most stimulating. Over 250 plants are named. Many are now firmly in cultivation – *Colquhounia coccinea*, and some *Correa* and *Echium* species; others remain ephemeral – *Entelea arborescens*, some *Boronia* and *Melaleuca* species. Another sizeable group is at best rarely cultivated, or not outdoors – *Jacaranda mimosifolia*; genus *Aotus* (around 15 species – even Elliot and Jones' *Encyclopaedia of Australian Plants* [1981] states that, 'Little is known about cultivation as only one species *A. ericoides* has been grown to any extent'), and *Carrierea calycina*. The latter was noted in *Plantae Wilsonianae* (Sargent, 1913) as 'this handsome tree', and so it is at Abbotsbury, if only 1.5m tall currently, with long, dark green, red-petioled leaves. In 1930, Edgar Thurston recorded it in *British and Foreign Trees and Shrubs in Cornwall* as having reached '25 feet high at Lanarth'.

Left: *Puya alpestris*. (See pages 226–7.)

Fifty years on, we can name 2,500 plants in such a chapter. We do not have the professional, dedicated plant hunters of 75–150 years ago, living, working, and dying in appalling conditions, but gardeners of a new millennium are overwhelmed by choice of plants. Sources are legion. Intrepid amateurs travel and introduce new species: two such currently garden near Truro, Cornwall. Professionals still brave remote areas to collect seed, such as the husband and wife team active in western South America, and the family collecting for their South African seed firm, especially in the high Drakensberg. National media figures explore and write about India and south-east Asia, returning with valuable plant material. Several British nurserymen supplement interest and business by collecting in many areas. We are indeed fortunate.

Some of the 'new' plants have appeared in previous chapters. This chapter concentrates on a tiny, eclectic fraction from other assorted groups, not mentioned by Arnold-Forster, which should be tried by those 'gardening on the edge'.

Oceania

To begin as far away as possible from Cornwall. Landfall is, on Antipodes Island, at 50°S and near longitude 180° – one of New Zealand's sub-Antarctic islands. It is a harsher climate than southwest Britain, with rain or snow on 300 days a year (*c.*1,450mm precipitation); average sunshine less than two hours daily, and very windy. The bleak landscape over 60sq km supports around 60 species, which are low and 'grassy'. The one endemic, *Senecio antipodus,* sounds interesting, but is a short-lived biennial at best.

Further north-east are the Chatham Islands, home of the famed *Myosotidium hortensia,* apparently grazed to near extinction in the wild. Another native is the beautiful *Senecio huntii,* a shrub or tree up to 6m high, from Pitt Island. It is always elegant, the downy young leaves becoming glossy pale green, and up to 8cm long. It is particularly striking when covered in terminal panicles of golden-yellow flowers.

The Nikau palm (see page 101) has an outpost here – a so-called hardier form named *Rhopalostylis sapida 'oceania'* – though whether it is hardier than the plants of the sunless valleys of extreme South Island is questionable. *Hortus Third* (Bailey, 1976) gives *R. sapida* Zone 10a, with allied species *R. baueri* and *R. cheesmanii* Zone 9B. However, *R. sapida,* given its preferred sunless, shaded (canopied) position, copes with screen temperature of -3°C.

Still further north, Poor Knights Island supplies *Xeronema callistemon.* The major support of the plants celebrated here is the proximity of an equable sea. This lovely member of Liliaceae is best treated as an orchid, with nutrient-poor, well-drained compost; protection from frost, and a bright, but not overly sunny position. The reward is horizontal spikes of glowing red stamens, amidst glossy, irid leaves. It is suggested that dilute seaweed extract feeds help in culture, but that glasshouse treatment reduces its chance of success.

New Zealand

Climatologists tell us that global warming may mean marginally hotter summers for Britain, with wetter, windier, and milder winters. This sounds ideal for New Zealand plants – *Cordyline, Metrosideros,* and *Panax.* Others warn that melting of the polar ice could lead to the cessation of the North Atlantic drift, when Britain would develop a Labrador-like climate, rendering this and other books of historical interest!

Metrosideros robustus.

Of the cordylines, there are now several species and fascinating cultivars. A favourite is *Cordyline pumilio.* Edgar Moore's *The Flora of New Zealand* (1976) lists just five native species – *C. australis, C. banksii, C. indivisa, C. kaspar,* and *C. pumilio* – but acknowledges many ill-understood names and hybrids. Some refer to *C. pumilio* as stemless; others accept the 0.6–1.2m stems found in early introductions from New Zealand nurserymen Duncan

Cordyline pumilio.

Hibbertia aspera.

and Davies. From the same source, *C. kirkii* (nom. nud.) does not make a stem and flowers, as does young *C. pumilio*, in a sessile state. Though native to North Island, north of latitude 38°, in experience it is hardier than *C. australis*, although some of the purple-red foliage forms of this latter species can be seen well established in the windy, cold

Cordyline indivisa.

gardens of inland Durham and Northumbria. The freely produced, off-white flowers have a pervasive, sweet perfume.

Also a North Islander, *Senecio kirkii* grew some years ago as an epiphyte on *Phoenix canariensis* on Tresco, Isles of Scilly. When terrestrial, it can reach 30m, but, as an epiphyte, stems are shorter, with large, fleshy leaves and sparse, but large flowers, with long white ligules of 2.5cm.

Panax and allied genera of the Araliaceae were not mentioned by Arnold-Forster. Two outstanding species now established are *Pseudopanax crassifolia* and *P. ferox*. The latter, at 5m, makes a small tree only one-third the height of the former. At

maturity they are both round-headed, with leathery, varied-shaped leaves. In the juvenile state they are dramatic, with deflexed, rigid 1m leaves, 0.5–1cm wide, sage-green to brown, with raised orange midribs. Additionally, the leaves of *P. ferox* are hooked at thorned edges.

Australia

Australia offers a much larger, even bewildering flora. We look mainly to the cool, warm temperate, and Mediterranean zones as plant sources; and the south-east and south-west of the continent, plus Tasmania, provide hundreds of subjects. Acacias and eucalyptus species are well known, but new species and genera become available yearly. *Hibbertia aspera* is an example of the green and gold of 'Oz' at its most powerful. Growing against a low stone wall at Coleton Fishacre, Devon, its nearly orbicular 0.5–1cm leaves, on reddish-brown, rough (hence 'aspera') stems, are sufficiently attractive, but when liberally spangled with 1cm, bright yellow 'buttercups', it is beautiful. If anything, the scrambling bush can be too exuberant, needing careful thinning and training once or twice a year. Stems can layer, and young, firm shoots will strike as cuttings.

Well over 100 'Guinea Flowers' occur in Australia – 30 species in Victoria alone – and, as common with Gondwanaland remnants, a few species occur in New Guinea, Fiji, and Madagascar. More should be tried: *Hibbertia fascicularis*, *H. linearis*, and *H. procumbens*, for example. *Hibbertia fascicularis*, though a coastal plant, ascends to altitudes of 900m in Tasmania. From the same source, *H. procumbens* grows between sea level and 1,200m.

The Dilleniaceae has four genera in Australia – *Dillenia*, *Hibbertia*, *Pachynema*, and *Tetracera* – and, in general, it has tropical or subtropical species, but *Hibbertia* provides some exceptions.

Also Tasmanian is one of the superb *Dianella* species. There are around 25 *Dianellas*, mostly with mid-green, iris-like leaves, though there are striking variegated leaf forms. As with others of the genus, widespread from East Africa and Madagascar to China, Australia to Polynesia, to South America, *D. tasmanica* has relatively insignificant pale blue flowers, and, in this species, leaves 1–2m long, by 4cm wide. It is the indigo-blue berries that are truly decorative, especially in the long, persisting sprays of the smaller New South Wales *D. caerulea*, which always attracts attention as ground cover under light shade.

Dianella caerulea and *Aloe striatula*.

In recent years, Grass trees have become fashion accessories, or 'garden make-over necessities'. Bizarre *Xanthorrhoea* (from *xanthos* – yellow – and *rheo* – flow – because of the resins produced) species are being imported under licence as mature specimens, like the tree-ferns, *Dicksonia antarctica*. Maturity gives a pampas grass on a pole several feet high: *X. australis* may have a 3m trunk. *Xanthorrhoea johnsonii* seems to be the most common import. Seed is available for the patient – and young. It is said that *Xanthorrhoea* are best regarded as pot plants for the first 50 years. At this stage the trunk should become evident, and after planting out, flowering should start in another 50 years. Part of the fire economy, bush blazes are implicated in initiating flowering, when 2–2.5m-tall spikes of dense white flowers appear. (Honey produced from the flowers is said to be foul!) Hardiness is an issue until more evidence is available. To date, *X. hastilis* from seed has formed 1m-high

clumps of hundreds of coarse, dark green, reed-like leaves after 18 years. The severe winter of 1987 in west Cornwall did not damage it at all.

The British group of the Society for Growing Australian Plants (Secretary Jeff Irons is a co-author of *Australian Plants* [Ross & Irons, 1997], devoted to culture in Europe) aims to expand the range of Australian plants in cultivation. Some genera are now common; *Callistemon*, *Grevillea*, *Kunzea*, and others are just becoming established. *Casuarinas*, the graceful sheokes, have been represented by *C. littoralis*, but not by Tasmanian species *C. monilifera*, *C. paludosa*, and *C. stricta*, which are proving hardier. Yet Thurston (1930) recorded *C. stricta*, growing at Trevaylor, and three other species – *C. cunninghamiana*, *C. glauca*, and *C. suberosa*.

Of the ubiquitous olearias, one to add to Arnold-Forster's list is the Bogona Daisy Bush, *Olearia frostii*. Reminiscent of *O. semidentata*, it is smaller – 0.6–1m – and rather straggling. Native to Bogong High Plains in Victoria's alpine zone above 1,500m, it is very hardy, but short-lived in Britain, and needs regular renewal from cuttings. The beauty is in the soft, grey, furry foliage, and the 3cm-diameter mauve flowers. There are many more in the genus when material becomes available – (Australia) *O. adenophora*, *O. imbricata*, *O. incana*, *O. magniflora*; (New Zealand) *O. angustifolia* – all stunning in flower.

The RHS Plant Finder 2003–2004 lists eight *Pandorea* – *P. jasminoides* and *P. pandorana* with varieties – but there are six species native to Australia. The former, 'Bowervine', is a vigorous, twining climber, often attaining the tops of rain-forest trees. They also cover ground well, and have been

Olearia frostii and *Callistemon citrinus* 'White Anzac'.

recommended for hanging baskets, responding well to pruning. The pinnate foliage is evergreen and, once hardwood is made, plants seem quite hardy. With many varieties, the 4–5cm trumpet flowers vary in colour – white, pale yellow, pale or deep pink – appearing in profusion in sunny positions. Some forms of *P. pandorana* can be tender. With a wide natural distribution, inland and southern forms are hardy to moderate frosts, while Queensland and Northern Territory variants are easily damaged. Flowers are smaller than the first species, but are even more variable in colour – white through yellow, to brown and pink, usually with purple blotches or streaks in the bell.

Papua New Guinea

The Highlands of Papua New Guinea are reported to hold many exciting possibilities for gardeners. Examples in the Vireya section of rhododendrons and tree-ferns are described in Chapter 2. Hopefully more genera will become available for trial.

Taiwan

Further north, Taiwan (formerly Formosa) has an intriguing flora. Bowring – a former Governor of

Tetrapanax papyrifer 'T. Rex'.

Hong Kong – introduced *Tetrapanax papyrifer* to Kew Gardens in 1850. As the specific name suggests, the pith is a source of rice-paper used in artificial flowers in China (it is also native to south-east China). Bailey's *Hortus Third* (1976) gives a Zone 8 rating. Young, thin stems are cut to the ground by one or two degrees of frost, but once established, the roots and mature corky-barked stems – up to 4.5m tall, and 7.5–10cm in diameter – are frost-hardy, certainly to -3°C. Bailey (1976) notes 'orbicular leaves 10–15 inch [25–38cm] diameter', but, in fact, 1m is common, and gives a 'tropical jizz'. In slightly warmer conditions, '3ft [1m] panicles of white flowers' are an additional feature, but observation suggests that temperatures of just -2°C damage the flowers appearing in early winter. A four-shaded, variegated leaf form is in cultivation. Two minor problems have been noted. First, the extensive root system produces suckers frequently, though these are easily detached and root with a little bottom heat. Second, the huge leaves die, become detached, and invariably lodge themselves just out of reach in the branches of neighbouring trees, where they sag and flap feebly like small, dead pterodactyls.

Also in the Araliaceae, *Schefflera* are now gaining a cultivation foothold. These too recover from established roots, even if tops are frosted (Zone 9). *Schefflera arboricola*, S. *octophylla*, and S. *taiwanianum* are recommended, for the large, digitate, compound leaves add instant tropical effect. *Schefflera delavayii*, from mainland China, is similarly half-hardy, reaching 6m in a robust fashion. The Australian (Queensland) representative, S. *actinophylla*, has been transferred to the genus *Brassaia*, which has 40 species between India and (eastward) Hawaii. It is allocated to Zone 9b.

Cinnamomum camphora is one of 250 aromatic *Cinnamomum* trees and shrubs, eight of which are found on Taiwan (five are endemic). The tree can reach 30m, and grows at altitudes of up to 1,830m. Thurston (1930) recorded a 15m specimen at Penjerrick in 1930, with sizeable specimens at five other locations. This elegant species has 13cm ovate-elliptic, glossy yellow to pale green leaves, white beneath; in autumn, and occasionally throughout the year, some turn orange to scarlet. It seems hardy to salt winds.

Cinnamomum camphora belongs to the *Lauraceae*, whereas *Trochodendron aralioides* has its 'own' family. Also found in Japan, the latter tree reaches

Cinnamomum camphora.

4.5–6m, and forms pure stands on Taiwan. Evergreen, with dark red tints in the leaves, it is oddly attractive, and rare in cultivation, although Thurston (1930) recorded plantings at Bosahan and Lanarth. Like *Metrosideros*, seedlings may start life as epiphytes – in this case on *Cryptomeria* – and make slow growth to achieve tree-like status.

Hong Kong

Westward, Hong Kong island and territories provide many plant challenges in cultivation. Temperatures are higher than in Britain. An account of their 'great frost of 1893' records icy roads and icicles, 'although only one day was 32°F/0°C registered' in Kowloon (31m above sea level).

As a measure of the limitations, *Hoya carnosa* – common on Lugard Road, Victoria Peak – has been attempted outdoors in Cornwall on several occasions, with little success. However, Compton Mackenzie (who started living in Cornwall at Cury Vicarage in 1907, taking a house at Phillack, on

the Hayle Estuary, the following year), visited a garden on The Lizard cliffs at Halzephron, where he saw 'a *Hoya carnosa* apparently as much at home as in its native Queensland'.

Rhodoleia championii (recorded by Thurston in 1930 at Trewithen and Lanarth, but not in the current *RHS Plant Finder*) is rare and superb, some saying it is the most beautiful of the region's flowering trees. In 1849, Champion, a career soldier – eventually wounded and dying a Lt.-Col. at Inkerman – found two trees growing together above Little Hong Kong village. Although a few more were noted later in Happy Valley woods, these disappeared, and the cultivated plants derive from the original two. Of the Hamamelidaceae, the flowers show the family characteristics, but the petals are bright rose with black anthers. Downy bracts are shades of gold and pinky-white. The 8cm leaves are ovate, with blue-white undersides. Champion formed an extensive herbarium in Hong Kong, and sent nearly 600 plants to Kew. Several plants were named for him, including a *Magnolia* and a *Mucuna*. *Rhododendron championae* was named by Sir William Hooker, 'in compliment to his amiable and accomplished lady, whose partiality for plants equals that of her husband'. It sounds a very beautiful rhododendron, from Victoria Peak, having 10cm pale pink flowers in clusters of five.

China

The major social event of the late twentieth and early twenty-first centuries has been the advent of information technology in relation to the world-wide net, and email, grafted on to the personal computer explosion. Horticulture is no less involved than any other human activity with, as ever, advantages (increased information and product availability) and disadvantages (no effective screening of misleading 'knowledge' and noxious products). Growers are increasingly 'on-line', and those of the emerging economies are gaining niches in the global plant market. Where William Hooker, Robert Fortune, and others bravely struggled to collect and send new specimens to Europe, the nurserymen of China and India now use electronic highways to expand their businesses.

China remains a major source of new plants. *Citrus* species and numerous cultivars provide a huge world product, with 60 million tons of fruit being produced annually. Mainly subtropical, at best they are borderline for us. A very hardy lemon

Citrus × meyeri in January.

was introduced by Frank Meyer in 1908, and he wrote that it is hardy down to -5°C, though associated climatic features of summer temperatures and sun hours are important in culture. Meyer's lemon is possibly not a true *Citrus limon*, but a hybrid, lemon with orange. In very cold spells, a temporary fleece cover will protect swelling fruits in winter and early spring. The flowers of summer and autumn are beautifully scented.

Citrus ichangensis is a challenge – and a mystery. Listed in *The RHS Plant Finder*, and found in the Hillier catalogue *c.*1970, apparently it was introduced from central and south-west China in 1907, yet references at that time are rare, and indeed *ichangensis* is little mentioned in *Citrus* (Rutaceae) accounts. It is certainly very hardy, and has excellent foliage, with markedly winged petioles, but the phrase in Hillier's list – 'Flowers when produced white' – is telling. If a healthy, 30-year-old bush on a south-facing wall has flowered, the flowers have been missed, yet the lemons 'when produced' are said to have excellent flavour.

Although Bailey (1976) gives Zone 10 to most citrus species, the oranges *Citrus aurantiaca* (seville), *C. reticulata* (mandarin/satsuma), and *C. sinensis* (sweet) appear considerably hardier than lemons (estimate Zone 8), but Bailey notes Zones 10:9:10 respectively. Given wall shelter, acid soil, and feeding, they grow and look well, but need sun for ripening and flowering.

Rehderodendron – Alfred Rehder's trees – form a nine-strong genus in the quietly elegant Styracaceae. *Rehderodendron macrocarpum* (Zone 8) is a shrub or small tree, and is available commercially (hardy, briefly deciduous, and has white, lemon-scented flowers); but *R. huii* (Zone 9) and *R. macrophyllum* apparently are not. It seems that these – and perhaps any of the other six – would be worth growing when available.

Firmania simplex (Zone 9) is a superb, monoecious tree, with large, shiny, maple-like leaves. An example with a good 4.5m of smooth-barked trunk can be seen at Fox Rosehill Gardens, Falmouth. Given sun, showy yellow calyces of the flowers add beauty to the tree.

Japan and Burma

Japan shares many plants with mainland east Asia. *Rhus (Toxicodendron) succedanea* seems to be a very hardy shrub or small tree, up to 9m tall. Its flowers are yellow-green, but the main glory is in the large, compound leaves, with glossy upper surfaces, which are amazing in spring, and take long-lasting yellow, orange, and red hues in autumn.

From Burma – much travelled by Frank Kingdon Ward, a friend and frequent visitor to Mary Williams at Trewidden, Penzance – came two more wonders. One is *Saurauia subspinosa* (Roy Lancaster records another species, *S. napaulensis*, in *Plant Hunting in Nepal* [1981]; Stainton in *Forests of Nepal* [1972] illustrates the latter and records another species, *S. roxburghii*) – a beautiful, large shrub with *Eriobotrya*-like leaves. The flowers are a superb bonus. Panicles of bright, rose-pink, campanulate blossoms persist for months. It is worth visiting Tresco Abbey Garden to see this plant alone, and any effort in providing shelter, tree canopy, and warmth to reproduce that success will be rewarded. Cuttings and seed give experimental opportunities.

Saurauia subspinosa.

The second wonder is *Rosa gigantea*, from upper Burma, north-east India, and Yunnan. It is hardier and extremely vigorous – 4m annual growth is not unusual. Invaluable on walls, even north- and east-facing, or climbing into large trees, it is virtually evergreen. Twice a year (plus less sporadic flowerings), it is covered with masses of white flowers, staining deep pink with age. They are around 10cm in diameter, but are said to achieve 15cm. Once a full display took place in January – a marvel against a cold blue winter sky.

Rosa gigantea.

India and Nepal

Finds – or rediscoveries – continue in northern India and Nepal. Bananas are not mentioned by Arnold-Forster (1948), but Thurston, 18 years earlier, recorded *Musa basjoo* already 30 years old at Rosehill (now Fox Rosehill Gardens), and at Boslowick and Caerhays Castle. This, the hardiest of the bananas, is native to Japan's Ryukyu Islands, and is said to survive even in Zone 5, perhaps reasonably for the most northerly growing of these herbaceous perennials. Its rhizomes are the basis of winter stews in central China (the fruits are

Musa basjoo.

Ensete ventricosum.

inedible). The whole family is of nutritional value, in many guises. *Ensete ventricosum* (Zone 9) has rhizomes that form part of the staple diet of Ethiopia. Thurston (1930) recorded *Musa ensete (Ensete ventricosum)* at Rosehill (Fox Rosehill), Trewidden, and Morrab Gardens, Penzance. Plants of this species thrive at Abbotsbury, Dorset, and in several Cornish gardens. Mulching and fleece wrapping help them through most winters.

An influx of 'new' species is occurring ('new' because our fathers knew most of them!). J.D. Hooker, in *Flora of British India* (1894) recorded six species and ten varieties, including *Musa sikkimensis* (syn. *M. hookeri*), and six 'imperfectly known species', including *M. velutina*. These two are now available. Paxton, in his *Botanical Dictionary* (1868), named 14 species (adding that 'the tops of the young plants are eaten as a delicate vegetable. The fermented juice of the trunks produces an agreeable wine').

Musa sikkimensis.

Agapetes serpen 'Ludgvan Cross'.

Musa sikkimensis seems as hardy as *M. basjoo*, but has orange with purple tinges in the equally large leaves. *Musa velutina,* the 'Hot Pink Banana' (Zone 6 or 7) is recommended, as it develops its velvet pink fruit with black seeds in less than a year. The dramatic purple-red form of the Abyssinian banana, *Ensete ventricosum* – *E.v. maurelii* or *E.v. rubra* – grows at equally high altitudes in East Africa, including the Transvaal. It looks tender, perhaps rewards 'fleecing', and being tolerant of some shade would benefit from a radiation frost-protective canopy, but has persisted for several growers in Cornwall. Glendurgan has a fine example, as do Tremenheere, Ludgvan, and Avallon, Marazion.

Recently (since micropropagation increased production and reduced costs), in the same family, *Musella lasiocarpa* has become a major decorative feature. Short-growing, freely offsetting the 'yellow Chinese banana', Zone 7 gives a tropical effect, and bright yellow heads. The Chinese value it mainly as a food for pigs, but the root-hardy, decorative foliage plants are valuable in their own right to Western gardeners.

On hill walks, the first signs of epiphytes above are fallen flowers on the path. So it is with *Agapetes (Pentapterygium) serpens* and, though usually flame-red, Roy Lancaster introduced a new variety, 'Nepal Cream'. Easily raised from cuttings, experimental plantings in open ground or, more appropriately, tree cavities, thrive with sprawling stems, geometrically precise leaves, and tubular flowers, plus dahlia-like storage roots.

Dichroa febrifuga is a striking member of the hydrangea family, extending from Nepal east to Taiwan, and south to Malaysia. It seems very hardy. The Nepalese call it *Basali*: the dried leaves

are powdered and ingested to reduce high fevers. In Sikkim, it is collected in the Darjeeling area, and used to treat malaria. Shoots and the skin of the roots are made into an infusion, which has the same medicinal effect. Caution is required as too high a dose causes vomiting. From the gardener's point of view, the 2m rigid shrubs are excellent, with large, bold, hydrangea leaves. On acid soils, the numerous small, bright blue flowers are in evidence much of the year; in neutral or alkaline conditions, flowers can be a rather wishy mauve or pink. All sources agree the plant grows best in wet locations, and *Medicinal Plants of the Sikkim Himalaya* (Rai & Sharma, 1994) advises 'low light conditions', making it ideal for Cornwall!

Dichroa febrifuga.

Also from this fascinating botanical treasury comes *Jasminum dispermum*. Despite dire warnings of tenderness, it has proved as hardy as *J. mesnyi*, *J. odoratissimum*, and *J. polyanthum*. Rapidly growing stems, with decorative, pinnate leaves can be too exuberant. Given a sunny aspect, the pale pink/white, highly perfumed flowers make up for the effort to control the rampant plant. The pure,

Jasminum angulare.

dense white – and even the perfumes – of *J. angulare* (South Africa) and *J. azoricum* (Macronesia) may be preferable, but *J. dispermum* is a beauty.

Daphne species is extended from Arnold-Forster's listings by the superb *D. bholua,* its allies and forms. Dominating large areas, the sparsely branched bushes or small trees are generally around 2.5–3.0m, but can reach 6m. The flowers are highly perfumed, and range from white, through pale and dark pink, to rich purple. (*Daphne papyracea* has beautiful white, but scentless flowers.) Forms from higher levels are deciduous, like the established *D. b.* 'Gurkha'. Equally available are the evergreen *D. b.* 'Jacqueline Postill', with pink flowers, 'Darjeeling', 'Damon Ridge', and at least six other cultivars. *Daphne* species have a reputation for being miffy and short-lived, but this group seems reasonably sound. July cuttings – largish at 15–20cm – root fairly readily, with bottom heat, though grafting on *D. laureola* seedlings is possible.

Daphne bholua 'Deepak Gurung'.

Africa

'Africa' is difficult to condense into a few species! The Highlands of East Africa are a persisting and increasing challenge, with access to the plants of the ericacious (3,000–4,000m) and alpine (4,100m+) belts being achieved. From the former come *Ericas*; giant *Senecio* species, like *S. johnstonii* and varieties, and even *Protea*, like *P. caffra*, ssp. *kilimandscharica*. From slightly lower elevations are giant *Lobelias*, such as *L. gibberoa*. In the alpine zone are more *Senecio* and *Lobelia* species, with *Helichrysum* – for example, *H. newii* and *Euryops dacrydioides*. Cold may be a limiting factor in cultivation – the surface of the soil freezes every night of the year, with rapid daily thawing. Other limitations may lie in any or all of the following: day temperatures, sun hours, ultraviolet light, and soil structure.

Euryops pectinatus.

For the present, marginally easier accessions are from the south-west Cape and Drakensberg mountains. Kirstenbosch (South African Botanical Society) supplies an extensive seed range, and several private seed firms have even larger lists. One family firm collects in high, cool areas, and supplies estimated zone numbers for the species.

The wonderful 700 South African *Erica* species have excited European growers for centuries, initially protected by glass and lately with outdoor cultivation in the extreme south-west of Ireland and on the Isles of Scilly, with some extensions further north and east into the 'off island' – for example, *E. canaliculata* (Zone 8). Experimentation with many of the South African species is worthwhile, examples being *E. baccans* (Zone 8, pink/white); *E. caffra* (Zone 8, small tree; white with a subspecies on Mt Kilimanjaro); *E. cerinthoides* (Zone 8, red tubes); *E. patersonia* (Zone 8, yellow); *E. sessiliflora* (Zone 8, green-white); *E. straussiana* (Zone 7, pink tubes). The seed is very fine, seemingly over-abundant in packets. Seedlings are delicate, but at two years old may be planted out.

Acacia karroo is one of the large, flat-headed thorn trees beloved of tourist-guide photographers – elephants and giraffes eating them, and ants developing symbiotic relationships. It is said that a Dr Barker grew one outdoors for many years in the 1930s and 1940s at Salcombe, Devon. Given a bit of age and wood, it does seem hardy. The fine, pinnate leaves, and amazing 8cm, paired white thorns are enough, but given a hot summer, typical 1cm yellow, fluffy 'mimosa' spheres are a bonus, with a rich, fruity smell. Gum secreted from stems is a 'gum Arabic', and used as a sugar in cooking. Even the seed is used as a coffee substitute. *Acacia giraffae* should also behave like the 'sweet thorn'.

Gardenias have a special cachet, redolent of the 1920s and Good Time Charlies… Vast quantities of *G. jasminoides* are produced and sold, but few seem to survive long. The genus has 200 species, and a few may be tougher. One such is *G. thunbergii* (Zone 7), from the East Cape and Natal, which takes some frost, making a stiff, angular bush or small tree. Glossy, crenate leaves are decorative, but when – if – established, flowers should be single white, strongly scented, up to 8cm in diameter.

Gardenia thunbergii.

An interesting *Rubus*, *R. ludwigii* (Zone 7) is raised easily from seed in commerce. Eventually making a small tree, it has new branches as

white as *R. cockburnianus*. Flowers are pink, and the rather squat, dusky-red fruits have a good flavour.

Senecio grandiflorus (Zone 9) is a superb plant, with long (23cm), ovate leaves, and enormous heads of typical 'ragwort' flowers. It does need a very sheltered spot, or mild winters, but small trees of up to 4m+ are recorded through southern England.

Senecio grandiflorus.

There are many huge plant groups in the African florilegium. Succulent genera cannot be left out. Mesembryanthemums, the jewel-like midday flowers, have shrubby members in the very hardy *Ruschia*, and many *Lampranthus* species are cold-wet resistant.

Lampranthus banksia grandis.

Dramatic *Aloe* species have special claims to attention. *Aloe striatula* (Zones 6–7) is perhaps hardiest of all, and known to thrive in north to south-west Scotland and north-east England in Britain. It has simple, rarely branching stems, up to 1m in height, freely bearing large spikes of yellow or pale orange, tubular flowers. Green-brown seed-

Aloe striatula.

Aloe polyphylla.

Aloe saponaria.

pods of 2.5cm diameter often follow. These plants cope with quite wet soils. In general, several *Aloe* species are hardy to cold, though sunny aspects with good drainage help them through most winters; a south-facing bank or Cornish hedge, preferably with a wall or large rock behind for shelter and to radiate heat, is ideal. Research into optimal conditions for individual species pays.

Aloe polyphylla, from the Lesotho Drakensberg, has established on a 60° slope of peaty soil with excellent drainage (yet near-continuous flow of water through the roots), and the 76cm-diameter rosettes of spiralled leaves make superb features. A South African naturalist remarked in January 2003 that this species is now extinct in the wild. *Aloe broomii* (Zone 8) and *A. pratensis* (Zone 7) give a similar, if smaller, effect, but flower more readily. Available species *A. aristata* (Zone 7), *A. brevifolia* (Zone 8), *A. daveyana* (Zone 8), *A. mitriformis* (Zone 9), *A. reitzii* (Zone 7), and *A. saponaria* (Zone 7), are worth trying, as are a number of 'grass-aloes', like *A. ecklonis* (Zone 8). *Aloe arborescens* (Zone

9) has been grown for years, making large 'shrubs' if protected for the first few years to 'harden off'. Orange-red or yellow flowers add to the effect, and there is a slightly more tender, lovely variegated form.

'Strange' genera are appearing. *Tarchonanthus* is a small (two to four species, depending upon your taxonomist) genus from South Africa, South West Africa, and Botswana. *Tarchonanthus camphoratus* is a large, open bush for coastal exposure, as it grows well near Cape Town beaches but, being widespread, also tolerates the burning Kalahari and the serious cold of Free State. If necessary it will grow in pure sand. Young leaves, like the whole plant, are strongly camphor-scented, and are silvery-velvety. Mature leaves are varied in shape; leathery, and glabrous grey-green on top, velvety grey-white beneath. Velvet continues into the flowers: the males are greenish, mimosa-like balls; the females are larger, pure white, profuse, and very decorative. The whole plant is used locally – in medicines; as fodder for livestock (camphor-scented milk!); as a perfume; and as a source of hard, tough wood for boat-building, making bows and spears, and fencing posts that are durable for 30 years. Smoke of burning wood is said to resemble frankincense (*Boswellia* spp.). *Tarchon* derives from the Arabic name for *Artemesia dracunculus*, because of a similarity of the flowers of the two plants.

From South Africa, we go north to see a lovely small tree, with weeping, silvery branches. *Retama monosperma* was a *Genista*, and indeed now appears to be in the process of being changed yet again (when will taxonomists learn to modify academic enthusiasms with the reality of the need for consistent communication of knowledge and names?). Elegantly broom-like (i.e., *Cytisus*-like), scattered white, scented flowers occur throughout the year, and with major flushes in early spring and autumn. Cuttings and the one-seed pods make propagation simple. The species occurs across the straits in southern Spain.

Retama monosperma.

The Mediterranean basin

Plants from the 'four corners' are exciting, but the age-old source of the Mediterranean basin still contributes superb material. *Arbutus* species, *A. unedo* and *A. menziesii* are common in cultivation, but *A. andrachne,* as in Cyprus, is a beautiful small tree with a very tactile, smooth, pink to mahogany-coloured bark, which flakes to grey-green for part of the year. Hybrids occur with other species. From the same island, another lovely bush to small tree (3–9m) is *Quercus alnifolia.* Typical evergreen oak leaves – hard, glossy, dark green – the beauty lies in the golden, sometimes reddish indumentum of the lower surface. Revealed by wind, it gives the name to the Golden Oak. In 1937, W.J. Bean wrote in *The New Flora and Silva* of 'this oak, very rare at present' (although it had been introduced in 1885), and of 3m specimens at Kew and Borde Hill. Acorns are 4cm long, and 9–13mm in diameter.

Some plants are desirable, not because of size, rarity, enormous leaves, or flamboyant flowers – but because of a quiet presence, a serenity. Endemic to Crete is a beautiful elm relative, *Zelkova abeliacea.* Grey-barked and slow-growing, it has small, lobed, alternate leaves, and insignificant, but perfumed white flowers. A curio as a remote outlier in the west of a small genus, it has a further interest. In 1862, an Austrian botonist, Kotschy, reported the species from Esentepe, midway along the north Cypriot coast. It has never been found on that island since, and hence is regarded as Cretan endemic.

Olea europaea is much better known, but oddly is still rarely planted. The olive is not recorded by Arnold-Forster (1948), but Thurston (1930) has a lengthy, interesting note, in which he records the opinion, 'certainly hardy in Cornwall and the salt bearing gales by the sea do not trouble it'. This is of interest as Theophrastus indicated that the tree would not grow more than 65km from the sea. Perhaps the most famous tree in Britain is the Apothecary Garden Chelsea specimen. Long-lived, to 2,000 or 2,500 years, the stiff, silver-green trees are distinctive. They have small, delicately perfumed flowers, and will set fruit for us. (It was forecast by the International Olive Oil Council that in 2000–01, world production of olive oil would reach 2,070,100 tons – with Spain, Italy, and France expected to be the main producers.)

St Helena

Some plants are 'different' at first sight, having a distinctive 'jizz', as the 'birders' say. Such is a member of the cocoa family, Sterculiaceae. Already

'exotic', *Trochetiopsis ebenus* was perhaps first cultivated outdoors on Tresco, after reintroduction to
Cambridge Botanic Garden in 1980 from St Helena by Q.L.B. Cronk. An ebony – growing outdoors! It remains rare, with only two shrubs in the
wild on its native island. Evidence exists that in
earlier times there were many tree-size specimens
with a hard, black, valuable wood, so dense that
it sinks in water. Simple, funnel-like, five petalled
flowers are white, fading to pink, 4cm in diameter;
the leaves and whole plants are elegant. Cuttings
root fairly readily, and experimental plantings are
encouraging. Other trees from the island sound
interesting, and *Commidendrum* and *Melanodendron*
species would be worth trying if ever they become
available.

Isoplexis sceptrum.

Trochetiopsis ebenus.

The Macronesian islands

The Macronesian isles are closer, and better known
to European travellers. The flora is often common
to the Azores, Canaries, Cape Verde, Madeira,
and Salvages, but some species are endemic to
an island, or to a limited area. The 'usual' curious
distribution occurs with living relatives in South
and East Africa, and South America, and fossil
remnants throughout the Mediterranean basin to
southern Russia.

   Isoplexis is a genus of golden-orange 'fox-
gloves' (*Digitalis*-like), the commonest, *I. sceptrum*,
from Madeira, being around 1m high, and having
spikes of golden-brown flowers. Cuttings or seedlings are an insurance against a severe winter. *Isoplexis canariensis*, *I. isabelliana*, and *I. chalcantha* are
equally garden-worthy. The former reaches 1.4m
tall, and has rather more strident orange flowers.
The latter is a rarity, with copper-coloured flowers.
I. isabelliana is of more discreet beauty – but more

Isoplexis canariensis.

Isoplexis isabelliana.

readily available – and has dark, red-orange flowers, and small, dark green leaves.

A subspecies of *Retama monosperma* grows on the Canary Islands, as do the closely related *Spartocytisus filifera* and *S. supranubius*. Beautiful shrubs with large, strongly scented white flowers, they are worth seeking out. Of the *Euphorbias* from the islands, *E. mellifera* solely is well established in cultivation. Others, more succulent – *E. atropurpurea*, *E. bourgeana*, and *E. regisjubea* – need hot, well-drained situations. The cactiform *E. canariensis* (Zone 9 allocated by Silverhill Seeds of South Africa) is even more difficult to accommo-

Euphorbia clavarioides.

Euphorbia mellifera.

date. From the Azores, *E. stygiana* recently made an impact in gardens. Like a robust, refined *E. mellifera,* hybrids with it occur, one already named as *E.* 'Devil's honey'. The 'exotic garden' would be enhanced if more succulent euphorbias, especially from South Africa, could be acclimatized. One recommended is *E. clavarioides*, from Natal Drakensberg, between 1,500 and 1,800m, which forms a multi-headed, hardy cushion, and looks well between stones in a well-drained situation.

Argyranthemum – or are they returning to *Chrysanthemum?* – persist through most winters, and even if damaged by wind or cold, produce occasional flowers even in the winter months. Well

worth a set of insurance cuttings, which root easily, these are often best used to replace the rather gawky, woody shrubs that have come through the winters, but no longer look their best. Nevertheless the white, yellow, pink, puce, near red – single, semi-double, or double flowers – often clothe plants, young or old, for much of the summer. The simple white flowers of *A. foeniculaceum*, with blue, linear foliage, are quietly and persistently impressive. All 30 species, and numerous cultivars, especially of *A. frutescens*, have great presence, rapid growth, and dramatic colourful effect. Moreover, they are excellent as decorative nurse shrubs, to allow more permanent specimens to become established.

Attractive, short-lived umbellifer *Melanoselinum decipiens*, from the Azores, Cape Verde, and Madeira, achieves 2.5m and, though monocarpic, is statuesque. Woody stems, with yellow-green, palm-like leaves, and a huge inflorescence – 0.6–1m across – make a garden-visitor-stopper. Equally good in near-black seed, the show goes on.

Much smaller *Asteriscus sericeus* is a striking, short-lived shrub, with silky, silvery leaves setting off the golden-yellow composite flowers, 4cm across. *Asteriscus stenophyllus* is equally lovely, but insurance cuttings are worthwhile. *Asteriscus* seems to be in a state of taxonomic flux. The Madeiran endemic is an annual *Naupilus aquaticus*, with other species being introduced. Even these are variously referred to as *Pallensis* and *Odontospermum*.

From the 'laurel forests' come *Laurus azorica*, *Persea indica* (Madeiran mahogany), *Ocotea foetans*, and *Picconia excelsa* ('Palo Blanco' because of its whitish bark) – the latter currently 18m at Abbotsbury – giving solid forms to our gardens.

There are two curios from the archipelago and Europe. *Culcita macrocarpa* (previously *Dicksonia culcita*) is Europe's own tree-fern. Growing on Madeira, and possibly in Portugal, it is still scarcely in cultivation, with a few small specimens in the Jardim Botanico, Funchal. In the wild it is rare, with a sizeable population only in the remote and inaccessible Ribeira do Inferno. A 'trunk' rarely forms and is short – but it remains so desirable! The same curio-value lies in *Pittosporum coriaceum*. The genus is based in south-east Asia and Australasia, with the odd outlier in South Africa. But here, in Madeira, a European species! In cultivation, it grows into a small, smooth-barked tree, with large, dark green leaves (pale reverse) and large, fragrant, cream flowers. It tolerates a few degrees of frost.

Pittosporum coriaceum.

The Spanish and Portuguese used these islands as a springboard to explore the New World, returning with plants from the Americas to acclimatize in the same, equitable climate. It is fascinating that plants with which we still struggle today were known to our forefathers; the fabled melon-thistle, *Melocactus intortus* – still exercising today's cactophiles – was illustrated in 'The Garden at Eichstatt' (Basilius Besler, *Hortus Eystettensis*, 1613).

Plants flooded in at such a rate that provenance was often forgotten. *Opuntia bergeriana*, a lovely red-flowered, fairly hardy species, is known only from European cultivation.

North and Central America

Love them or hate them, the Cactaceae has thousands of representatives, a few of which add interest to the 'exotic garden'. All – apart from two or three *Rhipsalis* species found in south and west Africa – came from the Americas. *Selenicereus spinulosus* – from east Mexico to Texas (Zone 9) – proves very hardy, coming through the Penwith (Cornwall) 1987 winter with screen temperatures of -11°C, on a south wall. A scrambling, short-spined species, the 15cm-wide white flowers, with chestnut bracts, are not as large or showy as the West Indian species, but the 'moon-cereus' flowers are striking and have a fruity smell.

The more recognizably 'cactiform' *Opuntia phaeocantha* and varieties growing from California to Texas are exceptionally tough. They have typical discoid, jointed stems and unpleasant barbed spines; the mainly yellow flowers are quite large. For the brave and careful weeder (what do American cousins call those who remove 'volunteers' from their gardens?), they add a distinct addition to well-drained soils in full exposure.

Opuntia pheocantha minor.

North America provides statuesque if spiny plants in *Agave* and *Yucca* species. Just one or two make strong focal points and are easily grown

Yucca schidigera.

Yucca thompsoniana.

from seed, cuttings, or suckers. *Agave americana* and its variegated forms are said to take -9°C when acclimatized, but other species seem even hardier. *Agave celsii* syn. *A. micracantha* is said to stand -4°C, but in experience seems as hardy as, or hardier than, the first, especially as it prefers a light overhead canopy. The broad, glaucous, fine-toothed leaves make rosettes 1m across, and after the 2m, white-flowered, cylindrical inflorescence dies that rosette deteriorates, but offsets occur to build up a multi-headed plant. *Agave parryi* has smaller, even bluer, hardier (down to -6.5°C) rosettes. At maturity arises the astounding 6m yellow-flowered inflorescence to finalize the display. *Agave horrida* (tough, dependable, slate-blue), *A. salmiana* (enormous and tolerates tree-canopy cover), and *A. xylonacantha* (hard, small rosettes, with horny, broad-spined margins) are recommended.

Most species are sessile, or with very short stems. Yuccas, also of the Agavaceae, more frequently form trunks, and in general are depend-able in our wet climate. *Yucca glauca*, *Y. gloriosa*, and *Y. recurvifolia* are well known and thriving, but a wide range is available, and they grow reliably from seed. Some, like *Y. rostrata*, *Y. schidigera*, and *Y. thompsoniana*, make sturdy stems of up to 4–5m. *Yucca schottii* is even larger, but the rather slender trunk bends and, prostrate, the head starts to ascend again. All can take probably -18°C or lower. Although they are drought-resistant, more importantly for us, they are equally tolerant of our 100–127cm of annual rainfall. *Yucca schidigera* and *Y. thompsoniana* can be particularly recommended. The 20–23cm diameter trunks support massive heads of erect, steel-blue leaves, which eventually deflex and, in dying, adpress to the trunks in persistent straw colour. Flowers are large, campanulate, fleshy, and cream to white. Who cannot marvel at the huge spikes of the monocarpic *Y. whipplei*? Very colourful, variegated plants are found in *Y. aloifolia*, *Y. filamentosa*, and *Y. gloriosa*. Others worth growing, and equally available are *Y. baccata*, *Y. faxoniana*, and *Y. torreyi*. Only *Y. brevifolia* (the Joshua tree) and *Y. elephantipes* seem rather susceptible in wet, cold conditions – but there are some 40 species to try.

In the same family, *Calibanus*, *Dasylirion*, and *Nolina* species are available as seed or seedlings from specialists – all noteworthy, 'different', and rarely seen. The first, named for Shakespeare's grotesque Caliban, grows in dry, north Mexican hills, but is equally fine in wet west Cornwall. Memorably, the discoverer recorded that the caudex resembled 'a Volkswagen beetle', but it takes a long time to reach this size! The corky-barked, domed caudex has numerous ephemeral, reed-like leaves, and occasional sprays of whitish flowers rather like those of a *Cordyline*.

North America has far more to offer than xerophytes. Our gardens are resplendent with *Aesculus, Ceanothus, Pentstemon*, and other indispensable genera. Less well known are species from the southeastern USA, often with intriguing common names – Rabbit tobacco, Moose wood, Indian cigar (*Catalpa speciosa* – children smoke the long fruits), and Thunderwood, for example. *Xerophyllum asphodelus* (Turkey beard) and *X. tenax* (Bear grass) are woody-based, long-leaved members of the Liliaceae, having large racemes of small white flowers; in our climate they seem to require well-drained conditions, and are very slow to achieve their 1.5–2m potential.

Asimia triloba and *A. parviflora* – hardy pawpaws – are cold-tolerant, but need much sun to produce their curious, six-petalled, purple-brown flowers, and edible, aromatic fruit. It is almost enough to be able to grow one of the tropical Annonaceae outdoors.

Cherokee bean, *Erythrina herbacea*, is another curio. *Erythrina crista-gallii* is well known and striking, with large, scarlet pea flowers. Other members of this Old- and New-World genus worth trying, given a little protection, include *E. latissima, E. princeps*, and *E. zeyheri*. *Erythrina herbacea* has a perennial woody rootstock, and annual 1m stems, bearing the characteristic bright red flowers.

South America

The last stage of this superficial horticultural world journey enters the vastness of South America. Already genera from *Azara* (new species still being introduced) to *Zinnia* are established, but the potential in genera, and even families, barely known to us is enormous.

Solanaceae is a large, important family with 56 genera on the continent, 25 being endemic. Hundreds of varieties of potatoes, tomatoes, and other edibles are important for diets world-wide.

Brugmansia species and cultivars continue to provide challenges. The prolific 'angel trumpets'

Brugmansia sanguinea lutea.

flaunted in white, yellow, salmon, and pink are truly astounding. Wall protection and hot summers increase the chances of display, and though cut back by frosts, if well-established and mulched, many are root-hardy and resurgent in spring. Their vigour is often over exuberant, and they need regular, firm control, as do the allied *Iochroma* species.

Iochroma grandiflora from Brazil is worth a trial. A soft-wooded bush or small tree, its large, oval, downy, sticky leaves give a tropical effect, and the clusters of 8cm, bright, intense violet trumpets like small *Daturas* are charming. We in the North think of Brazil as tropical, but that vast country has myriad climatic variations. The hardiness of *Solanum jasminoides* is proven, and now becoming established is *Solanum rantonnetii*, from Argentina to Paraguay. The Blue potato bush, it thrives with us, presenting a multitude of 1–2cm dark violet, pale-eyed flowers late in the year to lighten the November gloom.

Verbenaceae is well represented. Mediterranean visitors are familiar with the brilliant colours of the poisonous *Lantana camara*. Insurance cut-

Iochroma grandiflora.

Solanum rantonnetii.

Lantana camara.

in late summer. Smaller growing, *C. montevidensis* (syn. *selloviana*) seems slightly hardier and has warm lilac pincushions.

Also Brazilian, a fabulous climber for a hot, sheltered wall is *Anemopaegma chamberlaynii*. Of the *Bignoniaceae,* the paired opposite, glabrous leaves are elegant, but the beauty lies in the 7.5cm pale yellow (streaks of purple in the throat) flowers in axillary racemes.

Alstroemeria, especially the dwarf species with their gorgeous, orchid-like flowers in cream, green, orange, vermilion, pink, and purple are amazing, and increasing in cultivation. 'Climbing alstroemerias' – *Bomarea* species – are also increasingly available. With at least 150 species, until recently only *B. caldasii* represented this soft-stemmed genus, with 4cm tubular, tawny with yellow flowers appearing in clusters throughout the year – even appearing in the annual Christmas Day flower count. *Bomarea hirtella* (see also pages 168, 172) has recently twined into prominence, with deep pink and yellow flowers. The large, tri-

Bomarea hirtella.

partite, sage-green seed pods are attractive, especially when the mitre cap opens to reveal pea-size, bright orange fleshy seeds. Several other species are intriguing, and worth trying when seeds can be obtained. All so far seem hardy, in that the white, fleshy tubers overwinter in light sandy soils. *Bomarea sanguinea* has, as expected, blood-red flowers; the plant grows exuberantly, but is shy to flower. *Bomarea* is the largest genus in the Amaryllidaceae in South America.

Once more raising their spiny heads, several cacti from the Andes are hardy, even under our

tings are required, but most winters leave these subshrubs barely damaged, allowing the production of yellow, white, pink, orange, and flame pincushions to delight butterflies and humans alike

Tephrocactus floccosus.

wet, cool conditions, despite their alternately hot and freezing natural habitat. *Tephrocactus* species, some thickly 'wool'-covered to protect their stems from high-altitude ultraviolet light, are proving hardy. *Tephrocactus floccosus* may be found in nature with its roots in snow-water-logged conditions, and copes with mild west Britain's rain, though here it is slow to make its thousand-head clumps and bright yellow flowers.

Cacti are notoriously the playthings of lumpers and splitters in taxonomy. *Soehrensia* has shifted variously within *Lobivia*, *Echinopsis*, *Trichocereus* and, however uneasily named, *S. formosa*, *S. ingens*, and *S. oreopepon* have proved very tough,

Soehrensia formosa.

giving a solid, spiny presence. Heads of 30cm-diameter bear large, brilliant red or yellow flowers for all too few days a year.

Many other members of the Cactaceae – *Lobivia*, *Echinopsis Cleistocactus*, *Trichocereus*, and *Eulychnia* species are worth experimentation to add exotic effect. From the far south comes *Maihuenia poeppigii*, a low, clump-forming opuntia, comparable with South Africa's *Euphorbia clavari-*

Cleistocactus strausii.

oides in appearance, apart from 4cm-wide yellow-white flowers. Like four others in the genus, it is very slow-growing, but cold-hardy.

Whoever first expressed the concept was right! Until a gardener has killed a plant four times, a species should not be regarded as 'unsuited' or 'tender'. The individual plant may have been a weakling, perhaps of inappropriate provenance, or the soil incorrectly prepared; it may not have had the optimal microclimate, or sufficient time to establish before the advent of extreme weather conditions.

Despite Arnold-Forster's encouragement to experiment, many still feel that 'puyas will not do' for them, even when admiring others' planting. A unique opportunity occurred in Marazion in the construction of a new Cornish hedge, which gave a growing area of around 50 sq m. The top was (over) planted with 200 *Puya alpestris*. Results after two winters are interesting in that, while perhaps 5 per cent have died, around the same number have grown very strongly, off-setting vigorously. The remainder have gained at varying rates, some

Puya alpestris planted on a Cornish hedge.

Puya chilensis.

Puya laxa.

with perfect rosettes, and others with variably severe leaf-tip damage (salt-laden south-westerly gales?). As conditions in terms of soil, drainage, and exposure have been uniform, it may be that the seedlings are hybrids (*Puya alpestris* pollinated by a less robust species), and this may become apparent at the hoped-for massed flowering.

If true *P. alpestris*, the flower would be dark blue with a metallic, green sheen. Of the 100 *Puya* species found in the Andes between Colombia and northern Chile, perhaps ten are reasonably available at this time. (Seven and a hybrid are listed in *The RHS Plant Finder 2003–4*.) *P. caerulea* (not *P. coerulea* [*Padilla*]) – metallic sea-green flowers – and *P. chilensis* – yellow-green – make up Arnold-Forster's trio, and are still the common ones in cultivation. A very beautiful plant with white leaves is occasionally met as *P. caerulea violacea* or *P.* 'violacea'.

A grower's problem is that there are many bromeliads in cultivation without names, or questionably named, and there are very few comprehensive reference works. Werner Rauh of Heidelburg, an outstanding botanist until his death in 2000, wrote one of the most practical available (1979), and the same-titled *Bromeliads* by Victoria Padilla (1973), is also very useful. Articles such as 'Notes on the Genus Quesnelia' by Clive Innes in *The Plantsman* (vol. 7, 1985–86) are invaluable when located.

The International Succulent Institute has been a major source of 'new' bromeliads in recent times. For example, in 1994 five *Puya* species were listed for sale: *P. ferruginea* and *P. humilis* (the former later proved not to be a *Puya*), and three unidentified.

Of other species, a very fine, silver-leaved form of *Puya chiliensis*, Linares form, has proved very

hardy, but is yet to flower. The unusual *P. strictiflora* is equally robust, as are the small *P. mirabilis* (few, large green-white flowers); larger, silver-leaved *P. laxa* (an odd, dingy inflorescence – until the individual flowers are closely examined, which are violet, flared, and with an external green stripe); and, bigger still, *P. venusta* (silver rosettes to 1m across, with red-stalked, purple-petalled flowers). Greater still – and available – are *P. berteroniana* from mid-Chile (like a *P. alpestris* on steroids!) – Victoria Padilla describes the flower colour as 'a vivid Kelly green'), and the largest of all bromeliads, Peruvian *P. raimondii*. Monocarpic, the 5m-high plant can double its height with its flower, but only after 80–150 years of growing. The inflorescence is covered in thousands of creamy-yellow flowers. Unfortunately, these resin-rich plants are endangered as they are vandalized, being deliberately and needlessly burned.

The name 'puya' derives from the word for 'point' in the language of the Mapuche Indians of Chile. Anyone working with the plants quickly gets the point! Apart from the sharp tip, the curved marginal spines on the leaf edges, in some species, change direction; on the outer half of the leaf, the spines project outward, while on the inner half the spines curve towards the heart of the rosette. It has been suggested that theses species may be regarded as carnivorous plants. Small birds and animals which, with difficulty, progress through the outer leaf defences, find themselves imprisoned by the incurved inner defence and die – eventually supplementing nutrition from the nitrogen-poor mountain soils. In cultivation, removing weeds near these 'cruel beauties' can be uncomfortable. It is worth considering planting through weed-suppressant plastic sheet, or similar mulch, to obviate the problem; covering this with stones, and/or coarse bark improves the aesthetic appearance, and hands are not lacerated.

This account has touched on but a small percentage of puyas, and an even smaller fraction of the 2,000 species in the 45-genera family – all endemic to this last continent on the journey, apart from one wayward African species.

Species from other genera should be tried in outdoor culture. *Billbergia nutans* – common enough as the houseplant 'Queen's tears' – is very persistent in semi-shaded, humus-rich soils, as are *B.* × *windii* and derivative hybrids. *Fascicularia bicolor* (see photo, page 26) and *F. pitcairnifolia* are

Fascicularia pitcairnifolia on a dead sycamore tree.

boringly dark green, seaside park border edging – until suddenly a rosette bursts into flame, with brilliant red inner leaves and a central boss of blue flowers. *Ochogavia* (five species) are similar with *O. carnea* and *O. elegans* most frequently seen. Their flower range is pink, red, and yellow – but unfortunately rabbits enjoy nibbling their leaves!

Dyckia and *Hechtia* species are generally smaller than the above and, being 'succulent'-leaved are often described in cactus and succulent reference works. Some will survive in well-drained, sunny

Ochagavia carnea.

spots, as do the still smaller and perhaps hardier Argentinian *Abromeitiella*. *A. brevifolia* and *A. loretziana* appear occasionally in 'cactus nurseries'. The latter is the larger growing, but the clumps formed by both species look rather 'mossy' or saxifrage-like, and both have interesting greenish flowers.

Several larger bromeliads are worth trying as epiphytes outdoors, including members of the genera *Aechmea*, *Quesnelia*, and *Vriesea*. Most of the family is easily propagated by division, so that losses in experiment are not serious. Still less susceptible to climatic damage are some members of the vast *Tillandsia* genus – the 'air plants' – which are generally epiphytic or epilithic. *Tillandsia bergeri* has lived outdoors in west Cornwall, suspended under trees, for 20 years, enduring the severe winter of 1987. Other small, silver-scaled species

Tillandsia bergeri.

(including *T. usneioides*, 'Spanish moss' – well! It is said to be 'perfectly hardy in Paris'!) can be tried in trees. Another good placement is in the fibrous 'cups' formed by the old leaf bases of *Trachycarpus fortunei* fans – this is good for some orchids, ferns and other epiphytes too.

South America has so many horticultural delights and challenges. Excitingly, we can only ever know and grow a tiny fraction of plants available. Now this journey concludes, following

many forgotten travellers westwards back across the Pacific to the starting point, but the last sentence must belong to Will Arnold-Forster: 'May this chapter, defective as it is, serve as a stimulus to that enterprise which has in the past proved so fruitful, especially in the "milder counties".'

The Contributors

Michael Bell is a founder member and President of the Bamboo Society (EBS Great Britain), and a regular contributor to its journal. He has been growing bamboos for over 40 years, and holds one of the National Collections of *Phyllostachys* (cultivated forms), which forms part of his collection of more than 260 temperate taxa, and is one of the most comprehensive in Europe. He is the author of *The Gardener's Guide to Growing Temperate Bamboos* (2000), and has contributed to several other books. In 2000 he was invited to the USA as guest speaker of the American Bamboo Society in Atlanta. His garden has been the subject of two television presentations, and several articles in garden journals.

Mark Brent trained in the gardens of the Rothschild family in north Buckinghamshire, and at the Royal Botanic Gardens, Kew, before settling in Cornwall in 1992 to assist with the development of Lamorran House Gardens at St Mawes. He has travelled widely around the Mediterranean, and in the Pacific North-West region of North America.

Les Cathery started to grow bamboos in the early 1980s, to augment a predominantly Himalayan garden in Surrey. In 1994 he moved to the far south-west coast to house the expanding bamboo collection, and to include less hardy species, but mainly to indulge a growing passion for Southern hemisphere plants, particularly Proteaceae and Restionaceae. He holds the NCCPG *Phyllostachys* cultivar joint collection.

Peter Clough's life in coastal gardens has led him up and down the west coast of Britain as head gardener of Achamore House on the Isle of Gigha; Tresco Abbey Garden, in the Isles of Scilly, and Inverewe Garden on the north-west coast of Scotland. He has advised on the provision of shelter on Ramsey Island off the Welsh coast; acted as consultant to the gardens of Colonsay House in the Hebrides, and contributed to the cliff gardens of St Michael's Mount in Cornwall. He has designed and planted private gardens by the sea, and now works a cliff farm in West Penwith, growing cut foliage, and plants suitable for coastal gardens in the 'milder counties'. He has lectured to garden societies all over Britain on the subject of 'gardening on the edge'.

Tom Hudson is a New Zealander by birth, and has been living and gardening at Tregrehan, Cornwall, since 1987. He is particularly interested in trying out plants with known source background, many of which seem to have little horticultural worth.

Philip McMillan Browse is a horticultural consultant, and has been Director of the Saratoga

Horticultural Foundation in California, and Director of the Royal Horticultural Society's Garden at Wisley. He is one of the originators of the Eden Project, and has been Horticultural Director of the Lost Gardens of Heligan since its modern beginnings. His publications include *Plant Propagation* (1979), and *Palms for Cooler Climates* (1993). He is co-author of *The Heligan Vegetable Bible* (2000).

Guy Moore was born and grew up on St Mary's, Isles of Scilly. He worked first as a landscape gardener, specializing in traditional woodworking techniques. Having developed a particular interest in proteaceous plants, since 2000 he has been specialist plant advisor at Trevena Cross Nurseries – the largest protea grower in the UK. He holds the RHS General Certificate, and the NVQ Level 3 in Amenity Horticulture.

Edward Needham: an early interest in the wild plants of his native Cotswolds soon grew to encompass the flora of Europe and beyond, and reached a high point with several trips to the Nepal Himalayas in the 1980s, and later to the parts of south-west China open to independent travel. Despite a growing awareness that plants are infinitely more attractive in their natural environment, where it still exists, than in captivity, he nevertheless maintains a garden of sorts in a small wooded valley near the Fal, dedicated almost exclusively to plants of natural origin.

Dr Chris Page, also originally from the Cotswolds, is a specialist in taxonomy, biology, ecology, and the evolution of ancient living plants. Former Principal Scientific Officer of the Royal Botanic Garden, Edinburgh (1969–94), he founded both the RBGE's International Conifer Conservation Programme, and the Conifer Specialist Group of the Species Survival Commission. He is a former Vice-President of the British Pteridological Society; Fellow of the Linnean Society, and Member Emeritus of the International Union for the Conservation of Nature (IUCN). His publications include *The Ferns of Britain and Ireland* (1982), and *Ferns: Their Habitats in the Landscape of Britain and Ireland* (Collins New Naturalist series, 1988). Now based in Cornwall, England, he writes on local natural history, and internationally on the interpretation of wider issues of plant evolutionary processes against the background of advancing fields of geological evolution and Earth Science.

Charlie Pridham owns and runs the Roseland House nursery, and holds the National Collection of *Clematis viticella*. He had no formal horticultural or botanical training, but gained his knowledge from growing and propagating plants, in particular climbing plants, coupled with the advice and help of other Cornish gardeners. His love of climbing plants stems from seeing the more flamboyant tender climbers all around the world while pursuing an earlier career in the Merchant Navy.

Dr Rob Senior was influenced more than he realized by his father's love of gardening. He was set to work in the vegetable garden, and a teenage interest in cacti was a reaction to potatoes and broad beans. Reading W. Arnold-Forster's *Shrubs for the Milder Counties* was a revelation of something of the magnificent scope of horticulture, and led him to leave the 'frozen north' and seek employment in the 'sunny south'. Through the ensuing 40 years, plantsmen, gardens, and plants helped him retain a degree of equanimity, despite the pressures of NHS bureaucracy. In retirement from general practice, they are a panacea for the trials of advancing age.

Nurseries, Specialist Suppliers, and Societies

Nurseries in Cornwall

This list is based on a list of nurseries in *The Cornwall Gardens Guide* (Douglas Ellory Pett, Alison Hodge, 2003). Nurseries asterisked contribute to *The RHS Plant Finder*. Those listed without postcodes do not usually trade by mail order.

Nurseries

Barracott Plants, Calstock Road, Gunnislake PL18 9AA. Tel: 01822 832234. *Herbaceous perennials and shrubs – especially shade-loving plants – and a good range of bamboos.*

Bay Tree Nurseries, Long Lane, St Hilary, Penzance TR20 9EF. Tel: 01736 763635. *Bay trees.*

B.J. Plants & Herbs, Killigarth, Paul, Penzance TR19 6TY. Tel/Fax: 01736 731356. *Speciality: camellias and herbs.*

Blackacre Nurseries, Blackacre, nr Indian Queens. Tel: 01637 881300.

*Bodmin Plant & Herb Nursery, Laveddon Mill, Lanival Hill, Bodmin PL30 5JU. Tel: 01208 72837. Fax: 01208 76491. Email: bodminnursery@aol.com.

Boskenna Nursery, St Buryan, Penzance. Tel: 01736 810384.

*Bregover Plants, Hillbrook, Middlewood, North Hill, nr Launceston PL15 7NN. Tel: 01566 782661.

Calamazag Nursery, East Taphouse, Liskeard. Tel/Fax: 01579 321799.

*Churchtown Nurseries, Gulval, Penzance TR18 3BE. Tel/Fax: 01736 362626.

Churchtown Nursery, Perranarworthal, nr Truro. Tel: 01872 863033.

Crankan Nurseries, Newmill, Penzance. Tel: 01736 362897. *Speciality: pelargoniums.*

Cross Common Nursery, The Lizard, Helston. Tel: 01326 290722. Web: www.crosscommonnursery.co.uk *Half-hardy, exotic, conservatory plants; trees and shrubs for coastal gardens.*

*Duchy of Cornwall Nursery, Cott Road, Lostwithiel PL22 0HW. Tel: 01208 872668. Fax: 01208 872835. Email: sales@duchyofcornwallnursery.co.uk. Web: www.duchyofcornwallnursery.co.uk. *Extensive range of all garden plants, including trees, shrubs, conifers, roses, perennials, fruit, and half-hardy exotics.*

Fentongollan Bulb Farm, Merther Lane, St Michael Penkivel, Truro TR2 4AQ. Tel: 01872 520209. Fax: 01872 520606. Email: bulbs@flowerfarm.co.uk. Web: www.flowerfarm.co.uk. *Bulb sales Aug–Dec.*

Fiveways Nursery, Pelean Cross, Ponsanooth, Truro.

Tel/Fax: 01872 865185.

Godolphin Hill Nursery, Godolphin, Helston TR13 9TQ. Tel/Fax: 01736 762124. Email: marshall@euphony.net. Web: www.godolphinhill.com. *Speciality: old-fashioned and species roses.*

Gweek Nurseries, Chapel Hill, Gweek, Helston. Tel: 01326 221311.

*Hardy Exotics Nursery, Gilly Lane, Whitecross, Penzance TR20 8BZ. Tel: 01736 740660. Fax: 01736 741101. Web: www.hardyexotics.co.uk. *Largest UK collection of trees, shrubs, and herbaceous plants for tropical and desert effects.*

Heather Lane Nursery, Back Lane, Canonstown, Hayle. Tel: 01736 740198. Fax: 01736 741294.

Illand Nurseries, Illand, Coads Green, Launceston. Tel: 01566 782521.

J.R. Nurseries, Rosenannon, St Wenn, Bodmin. Tel: 01637 880108.

Leire Nursery, Ruan High Lanes, nr Truro. Tel/Fax: 01872 501502. Email: leirenursery@aol.com.

Losowek Herbs, Treventon, Well Lane, St Keverne, Helston. Tel: 01326 280514. Email: losowek.herbs@btinternet.com.

Lower Kenneggy Nurseries,

Rosudgeon, Penzance. Tel: 01736 762959. *Speciality: agaves and other succulents.*

Medrow Nursery, Polyphant. Tel: 01566 86322. *Speciality: fruit and vegetables, bedding plants, and trees.*

Millennium Plants (Cornwall) Ltd., Newquay Road, Goonhavern, Truro TR4 9QQ. Tel: 01872 572310. Fax: 01872 572628.

Myrtle Nursery, High Lane, Manaccan. Tel: 01326 231604.

New Season Ltd., Green Lane Nurseries, Redruth TR15 1LH. Tel/Fax: 01209 313245. Email: newseason@lineone.net. Web: www.newseasonltd. com. *Spring bedding; shrubs; cottage garden plants, organically grown.*

*Old Withy Garden Nursery, The, The Grange, Gweek, Helston TR12 6BE. Tel: 01326 221171. Email: Withy Nursery@fsbdial.co.uk.

Pentewan Valley Nurseries, Pentewan Road, St Austell. Tel/Fax: 01726 842360.

Penventon Nursery, Cumford, Lanner, Redruth. Tel: 01209 820049.

Plantation Nursery, Bototoe Road, Baripper, Camborne TR14 0QS. Tel/Fax: 01209 714522.

*Quality Daffodils, 14 Roscarrack Close, Falmouth TR11 4PJ. Tel/Fax: 01326 317959. Email: rascamp@daffodils.uk.com. Web: www.qualitydaffodils. co.uk. *Speciality: narcissus hybrids and species. Mail order.*

Rainbow's End Nuseries, Trescowe Common, Germoe, nr Penzance TR20 9RX. Tel/Fax: 01736

850322.

*Rezare Nurseries, Rezare, nr Treburley, Launceston PL15 9NX. Tel: 01579 370969. Email: rezareurseries@aol. com.

*Rosewarne Collections, Duchy College, Rosewarne, Camborne TR14 0AB. Tel: 01209 722151. Fax: 01209 722159. Email: r.smith@cornwall.ac.uk. *Speciality: National Collection of escallonia hybrids and species.*

Sunny Corner Nurseries, Old Market Garden Centre, Chacewater, Truro. Tel: 01872 560084.

Tartendown Nurseries, Landrake, Saltash. Tel: 01752 851431.

Towan Camellia & Hydrangea Nursery, Carwinion Garden, Mawnan Smith, Falmouth. Tel/Fax: 01326 251115. Email: johnpricecam ellias@hotmail.com.

Trebarwith Valley Nursery, Trewarmett, Tintagel. Tel: 01840 770625. Email: tony@park-farm.freeserve. co.uk.

*Tregothnan Nursery, Estate Office, Tregothnan, Truro TR2 4AN. Tel: 01872 520325. Fax: 01872 520291. Email: bigplants@tregothnan.co.uk. Web: www.tregothnan.com. *Speciality: rare and unusual plants from own stock, with known-provenance, large specimens.*

Trenowth Nurseries, Lower Trenowth Farm, St Columb. Tel: 01637 881473. *Speciality: bedding plants, hanging baskets, and tubs.*

Treseders, Wall Cottage Nurseries, Lockengate, St Austell. Tel: 01208 832234.

*Tresidder Farm Plants, St Buryan, Penzance TR19 6EZ. Tel: 01736 810656. Email: janmilligan25@hotmail.com. *Speciality: Proteaceae, Aloeacae – large aloe collection, unusual succulents.*

*Trevena Cross Nurseries & Garden Centre, Breage, Helston TR13 9PS. Tel: 01736 763880. Fax: 01736 762828. Email: sales@trevenacross.co.uk. Web: www.trevenacross. co.uk. *Speciality: South African and Australian plants, aloes, proteas (largest grower in the UK), tree-ferns, palms, restios – wide range of other hardy exotics.*

West Coast Gardens, Dorminack, St Buryan, Penzance TR19 6BH. Tel. 01736 810087. *Plants of Cornish origin; coastal garden plants, ferns and historic daffodils. Mail order only.*

Nurseries associated with gardens

The following nurseries are associated with gardens open to the public. They are permanent, and open to the public even when not visiting the garden. Some are substantial.

*Bosvigo, Bosvigo Lane, Truro, TR1 3NH. Tel: 01872 275774. Fax: 01872 275774. Email: bosvigo. plants@virgin.net. Web: www.bosvigo.com.

*Burncoose Nurseries, Redruth TR16 6BJ. Tel: 01209 860316. Fax: 01209 860011. Email: burncoose@eclipse.co.uk. Web: www.burncoose.co.uk. *Over 3,000 ornamental trees and shrubs. Rare and unusual magno-*

lias and rhododendrons.

Carwinion Bamboo Garden, Mawnan Smith, Falmouth TR11 5JA. Tel: 01326 250258. Fax: 01326 250903.

Hidden Valley Gardens & Nurseries, Treesmill, Par PL24 2TU. Tel: 01208 873225. Web: www.hidden-valleygardens.co.uk. *Speciality: Siberian iris, crocosmias, and hardy geraniums.*

Japanese Garden & Bonsai Nursery, St Mawgan, Newquay TR8 4ET. Tel: 01637 860116. Fax: 01637 860887. Email: rob@thebonsainursery.com. Web: www.thebonsainursery.com.

***Lanhydrock Plant Nursery**, Bodmin PL30 5AD. Tel: 01208 265950. Fax: 01208 265959. Email: lanhydrock@nationaltrust.org.uk. Web: www.nationaltrust.org.uk.

***Old Mill Herbary**, Helland Bridge, Bodmin PL30 4QR. Tel/Fax: 01208 841206. Email: enquiries@oldmillherbary.co.uk. Web: www.oldmillherbary.co.uk.

***Pine Lodge Nursery**, Holmbush, St Austell PL25 3RQ. Tel: 01726 73500. Fax: 01726 77370. Email: garden@pine-lodge.com. Web: www.pine-lodge.co.uk.

Pinsla Garden & Nursery, Cardinham, Bodmin PL30 4AY. Tel/Fax: 01208 821339. Email: info@pinslagarden.co.uk. Web: www.pinslagarden.co.uk.

***Roseland House Nursery**, Chacewater, Truro TR4 8QB. Tel: 01872 560451. Email: clematis@roselandhouse.co.uk. *Speciality: climbing plants.*

***Trebah Enterprises Ltd.**, Mawnan Smith, Falmouth TR11 5JZ. Tel: 01326 250448. Fax: 01326 250781. Email: mail@trebah-garden.co.uk. Web: www.trebah-garden.co.uk.

***Tregothnan Nursery**, see above, under 'Nurseries'.

Tregrehan, Par. Tel: 01726 814389.

***Trewithen Nurseries**, Grampound Road, Truro. Tel: 01726 882764. Fax: 01726 882301. Email: gardens@trewithenestate.demon.co.uk. Web: www.trewithengardens.co.uk.

Specialist nurseries and suppliers

See *The RHS Plant Finder* for full details.

Palms

Suppliers of potted specimens or seed are listed below. Also, for palm seeds online, see www.rarepalmseeds.com.

Amulree Exotics, Tropical Wings, Wickford Road, South Woodham Ferrers, Essex CM3 6AD. Tel/Fax: 01245 425255. Contact: Simon Gridley. Web: www.turn-it-tropical.co.uk.

Architectural Plants, Cooks Farm, Nuthurst, Horsham, West Sussex, RH13 6LH. Tel: 01403 891772. Fax: 01403 891056. Contact: Angus White. Web: www.architecturalplants.com.

Brooklands Plants, 25 Treves Road, Dorchester, Dorset DT1 2HE. Contact: Ian Watt.

Mulu Nurseries, Longdon Hill, Wickhamford, Evesham, Worcs. WR11 7RP. Tel: 01386 833171. Fax: 01386 833136. Contact: Andy Bateman. Web: www.mulu.co.uk.

Palm Centre, Ham Central Nursery, Ham, Richmond, Surrey, TW10 7HA. Tel: 0208 2556191. Contact: Martin Gibbons. Web: www.palmcentre.co.uk.

Rosedown Mill Nursery, Hartland, Bideford, Devon EX39 6AH. Tel: 01237 441527. Contact: Huw Collingbourne. Web: www.rosedownmill.freeserve.co.uk.

Proteaceae

Silverhill Seeds, PO Box 53108, Kenilworth 7745, Cape Town, South Africa. Tel: +27 21 762 4245. Fax: +27 21 797 6609. Email: Rachel@silverhillseeds.co.za. Web: www.silverhillseeds.co.za. *Seed.*

Trevena Cross Nurseries & Garden Centre, Cornwall (see above, under 'Nurseries'). *Potted specimens.*

Bamboos

Special and rare bamboos may be obtained from all the national collections. (Pre-ordering is advisable.)

Duchy of Cornwall Nursery, Cornwall (see above, under 'Nurseries'). *Good selection of the more common varieties of bamboo.*

Michael Bell, Beecroft Park Road, Wadebridge, Cornwall PL27 7NG. *Phyllostachys cultivars.*

Tuckermarsh Gardens, Bere Alston, Yelverton, Devon PL20 7HN.

Tel: 01822 840721.

Restios

Silverhill Seeds (see above, under 'Proteaceae'). *South African seeds.*

Hedychiums and cautleyas

Hedychiums are being offered by an increasing number of suppliers, but the plants offered by the large bulb firms are of the imports from India. The following are recommended as supplying plants of known origin.

Crûg Farm Plants, Griffith's Crossing, Caernarfon, Gwynedd LL55 1TU. Contact: Bleddyn & Sue Wynn-Jones. *An astonishing array of plants from their own collection. Unfortunately no mail order, and the catalogue lists plants by name only.*

Fillan's Plants, Tuckermarsh Gardens, Tamar Lane, Bere Alston, Devon PL20 7HN. Contact: Mark Fillan. *Includes a number of hedychiums, and in time should be able to offer most of the forms mentioned in this book.*

Koba Koba, 2 High Street, Ashcott, Bridgwater, Somerset TA7 9PL. Tel: 01458 210700. Contact: Christine & David Constantine. *Issues a highly informative and interesting catalogue, and offers a selection of Tom Wood's many Hedychium hybrids, a few of which may have some potential in the open garden in Britain.*

Pan-Global Plants, The Walled Garden, Frampton Court, Frampton-on-Severn, Glocs. GL2 7EX. Contact: Nick Macer.

Climbers

J. Bradshaw & Son, Bushey-fields Nursery, Herne, Herne Bay, Kent CT6 7LJ. Tel: 01227 375415.

Hill House Nursery, Landscove, Ashburton, Devon. Contact: Mr & Mrs R. Hubbard.

Plantsman's Nursery, The, North Wonson Farm, Throwleigh, Okehampton, Devon EX20 2JA. Contact: Mr & Lady Sisson. Tel: 01647 231618.

Reads of Loddon, Hales Hall, Norfolk NR14 6QW. Tel: 01508 548395.

Roseland House Nursery, Cornwall (see above, under 'Nurseries associated with gardens'). Contact: Charlie Pridham.

Uncommon, untried, and tender plants

Australian Plant Society, Hon. Secretary: Jeff Irons, Stonecourt, 74 Brimstage Road, Heswall, Wirral CH60 1XG. *Australasian seed; information; occasionally plants.*

Flores & Watson, c/o M.J. Cheese, Silvercove, Lee Downs, Ilfracombe, North Devon EX34 8LR. *Wild collected seeds from Argentina and Chile.*

International Succulent Institute, Huntington Botanical Gardens, 1151 Oxford Road, San Marino, California 91108, USA. *Especially puyas. Orders can be routed by a UK agent.*

Koba Koba (see above, under 'Hedychiums and cautleyas'.) *Exotics, especially banana and ginger families.*

Plant World, St Marychurch Road, Newton Abbot, Devon TQ12 4SE. Tel: 01803 872939. *Dwarf alstroemeria, and many other species.*

Silverhill Seeds (see above, under 'Proteaceae'). *South African seeds.*

Specialist societies

Alpine Garden Society: AGS Centre, Avon Bank, Pershore, Worcestershire WR10 3JP.

Australian Plant Society: see above, under 'Uncommon, untried, and tender plants'.

Bamboo Society, (EBS Great Britain): c/o 39 West Square, London SE11 4SP.

Botanical Society of South Africa: Private Bag X10, Claremont, 7735, Republic of South Africa.

British Cactus and Succulent Society: Mr D.V. Slade, Secretary, 15 Brentwood Crescent, Hull Road, York YO10 5HU.

British Pteridological Society: c/o Department of Botany, The Natural History Museum, Cromwell Road, London SW7 5BD.

Half-Hardy Group of the Hardy Plant Society: The Administrator, Little Orchard, Great Comberton, nr Pershore, Worcestershire WR10 3DP.

Hebe Society: The Secretary, Rosemergy, Hain Walk, St Ives, Cornwall TR26 2AF.

International Palm Society: Libby Besse, Administrative Secretary, 6729 Peacock Road, Sarasota, Florida 34242, USA.

Mediterranean Garden Society: The Secretary, PO Box 14, Pania GR-19002, Greece.

Gardens to Visit and National Collections

Most plants mentioned in this book can be seen in Cornish gardens open to the public. For full details see *The Cornwall Gardens Guide* (D.E. Pett, Alison Hodge, 2003), and *Gardens of England and Wales Open for Charity* (The National Garden Scheme's 'yellow book': www.ngs.org.uk). The gardens below – in Cornwall and elsewhere – are of particular interest in relation to certain chapters of *Gardening on the Edge*.

Gardens at the edge of the sea

Abbotsbury Subtropical Gardens, Dorchester, Dorset
Achamore House, Isle of Gigha, Argyll
An Cala, Isle of Seil, Argyll
Arduaine, By Oban, Argyll
Bosahan, Manaccan, Cornwall
Brodick Castle, Isle of Arran
Cadland House, Fawley, Hampshire
Caerhays Castle Gardens, Gorran, St Austell, Cornwall
Coleton Fishacre, Kingswear, Devon
Colonsay House, Isle of Colonsay, Argyll
Dereen, Lauragh, Ireland
Fox Rosehill Gardens, Falmouth, Cornwall
Greencombe, Porlock, Somerset
Headland Garden, Polruan by Fowey, Cornwall
Ilnacullin, Glengarriff, Ireland
Inverewe, Poolewe, Ross-shire

Kerrachar Gardens, Kylesku, Sutherland
Lamorran House Gardens, St Mawes, Cornwall
Lochalsh Woodland Garden, Balmacara, Kyle, Ross-shire
Lost Gardens of Heligan, Pentewan, Cornwall
Morrab Gardens, Penzance, Cornwall
Overbecks, Salcombe, Devon
Owl Cottage, Newport, Isle of Wight
Pencarreg, Anglesey, Gwynedd
Queen Mary Gardens, Falmouth, Cornwall
St Michael's Mount, Marazion, Penzance, Cornwall
Southsea Common & Esplanade, Southsea, Hampshire
Tongue House, Tongue, Sutherland
Trebah, Mawnan Smith, Falmouth, Cornwall
Tresco Abbey Garden, Tresco, Isles of Scilly
Ventnor Botanic Garden, Ventnor, Isle of Wight
Yaffles, Ventnor, Isle of Wight

Conifers

Bicton College Gardens, Sidmouth, Devon
Endsleigh House, Milton Abbot, Tavistock, Devon
Killerton, Broadclyst, Devon
Pine Lodge Gardens, Holmbush, St Austell, Cornwall
Tregrehan, Par, St Austell, Cornwall
Trevarno Estate Gardens, Helston, Cornwall

Palms

Abbotsbury Subtropical Gardens, Dorchester, Dorset
Fox Rosehill Gardens, Falmouth, Cornwall
Glendurgan, Mawnan Smith, Falmouth, Cornwall
Jardin Georges Delaselle, Ille de Batz, Roscoff, Brittany, France
Lamorran House Gardens, St Mawes, Cornwall
Lost Gardens of Heligan, Pentewan, Cornwall
Penlee Memorial Gardens, Penzance, Cornwall
Royal Botanic Gardens, Kew, Richmond, Surrey
Trebah, Mawnan Smith, Falmouth, Cornwall
Tresco Abbey Garden, Tresco, Isles of Scilly

Proteaceae

Genera such as *Lomatia* and *Embothrium* may be viewed in gardens throughout Cornwall, notably at **Trengwainton**, Penzance, and **Fox Rosehill Gardens**, Falmouth

Genera such as *Banksia* and *Protea* may be viewed at **Tresco Abbey Garden**, Tresco, Isles of Scilly, and at **Kirstenbosch Botanic Garden**, Cape Town, South Africa (www.nbi.ac.za)

Bamboos

Bicton College Gardens, Sidmouth, Devon
Carwinion Bamboo Garden, Mawanan Smith, Falmouth, Cornwall

Endsleigh House, Milton Abbot, Tavistock, Devon
Fox Rosehill Gardens, Falmouth, Cornwall
Lost Gardens of Heligan, Pentewan, Cornwall
Penjerrick Garden, Mawanan Smith, Falmouth, Cornwall
Trebah, Mawnan Smith, Falmouth, Cornwall

Climbers

Greenway Gardens, Churston Ferrers, Brixham, Devon
RHS Garden Wisley, Wisley, Woking, Surrey
RHS Garden Rosemoor, Great Torrington, Devon
Crug Farm, Griffiths Crossing, Gwynedd

Ferns

Dereen, Lauragh, Ireland
Fota, Kerry, County Cork, Ireland
Penjerrick Garden, Mawnan Smith, Cornwall
Trebah, Mawnan Smith, Cornwall
Trewidden Garden, Penzance, Cornwall
RHS Garden Rosemoor, Great Torrington, Devon

National Collections

Comprehensive collections of groups of plants are made and held under the auspices of the National Council for the Conservation of Plants and Gardens. For details, contact: The Plant Conservation Officer, NCCPG, The Stable Courtyard, Wisley Garden, Woking, Surrey GU23 6QP. The current *National Plant Collections Directory* may be ordered from NCCPG Publications Ltd., at the same address. National Collections are open by appointment. They are not obliged to supply material to individual gardeners.

Seaside plants
Olearia and Brachyglottis
National Trust for Scotland, Inverewe Garden, Poolewe, Ross-shire IV22 2LG

Bamboos
General collection
D. Crampton, Drysdale Garden Exotics, Bowerwood Road, Fordingbridge, Hants SP6 1BN. Tel: 01425 653010

Phyllostachys cultivars
(joint collection)
Les Cathery, Gwarackewenbyghan, Boskennal, St Buryan, Penzance, Cornwall TR19 6DF
Michael Bell, Beecroft, Park Road, Wadebridge, Cornwall PL27 7NG

Hedychiums and others
Hedychium
Bristol Zoological Society, Gutherie Road, Clifton, Bristol

Roscoea
Roland Bream, Cruckmeole House, Cruckmeole, Shrewsbury SY5 8JN

Climbers
Aristolochia
Mr and Lady Sisson, The Plantsman Nursery, North Wonson Farm, Throwleigh, Okehampton, Devon EX20 2JA

Clematis
Raymond J. Evison, Domarie Vineries, Les Sauvages, St Sampson, Guernsey GY2 4FD

There are a number of other *Clematis* collections based on smaller sections of the genus, one of which, *Clematis viticella* cvs., is held at Roseland House, Chacewater, Truro TR4 8QB

Lathyrus
Miss S. Norton, Weavers Cottage, 35 Streetly End, West Wickham, Cambridge, CB1 6RP

Lonicera
(species and primary hybrids)
Mr T. Upson, University Botanic Garden, Cory Lodge, Bateman Street, Cambridge CB2 1JF

Passiflora (species)
Mr R. Vanderplank, Greenholm Nurseries, Lampley Road, Kingston Seymour, Somerset BS21 6XS

Passiflora (cvs)
Miss J. Lindsay, 111 Clevedon Road, Tickenham, North Somerset BS21 6RE

Rosa
Peter Beales Roses, London Road, Attleborough, Norfolk NR17 1AY

Trachelospermum
Mr James McCulloch, Superintendent of Parks & Gardens, West Ham Park, Upton Lane, Forest Gate, London E7 9PU

Tropaeolum
Ms C. Reaney, Head Gardener, Inveresk Lodge Garden, Musselburgh, East Lothian EH21 7TE

Further Reading

Below is a selection of general and specialist books related to the subject of 'gardening on the edge'.

General

Arnold-Forster, W. (1948), *Shrubs for the Milder Counties*. London: Country Life. Reprinted, Penzance: Alison Hodge, 2000.

Bean, W.J. (1937), in Cox, E.H.M. (ed.), *The New Flora and Sylva*, 9. London: Dulau.

Bean, W.J. (1980), *Trees and Shrubs Hardy in the British Isles*, 8th edn. London: John Murray.

Griffiths, M. (1994), *The New Royal Horticultural Society Index of Garden Plants*. London: Macmillan.

Davey, F.H. (1897), 'Acclimatisation of exotics in Cornwall, Falmouth–Truro District', *Journal of the Royal Institute of Cornwall*, 13, pp. 313–43.

Heywood, V.H. (1978), *Flowering Plants of the World*. Oxford: Oxford University Press.

Hillier, J. & Coombes, A. (2002), *The Hillier Manual of Trees and Shrubs*. Newton Abbot: David & Charles.

Hunkin, J.W., ed. D.E. Pett (2001), *From a Cornish Bishop's Garden*. Penzance: Alison Hodge.

Huxley, A. (ed.) (1992), *RHS Dictionary of Gardening*. London and Basingstoke: Macmillan.

Miles, T. & Rowe, D. (2003), *The New Cornish Garden*, Truro: Truran.

Pett, D.E. (2003), *The Cornwall Gardens Guide*. Penzance: Alison Hodge.

Pring, S., ed. (1996), *Glorious Gardens of Cornwall*. Truro: Cornwall Gardens Trust.

Royal Horticultural Society (2002), *The RHS Plant Finder 2003–2004*. London: Dorling Kindersley.

Thurston, E. (1930), *British and Foreign Trees and Shrubs in Cornwall*. Cambridge: Cambridge University Press.

Conservation Press (1998), *World List of Threatened Trees*.

Specific

Gardening at the edge of the sea

Allan, H.H. (1961), *Flora of New Zealand*. Wellington: R.E. Owen.

Caborn, J.M. (1965), *Shelterbelts and Windbreaks*. London: Faber.

Cave, Y. & Paddison, V. (1999), *The Gardener's Encyclopaedia of New Zealand Native Plants*. Auckland: Random House.

Clough, P. (1995), 'Daisy bushes – a journey through a beautiful minefield', *The Cornish Garden*, 38.

Ingerwersen, W.E.T. (1951), *Wild Flowers in the Garden*. London: Geoffrey Bles.

Kelway, C. (1962), *Seaside Gardening*. London: Collingridge.

Kelway, C. (1965), *Gardening on Sand*. London: Collingridge.

Kelway, C. (1970), *Gardening on the Coast*. Newton Abbott: David & Charles.

Le Sueur, A.D.C. (1951), *Hedges, Shelter-Belts and Screens*. London: Country Life.

MAFF/ADAS (1950–84), *Annual Reports of Rosewarne, Ellbridge and Isles of Scilly Experimental Horticultural Stations*. London: HMSO.

Shepherd, F.W. (1990), *Seaside Gardening*. London: Cassell, RHS Handbook.

Wyman, D. (1938), *Hedges, Screens and Windbreaks*. London: McGraw Hill.

Recent woody plant arrivals in Cornwall

Bailey, L.H., Bailey, E.Z. & Bailey, L.H. (1976), *Hortus Third: A Concise Dictionary of Plants Cultivated in the United States and Canada*. New York: Macmillan.

Bramwell, D. (1997), *Flora of the Canary Islands*. Madrid: Editorial Rueda, SL.

Cameron, M., ed., & Launceston Field Naturalists Club (1986), *Guide to Flowers and Plants of Tasmania*. Sydney: Reed Books.

Chamberlain, D. (1982), 'Revision of *Rhododendron* II', in *Notes from the Royal Botanic Garden Edinburgh*, 39, 2. London: HMSO.

Chamberlain, D.F. & Cullen, J. (1980), 'A revision of *Rhododendron*' in *Notes from the Royal Botanic Garden Edinburgh*, 39, 1, 2. London: HMSO.

Costermans, L. (1996), *Native Trees and Shrubs of South-Eastern Australia*. Adelaide: Rigby. Reprinted, Sydney: New Holland, 2000.

Cox, P.A. & Cox, K.N. E. (1997), *The Encyclopedia of Rhododendron Species*. Perth: Glendoick.

Foster, R. (1983), *Rare, Exotic and Difficult Plants*. Newton Abbot: David & Charles.

Frodin, D. & Govaerts, R. (1996), *World Checklist and Bibliography of Magnoliaceae*. London: Royal Botanic Gardens, Kew.

Gentry, A. (1996), *Field Guide to the Woody Plants of Northwest South America*. Chicago: University of Chicago Press.

Grierson, A.J.C. & Long, D.G (1983), *Flora of Bhutan including a record of plants from Sikkim and Darjeeling*. Edinburgh: Royal Botanic Garden, Edinburgh.

Hillier, H. (1981), *Hillier's Manual of Trees and Shrubs*. New York: Van Nostrand Reinhold.

Keng,. H., Hong, D-Y. & Chen, C.-J. (1993), *Orders and Families of Seed Plants of China*. Singapore: World Scientific Publishing Co.

Li, H-L. (1963), *Woody Flora of Taiwan*. Philadelphia, Pennsylvania: Morris Arboretum.

Mabberley, D.J. (1987), *The Plant-Book*. Cambridge: Cambridge University Press. Reprinted, CUP, 1997.

Ohwi, J. (1984), *Flora of Japan*. Washington, DC: Smithsonian Institution Press.

Paton, V.S. & Paton, J.A. (2001), *Magnolias in Cornish Gardens*. Fowey, Alexander Associates.

Polunin, O. & Stainton, A. (1984), *Flowers of the Himalayas*. Oxford: Oxford University Press.

Poole, A.L. & Adams, N. (1963), *Trees and Shrubs of New Zealand*. Wellington: Government Printer.

Ruiz, H. (1998), *The Journals of Hipólito Ruiz: Spanish Botanist in Peru and Chile, 1777–1788*. Portland, Oregon: Timber Press.

Sargent, C.S. (1913–17), *Plantae Wilsonianae: An Enumeration of the Woody Plants Collected in Western China for the Arnold Arboretum of Harvard University During the Years 1907, 1908 and 1910 by E.H. Wilson*. 3 vols, Cambridge. Reprinted, Portland, Oregon: Dioscorides Press, 1988.

Stainton, A. (1988), *Flowers of the Himalayas: A Supplement*. Oxford: Oxford University Press.

Treseder, N.G. (1978), *Magnolias*. London: Faber.

Walker, J. & Kenyon, J. (1997), *Vireyas: A Practical Gardening Guide*. Portland, Oregon: Timber Press.

Wang, C-W. (1961), *The Forests of China*. Harvard: Maria Moors Cabot Foundation.

Conifers

Farjon, A. (1998), *World Checklist and Bibliography of Conifers*. London: Royal Botanic Gardens, Kew. (Information on wild conifers, including a checklist of the world's conifer species.)

Farjon, A. & Page, C.N. (1999), *Conifers – Status Survey and Conservation Action Plan*. Gland, Switzerland, and Cambridge, UK: International Union for the Conservation of Nature. (Threatened species and conservation issues.)

Farjon, A. & Page, C.N. (2000), 'An action plan for the world's conifers', *Plant Talk*, 22/23, pp. 43–7. (Threatened species and conservation issues.)

Gardner, M.F. & Thomas, P. (1996), 'The Conifer Conservation Programme', *The New Plantsman*, 3, pp. 5–21.

Gelderen, D.M. van & Hoey Smith, J.R.P. van, *Conifers: The Illustrated Encyclopedia*. 2 vols. Portland, Oregon: Timber Press.

Hillier, H.G. (1972), 'Conifers for different soils and exposures', in Fletcher, H.R. *et al.* (eds), *Conifers in the British Isles*. London: Royal Horticultural Society, pp. 105–8.

Hunt, D.R. (1972), 'Reference list of conifers and conifer allies grown out of doors in the British Isles', in Fletcher, H.R. *et al.* (eds), *Conifers in the British Isles*. London: Royal Horticultural Society, pp. 109–22. (Conifers in Britain and Ireland, including data on some of the species mentioned.)

James, N.D.G. (1969), *The Trees of Bicton (East Devon)*. Oxford: Blackwell. (Account relating to woody plants of one extreme of the south-west peninsula. See also Nellhams, M., below.)

Magor, E.W.M. (1988), 'Origins of conifers grown in Cornwall', *The Cornish Garden*, 31, pp. 65–74.

Mitchell, A. (1972a), 'Conifer statistics', in Fletcher, H.R. *et al.* (eds), *Conifers in the British Isles*. London: Royal Horticultural Society, pp. 123–293. (Conifers in Britain and Ireland, including data on some of the species mentioned.)

Mitchell, A. (1972b), *Conifers in the British Isles: A Descriptive Handbook*. Forestry Commission booklet, 33. London: HMSO. (Conifers in Britain and Ireland, as above.)

Mitchell, A. (1981), *The Gardener's Book of Trees*. London: Dent. (Conifers in Britain and Ireland, as above.)

Nellhams, M. (2000), *Tresco Abbey Garden: A Personal and Pictorial History*. Truro: Truran. (Account relating to woody plants of one extreme of the south-west peninsula. See also James, N.D.G., above.)

Page, C.N. (1986) (ed.), 'Gymnospermae', in Walters, S.M., *et al.*, *The European Garden Flora*. Cambridge: Cambridge University Press, pp. 68–107. (Conifers in Britain and Ireland, including data on some of the species mentioned.)

Page, C.N. (1989), 'The role of Edinburgh Royal Botanic Garden in the international conservation of conifers', *International Dendrology Society Yearbook, 1989*. Cambridge: International Dendrology Society, pp. 112–15. (Threatened species and conservation issues.)

Page, C.N. (1990), 'Conifers', in Kubitsky, K. (ed.), *The Families and Genera of Vascular Plants*. Berlin: Springer-Verlag, pp. 277–361. (Account of the world's conifer genera.)

Page, C.N. (1991), 'A Cornwall-linked botanic garden and temperate rainforest tree conservation strategy into the 21st century', *The Cornish Garden*, 35, pp. 69–75. (Threatened species and conservation issues. An evolving perspective of how exotic trees might be structured into arboretum plantings in Cornwall, with conservational and educational objectives.)

Page, C.N. (1992), 'Cornish gardens as potential green banks for the survival of threatened temperate rainforest trees', *The Cornish Garden*, 35, pp. 5–9. (Threatened species and conservation issues, as above.)

Page, C.N. (1994), 'The ex-situ conservation of temperate rainforest conifer tree species: a British-based programme', *Biodiversity and Conservation*, 3, pp. 191–9.

Page, C.N. & Gardner, M.F. (1994), 'Conservation of rare temperate rainforest conifer tree species: a fast-growing role for arboreta in Britain and Ireland', in Perry, A. & Gwynn Ellis, R. (eds), *The Common Ground of Wild and Cultivated Plants*. Cardiff: National Museum of Wales, pp. 119–44. (Threatened species and conservation issues nationally.)

Rushforth, K.D. (1987), *Conifers*. London: Christopher Helm. (Conifers in Britain and Ireland, including data on some of the species mentioned.)

Palms

Blombery, A. & Rodd, T. (1988), *Palms of the World: Their Care, Cultivation and Landscape Use*. London: Angus & Robertson.

Corner, E.J.H. (1966), *The Natural History of Palms*. London: Weidenfeld & Nicholson.

Drescher J. & Dufay A. (2002), 'Importation of Mature Palms: A Threat to Native and Exotic Palms in Mediterranean Countries?', *Palms* (formerly *Principes*): *Journal of the International Palm Society*, 46, 4.

Francko, D.A. (2003), *Palms Won't Grow Here and Other Myths: Warm-Climate Plants for Cooler Areas*. Portland, Oregon: Timber Press.

Gibbons, M. (1993), *Palms*. London: Apple Press.

Griessen, A. (1899), *The Book of Gardening*. London: Upcott Gill, pp. 807–64.

Henderson, A., Galeano, G. & Bernal, R. (1995), *Field Guide to the Palms of the Americas*. Princetown, USA: Princetown Press.

Hunkin, J.W. (1950), 'Ninety Years a Gardener: Captain W.S.C. Pinwill of Trehane', *Journal of the Royal Horticultural Society*, pp. 326–31.

Jones, D. (1984), *Palms in Australia*. Sydney: Reed.

King, R. (1985), *Tresco: England's Island of Flowers*. London: Constable.

McMillan Browse, P. (1993), *Palms for Cooler Climates*. Falmouth: Trebah Enterprises.

Meerow, A.W. (1992), *Treating Cold Damaged Palms*. Florida: University of Florida, Institute of Food and Agricultural Sciences fact sheet.

Menninger, E.A. (1964), *Seaside Plants of the World: A Guide to Planning, Planting, and Maintaining Salt-Resistant Gardens*. New York: Hearthside Press.

Pacific Northwest Palm Society (1996–2003), *Journals*. Vancouver: PNWPS.

Richardson, P. (1996), 'The Beautiful South', *Chamaerops*, 22, Spring. Richmond, Surrey: EPS, UK. (www.palms.org.)

Riffle, R.L. & Craft, P. (2003), *An Encyclopedia of Cultivated Palms*. Portland, Oregon: Timber Press.

Royal Horticultural Society (*c.*1962), 'Frost and Wind Damage Survey 1961–62' London: Royal Horticultural Society.

Tollefson, D. (1997a), 'Palms for Europe's Zone 8', *Chamaerops*, 25, Winter 1996/7. Richmond, Surrey: EPS, UK. (www.palms.org.)

Tollefson, D. (1997b), 'Pot Planting: A Revolutionary New Advance in Gardening',

Chamaerops, 28, Autumn. Richmond, Surrey: EPS, UK. (www.palms.org.)

Uhl, N.W. & Dransfield, J. (1987), *Genera Palmarum: A classification of palms based on the work of Harold E. Moore Jr.* International Palm Society and L.H. Bailey Hortorium, Cornell University.

Proteaceae

Cowling, R. &. Dave, R. (1995), *Fynbos: South Africa's Unique Floral Kingdom.* Cape Town: Fernwood Press.

Cronin, L. (n.d.), *Australian Flora.* Sydney: Reed.

Eliovson, S. (1965), *Proteas for Pleasure.* Cape Town: Howard Timmins. 5th edn, Johannesburg: Macmillan, 1979.

George, A.S. (1983), *The Banksia Book.* Kenthurst: Kangaroo Press.

Matthews, L. (2002), *The Protea Book: A Guide to Cultivated Proteaceae.* Portland, Oregon: Timber Press.

Rebelo, T. & Paterson-Jones, C. (1995), *A Field Guide to the Proteas of South Africa.* Vlaeberg, South Africa: Fernwood Press.

Vogts, M.M. (1958), *Proteas: Know Them and Grow Them. On the Cultivation of South African Proteaceae.* Johannesburg: Afrikaanse Pers-Boekhandel.

Bamboos and Restios

Bamboos

Bell, M. (2000), *The Gardener's Guide to Growing Temperate Bamboos.* Newton Abbot: David & Charles.

Meredith, T.J. (2001), *Bamboos for Gardens.* Portland, Oregon: Timber Press.

Recht, C. & Wetterwald, M.E. (1992), *Bamboos.* Portland, Oregon: Timber Press.

Stapleton, C.M.A. (1994a), *Bamboos of Nepal.* London: Royal Botanic Gardens, Kew.

Stapleton, C.M.A. (1994b), *Bamboos of Bhutan.* London: Royal Botanic Gardens, Kew.

Restios

Brown, N., Jamieson, H. & Botha, P. (1998), *Grow Restios: A Guide to the Propagation of South African Restios.* Cape Town: National Botanical Institute.

Cowling, R. &. Dave, R. (1995), *Fynbos: South Africa's Unique Floral Kingdom.* See

above:'Proteaceae'.

Darke, R. (1999), *The Colour Encyclopedia of Ornamental Grasses: Sedges, Rushes, Restios, Cat-Tails, and Selected Bamboos.* London: Weidenfeld & Nicolson.

Haaksma, E.D. & Linder, H.P. (2000), *Restios of the Fynbos.* Cape Town: Botanical Society of South Africa.

Linder, P. (n.d.), *Bothalia* , 15: 1–4. Pretoria: Botanical Research Institute.

Meney, K.A. & Pate, J.S. (1999), *Australian Rushes: Biological Identifications and Conservation of Restionacae and Allied Families.* Nedlands: University of Western Australia Press.

Hedychiums and others

A much-needed revision of the genus is currently being undertaken by Tom Wood, a botanist and grower based in Florida, USA, who has also collected in eastern India and Yunnan. He says, 'My monograph … will eliminate many customary species as well as resurrect a number of species which were buried by Turril.' Date of publication to be announced.

Alpine Garden Society Centre, *Bulletin of the Alpine Garden Society.* Avon Bank: AGS Centre. (Frequent references to the genus, with photographs.)

Cowley, E.J. (1982), 'A revision of Roscoea', in *Kew Bulletin*, 36, 4, pp. 747–77. (A scientific paper based on the herbarium material available at the time.)

Hooker, J.D. (1894), *Flora of British India.* Reprinted, Delhi: Periodical Expert Book Agency, 2001, and Dehradun: International Book Dist., 2002.

Polunin, O. & Stainton, A. (1984), *Flowers of the Himalayas.* See above: 'Some recent woody plant arrivals in Cornwall'.

Climbers

Johnson, M. (2001), *The Genus Clematis.* Stockholm: A.B. Sodertalje.

McMillan Browse, P.D.A. (1981), *The Commercial Production of Climbing Plants.* London: Grower Books.

Quest-Ritson, C. (2003), *Climbing Roses of the World.* Portland, Oregon: Timber Press.

Toomey, M.K. & Leeds, E. (2001), *An Illustrated Encyclopedia of Clematis.* Portland, Oregon: Timber Press.

Ferns, clubmosses, and horsetails

Allen, D.E. (1969), *The Victorian Fern Craze: A History of Pteridomania*. London: Hutchinson.

Camus, J.M. (ed) (1991), *The History of British Pteridology, 1891–1991*. London: British Pteridological Society.

Camus, J.M., Jermy, A.C. & Thomas, B.A. (eds) (1991), *A World of Ferns*. London: Natural History Museum.

Dyce, J.W. (1991), *The Cultivation and Propagation of British Ferns*. London: British Pteridological Society.

Hoshizaki, B.J. (1975), *Fern Growers' Manual*. New York: Alfred A. Knopf. 2nd edn., Portland, Oregon: Timber Press. (Includes details of many of the genera and their species.)

Ide, J.M., Jermy, A.C. & Paul, A.M. (eds) (1992), *Fern Horticulture: Past, Present and Future Perspectives*. Andover: Intercept Publishing.

Page, C.N. (1975), 'Some British ferns and their cultivation', *Journal of the Scottish Rock Garden Club*, 14, pp. 263–76.

Page, C.N. (1979), 'The diversity of ferns – an ecological perspective', in Dyer, A.F., *The Experimental Biology of Ferns*. London: Academic Press.

Page, C.N. (1982), *The Ferns of Britain and Ireland*. Cambridge: Cambridge University Press.

Page, C.N. (1988), *Ferns: Their Habitats in the Landscape of Britain and Ireland*. London and Glasgow: Collins, New Naturalist, 74.

Page, C.N. (1997a), 'Pteridophytes as field indicators of natural biodiversity restoration in the Scottish flora', *Botanical Journal of Scotland*, 49, pp. 405–14.

Page, C.N. (1997b), *The Ferns of Britain and Ireland*. 2nd edn. Cambridge: Cambridge University Press.

Page, C.N. & Bennell, F.M. (1986), 'Ferns and Fern Allies', *The European Garden Flora*, 1, pp. 1–67. Cambridge: Cambridge University Press. (Includes details of many of the genera and their species.)

Page, C.N. & Brownsey, P.J. (1986), 'Tree fern skirts: a defence against climbers and large epiphytes', *Journal of Ecology*, 74, pp. 787–96.

Page, C.N. & Hollands, R. (1992), 'The taxonomy and identification of Australian and New Zealand *Dicksonia* tree ferns in cultivation in Britain', *Pteridologist*, 2, pp. 102–3.

Perl, P. (1979), *Ferns*. The Netherlands and New York: Time Life International. (Includes details of many of the genera and their species.)

Poole, I. & Page, C.N. (2000), 'A fossil fern indicator of epiphytism in a Tertiary flora', *New Phytologist*, 148, pp. 117–25.

Rickard, M. (2000), *The Plantfinder's Guide to Garden Ferns*. Newton Abbot: David & Charles.

Swindells, P. (1971), *Ferns for Garden and Greenhouse*. London: Dent.

Some uncommon, untried, or tender plants

Allan, H.H., Moore, L.B. & Edgar, E. (1961, 1976, 1980), *Flora of New Zealand*. 3 vols. Wellington: Government Printer.

Bailey, L.H. & E.Z. (1976), *Hortus Third*. See above: 'Some recent woody plant arrivals in Cornwall'.

Bramwell, D. & Bramwell, Z. (2001), *Wild Flowers of the Canary Islands*. 2nd edn. Madrid: Editorial Mulda S.L.

California Horticulture Society, *Pacific Horticulture*. Quarterly journal: PO Box 680, Berkeley, California 94701, USA.

Cave, Y. (2003), *Succulents for the Contemporary Garden*. Portland, Oregon: Timber Press.

Costa, A. da & Franquinko, L. de O. (1990), *Madeira: Plantas e Flores*. 11th edn. Funchal: Francisco Ribeiro.

Cronk, Q.C.B. (2000), *The Endemic Flora of St Helena*. Oswestry: Anthony Nelson.

Elliot, W.R. & Jones, D.L. (1980), *Encyclopaedia of Australian Plants*. Melbourne: Lothian Publishing Co. Reprinted 1981.

Fisher, M.E., Satchell, E. & Watkins, J.M. (1970), *Gardening with New Zealand Plants, Shrubs and Trees*. Auckland: Collins.

Hereman, S. (1868), *Paxton's Botanical Dictionary*. London: Bradbury, Agnew & Co.

Herklots, G.A.C. (1951), *The Hong Kong Countryside*. Hong Kong: South China Morning Post. 6th impression, 1965.

Herklots, G.A.C. (1976), *Flowering Tropical Climbers*. Folkstone: W.M. Dawson.

Hoffman, J. (1991), *Flora, Sylvestre de Chile: Zona Araucana*. 2nd edn. Santiago de Chile: Fundacion Claudio Gay.

Hooker, J.D. (1894), *Flora of British India*. See above: 'Hedychiums and others'.

Irish, M. & G. (2000), *Agaves, Yuccas and Related*

Plants. Portland, Oregon: Timber Press.

Jacobsen, H. (1970), *Lexicon of Succulent Plants.* Jena: Gustav Fischer Verlag; London: Blandford, 1974.

Jeppe, B. (1969), *South African Aloes.* Cape Town, South Africa: Purnell. 3rd impression 1970.

Kohlein, F. (1997), *Freiland Sukkulenten.* Stuttgart, Germany: Ulmer.

Lancaster, R. (1981), *Plant Hunting in Nepal.* London: Croom Helm. Reprinted, Croom Helm, 1983. Enlarged, revised edn, Antique Collectors' Club, 1995.

Lancaster, R. (1989), *Travels in China.* Woodbridge: Antique Collectors' Club.

Metcalf, L.J. (1972), *The Cultivation of New Zealand Trees and Shrubs.* Wellington: A.H. & A.W. Reed. 2nd edn. 1975.

Moore, L.B. & Edgar, E. (1976), *The Flora of New Zealand.* Vol. 2. Wellington: A.R. Shearer for the Government of New Zealand.

Padilla, V. (1973), *Bromeliads.* New York, USA: Crown Publishers.

Paxton, Sir J. (1868), *Botanical Dictionary.* London: Bradbury Evans.

Praeger, R.L. (1932), *An Account of the Sempervivum Group.* London: Royal Horticultural Society.

Press, J.R. & Short, M.J. (1994), *Flora of Madeira.* London: HMSO.

Rai, L. & Sharma, E. (1994), *Medicinal Plants of the Sikkim Himalaya: Status, Usage and Potential.* Dehra Dun: Shri Gajendra Singh Gahlot for Bishen Singh Mahendrapal Singh.

Rauh, W.A.O. (1979), *Bromeliads for Home, Garden and Greenhouse.* Poole: Blandford Press.

Reynolds, G.W. (1950), *The Aloes of South Africa.* Cape Town: Aloes of South Africa Book Fund.

Rosenblum, M. (1997), *Olives: Life and Lore of a Noble Fruit.* New York: North Point Press.

Ross, T. & Irons, J. (1997), *Australian Plants.* Frankfurt/Main.

Sargent, C.S. (1913–17), *Plantae Wilsonianae.* See above: 'Some recent woody plant arrivals in Cornwall'.

Schäfer, H. (2002), *Flora of the Azores: A Field Guide.* Weikersheim: Margraf Verlag.

Span, J.N. (1994), *Growing Winter-Hardy Cacti.* Watertown, Conneticut: Elisabeth Harmon.

Stainton, D.D.A (1972), *Forests of Nepal.* London: John Murray.

Sudworth, G.B. (1967), Forest Trees of the Pacific Slope. New York: Dover.

Synge, P. (1938), *Mountains of the Moon.* London.

Waddick, J.W. & Stokes, G.M. (2000), *Bananas You Can Grow.* Louisiana: Stokes Tropical Publishing Co.

Index

Acknowledgements

Photographs are reproduced by kind permission of: Neil Armstrong, pp. 4, 7 (top), 130, 132, 143 (top left), 144 (top left), 148 (bottom left), 150, 151, 211, front and back endpapers; Michael Bell, pp. 133–7, 138 (right), 139–42, 143 (top right), 144 (bottom left, right), 145–6; Mark Brent, pp. 88 (top), 89–99, 101, 103, 105–6; Ian Browne, p. 107; Les Cathery, pp. 148 (top left, right, bottom right), 149, 152 (left, bottom right); Churton Inge Associates, facing title page, p. 14 (top); Alison Clough, pp. 18 (bottom), 19, 20 (top); Peter Clough, pp. 15, 17 (bottom), 21 (bottom), 24, 25 (top), 27; John Eddy, pp. 112, 115, 118 (bottom), 120 (bottom left), 123, 124 (left), 125 (left), 126, 128 (bottom); Alison Hodge, p. 88 (bottom); James Hodge, pp. 7 (bottom), 9–11, 122, 154; Tom Hudson, pp. 28, 30–32, 34–52, 54–8; Christopher Laughton, pp. 20 (bottom), 26 (top); Freya Laughton, p. 8 (bottom); C.A.E. Moore, pp. 110, 113, 117, 118 (top), 119, 120 (top, bottom right), 121, 124 (right), 125 (right), 128 (top), 129; John Packer, pp. 156, 158–61, 164 (top left, right), 165, 167–8; Chris Page, pp. 60, 62–71, 73–85, 186, 188–202, 204–5; Douglas Pett, p. 6; Charlie Pridham, pp. 163, 170–84; Rob Senior, pp. 17 (top), 21 (top), 22 (bottom), 23, 25 (bottom), 26 (bottom), 108, 138 (left), 143 (bottom), 144 (top right), 147, 152 (top right, mid right), 157, 163 (top), 164 (bottom), 206, 208–10, 212–29; Trebah Garden Trust, p. 86. Pages 8 (top), 12, 14 (bottom), 16, 18 (top), 22 (top), cover: Susanna Heron ©.